Essential Series

Springer

London
Berlin
Heidelberg
New York
Barcelona
Hong Kong
Milan
Paris
Santa Clara
Singapore
Tokyo

John Cowell

Essential
Java 2 *fast*

How to develop applications and
applets with Java 2

 Springer

John Cowell, BSc(Hons), MPhil, PhD
Department of Computer and Information Sciences, De Montfort University
Kents Hill Campus, Hammerwood Gate, Kents Hill
Milton Keynes, MK7 6HP, UK

ISBN 1-85233-071-6 Springer-Verlag London Berlin Heidelberg

British Library Cataloguing in Publication Data
Cowell, John, 1957-
    Essential Java 2 fast : how to develop applications and
    applets with Java 2. – (Essential series)
    1.Java (Computer program language)
    I.Title
    005.2'76'2
    ISBN 1852330716

Library of Congress Cataloging-in-Publication Data
Cowell, John, 1957-
    Essential Java 2 fast : how to develop applications and applets
  with Java 2 / John Cowell.
      p.   cm.
    ISBN 1-85233-071-6 (alk. paper)
    I. Title.
    QA76.73.J38C694 1999   99-25430
    005.2'762--dc21   CIP

© Springer-Verlag London Limited 1999
Printed in Great Britain
2nd printing 2000
3rd printing 2001

Typesetting: Camera-ready by author
Printed and bound by the Athenæum Press Ltd., Gateshead, Tyne & Wear
34/3830-5432 Printed on acid-free paper SPIN 10786551

Contents

1

Why Java 2 Is Special

Introduction

Over the past five years, the World Wide Web has changed from a resource which was known about and used by a small elite of computer scientists and researchers to a tool which millions of people use every day. The World Wide Web has remained a powerful research tool, but is now also used to find any information we wish, from the weather report on the island of Java to documentation on the Java language. You can even buy this book on-line or order a pizza!

Web pages are written in a language called HTML. As more people started to use the Web there was a demand for extra facilities and the limitations of HTML became apparent. Businesses wanted to do business over the Web and many people wanted Web pages to be more interactive and dynamic. Java is the most powerful way of doing this; other technologies such as dynamic HTML and ActiveX offer some of these facilities but Java is still the most flexible and powerful tool for creating great Web pages. Java applications which can be run within a Web browser are called applets.

The development of Java is closely linked with the growth of the Web, but you are not limited to writing Web-based applications in Java. It is increasingly being used to write stand-alone applications. One of the great benefits of Java is that a Java program can be run on any platform, so if you want to write applications which will run on a Sun workstation, an IBM mainframe and a PC, Java is the obvious choice.

This book is about Java 2, the latest version of Java produced by Sun Microsystems, formerly called the Java Development Kit (JDK)1.2. It represents a significant improvement over previous versions of the JDK. This book does not cover the Microsoft development environment Visual J++ 6.0 which does not have all of the facilities of Java 2 although it has many features for creating applications specifically for PCs running Windows. There is much overlap between these two platforms, but this book focuses specifically on Java 2.

Is this book for you?

This book assumes that you have used a high level programming language before, such as Pascal. A knowledge of C or especially C++ will be an even greater help, but this is not essential. It assumes that you have some experience of using a Web browser such as Netscape Communicator.

This book provides a complete introduction to Java 2. It not only describes the language and many of its class libraries but shows how they are used. The key concepts of object orientation are described and the examples show how to apply the theory.

If you are already a Java programmer who has used earlier versions of Java, it is worthwhile making the switch to Java 2. Many of the bugs in earlier versions have been fixed, which will make your applications more reliable.

There are many changes to the class libraries and their methods; not only have new classes and methods been added, but many may not be supported in the future (they have been "deprecated"). This means that they are still available but may not be in the later versions of Java. Sun are really giving you notice that you should change your applications to be compatible with Java 2 as soon as possible.

There have been extensive additions to the Java classes, in particular the introduction of the Swing classes which provide a new set of GUI components that are implemented in Java. You can change the look and feel of these components to give the appearance of Motif, Windows, Mac or cross platform Java.

The aim of this book is to cover all of the most important elements of the Java language and many of the classes and methods in the Java API. There are many examples, so that you can see them in action. The best way to learn a programming language is to try the examples for yourself.

This book is not intended to give exhaustive coverage of Java - several thousand pages would be needed to do that - it is intended to give you everything that you need to write Java applications and applets quickly.

What you need to run Java 2

You need Sun's JDK 1.2 now called Java 2 and some essential documentation on the class libraries. These can be downloaded free from the Sun Web site.

The browser used to test all the applets was Netscape Communicator V4.5, however you can also use Internet Explorer 4.01, although there are some differences between these two browsers, for example in their capabilities for displaying different types of image files. Sun also supply an applet viewer which you can use, but it does not seem to be as robust as the browsers. Most of the applets will work with earlier versions of these browsers, but the latest browsers are available free or at very low cost, so it is worthwhile using the latest versions.

Java 2 will run on a variety of platforms, however the most popular platform is likely to be a PC. All applets and applications were written and tested in a Windows 98 environment, using a Pentium II 400 processor with 128 MB of memory. This gave excellent performance, but you can develop and run applets successfully on a less powerful computer – it just takes longer. The minimum computer that you need so that the performance is adequate is:

- Pentium 200.
- 32 MB or more of memory.
- 50 MB of disk space for a full installation.

If you want to run other applications at the same time as using Java 2, more memory will give a significant improvement in performance. The Java 2 compiler is faster than previous versions, but it is still slow.

How to use this book

If you are new to Java or your programming skills are rusty the best way to use this book is to work through the first six chapters which give an introduction to object orientation, cover the syntax of the language and look at how to create and run applications and applets. Depending on the aspects of Java in which you are interested you can look at the specific chapters which follow. Where possible the chapters have been written to be self-contained; all of the examples are fully developed within a single chapter rather than being developed over a number of chapters to help this. There is inevitably some link between chapters, for example, to read chapter 16 on files and streams you need to understand chapter 14 on exceptions, but this has been kept to a minimum. If you are not interested in particular aspects of Java 2, such as using the Swing components or writing threaded applications, you do not have to read those chapters.

If you are an experienced programmer and know C or C++ you will be able to move through the earlier chapters fairly quickly, however there are some surprises in Java which can catch out even experienced programmers. When you are familiar with the basics, you can move to the more advanced features.

If you are an experienced Java programmer, but still using earlier versions of the JDK you will find some significant improvements in Java 2, in particular the Swing components.

This book is a practical, pragmatic introduction to Java, and the best way to improve your skills is to try the examples as you read. Wherever possible, new ideas are illustrated with examples to show how to implement the theory.

The best way to learn Java is to try the example programs on your own computer. If you do want to develop more complex applications or you are interested in a particular aspect of Java, you can go directly to the relevant chapters after you have read the earlier introductory material.

This book is not intended to be a definitive description of Java, if it was it would be about ten times as long and take twenty times as long to read. The philosophy of this book is to cover the key features of Java so that you can write applications as fast as possible. You do not need to read a book which is over a thousand pages long to write Java applications and applets, in fact you do not even need to read all of the chapters in this book before you can begin to develop powerful applications and applets in Java 2.

An object-oriented approach

Designing, writing and testing software is a difficult skill. It is worrying that every application we use contains bugs, in fact even if an application does not contain bugs it is impossible to prove it. To try and reduce the number of bugs in software many different design methodologies have been tried; the latest is object orientation. Many experts agree that it will be the most successful.

A lot of people are put off object orientation by the jargon which surrounds it, but when you get beyond that (this book will help you to do that), you will see that it has significant benefits over any other technique. Object orientation is a powerful way of modelling real-world problems and it has deservedly become the preferred way of designing applications. It is worthwhile gaining an understanding of the key concepts of object orientation before starting to use Java, as it will make it easier for you to develop successful applications.

One of the greatest benefits of object orientation is that when you are writing an application you can use libraries of classes. If you have programmed for a few years you have probably found that there are some programs or program fragments that you have written several times, perhaps for sorting numbers in order of size, or retrieving a list of names and addresses from a file. You may have written these programs in different languages or for different types of computer, or it may just have been too difficult to extract the portion of the program that you wanted to re-use. One of the great features of an object-oriented language is that you can create classes which carry out these common operations and re-use them as often as you want. Since you have already tested these classes you can use them with a high degree of confidence that they will work correctly. This means that you can develop applications more quickly, probably with fewer bugs.

Java 2 has an extensive set of class libraries which provide you with many capabilities, in addition you can build your own class libraries for operations that you often carry out.

To appreciate just how good an object-oriented language Java is, you need to know the concepts behind object-oriented programming. This book describes the essential principles of object-oriented design and after even after the first few chapters you will be able to develop substantial applications. The later chapters look at more complex aspects of Java.

Becoming fluent in a new programming language is difficult and time consuming. Fortunately you do not have to be fluent to produce useful applications. It is best not to try and learn every aspect of the language before you write your first Java program. The best way to learn Java is to read the early chapters and to try the examples for yourself.

Conventions

There are a few conventions used in this book which make it easier to read:

- All program examples are in *italics.*
- Java reserved words, classes, methods and variables defined in the Java API are in **bold**, for example, **float.**
- File names and user-defined identifiers are in *italics,* for example, *myFile.*

2
An Object-Oriented Application

Introduction

The ideas behind object orientation are ones that most people are already familiar with. Most pieces of hardware such as the computers we use are made up of a relatively small number of parts. If these parts are fitted together in the right way you can build a complex piece of equipment very quickly. If you want to build your own PC you can buy a few components such as the mother board, processor, memory, graphics card, and disk drive and plug them together. You do not need to buy individual chips and a soldering iron. If you want to increase the size of your disk drive you just replace it with another drive, you do not attempt to upgrade your existing drive. This idea is widely used to build most pieces of hardware from computers to videos to mobile phones. One of the key ideas behind object orientation is the idea that existing components or objects can be combined to produce complex products.

There are a lot of advantages to this approach. Since the components you are using have been thoroughly tested, you can use them with a high degree of confidence. They are likely to be more reliable than one-off custom-built components. The costs of producing standard components is high, since they must be meticulously designed and tested, but since they are likely to be used by many people the cost per person is low. These components are often straightforward to use. Many people have successfully changed the disk drive in their computer without knowing how the drive works internally.

Unfortunately software is usually not built like this, that is by combining existing objects. Virtually every piece of software is custom made. This has many disadvantages and is very wasteful of programmers' and designers' time. There are dozens of different word processors in use today; each of them took hundreds of man-years to write and each of them does roughly the same thing. It would be much simpler to build a word processor or any piece of software using a pool of existing software objects which are combined together. You would not need to test that each object worked correctly, just the interactions between them. One of the key ideas behind object orientation is that we can build software using a combination of standard existing objects and new objects we create ourselves.

In this chapter we are first going to create a simple Java application which displays a message on the screen, so that you can go through the process of creating, compiling and running an application before looking at more complicated problems. Secondly, we are going to use an object-oriented approach to designing a system for a library which will keep a record of the items stored in that library.

A first application

When learning a new language there is a lot to deal with. In addition to using Java you have to know how to create, compile and run your applications. The first application we are going to look at is only five lines long, but it will allow you to go through the mechanical process of producing an application.

It is a good idea to put every application or applet that you create into its own directory, or it can be difficult to remember which files you are working on.

The application that we are going to create is shown below. It displays the message *My first application* on the screen:

```
public class HelloApplication {                         // start of the class
    public static void main(String args[ ]) {           //start of the main method
        System.out.println("My first application");      //display the message
    }                                                    //end of the main method
}                                                        //end of the class
```

Type this into a text file called *HelloApplication.java* using your favourite editor. The text after // is comment and has no impact on how the application runs, it just helps the programmer.

The next stage is to compile this source file to produce a file called *HelloApplication.class*. If you are working on a Windows 95 or 98 computer you will need to go to the MS-DOS prompt and move to the directory where you have typed your Java source file. To compile the application type:

javac HelloApplication.java

If you have typed the program correctly, it will not display any error message. To run the program, type:

java HelloApplication

This will print the message *My first application* on the screen.

What can go wrong?

Writing and running your first Java application should have gone smoothly, but there are a number of mistakes which commonly occur:

- When you try to compile the application, your computer does not find the compiler *javac*. To correct this, change the path list for your computer to include the directory where the *javac* compiler is stored. If you do not know where it is stored, search for the *javac* file on your computer.
- Java is case-sensitive, so it is essential that you follow exactly the capitalisation of the program.
- The third line is terminated by a semicolon, which it is easy to miss.
- The name of the Java source file must be exactly the same as the name of the **public** class, that is *HelloApplication*.
- When you compile and run the application the name of the file you specify is case sensitive.

How does the application work?

We are not going to look at every aspect of the application, just some features that are common to all applications.

The first line states that we are creating a class called *HelloApplication*. The opening brace { indicates the start of the class definition. The last } in the application signifies the end of the class. All of the applications we are going to write will declare a **public** class at the start.

The second line marks the start of a method called **main**. A method is a collection of Java statements. The start of this method is also indicated by { and it is closed by } two lines further on. The text in brackets after the word **main** is used to pass any parameters from the command line. There are no parameters passed to this application when we run it. Every application has a **main** method declared in exactly the way it is used in this application. When the application starts to run, the **main** method is executed first. However many methods are in your application there will only be one **main** method and it is where the application always starts to run.

The third line of the application displays the text between the quote marks on the screen. If you want to display another line of text you can add another similar line below this one with the text enclosed in quotes.

It is important to note that the { and } are always paired. A common convention is to move the line after { one tab position to the right and to move it back one tab position after a } character. This makes the application easier to read and helps you to spot an opening or closing brace which is not paired.

We are now going to look at developing an object-oriented application. At this stage unless you have used Java before, you will not be familiar with all aspects of the application; the important feature to understand is the object-oriented approach used to design of the application. We will be looking in detail at every aspect used in this application in the next few chapters.

Classes and objects

One of the most common areas of confusion in object-oriented programming is between objects and classes. In the real world there are many objects which have the same characteristics, for example in a library there are many books. A library record system needs to store the same information on each book, such as the title, author, location and cost. The same operations are also performed on each book: its location in the library may change, its title may have been typed incorrectly and need to be changed. The information that is stored on each book and the set of operations that can be carried out on each book is called a class. Any particular book in the library is a member of this class; it is called an object or an instance of this class.

Let's see how we can create this class in Java and create an instance of it. The first stage is to decide what data we want to include in the class, that is what information needs to be saved for each book so that it can be identified and found:

- The author of the book.
- The title.
- The location in the library
- The publisher.

These pieces of data are called the instance variables of the class. Every instance of the class (that is every object) will have this information stored.

In addition to this information what operations do we want to carry out? In this example we are only going to carry out one operation, which will display the details of the book. Operations which are carried out on data in a class are called methods.

The class we are going to create is called *Library*. It can have any name you wish, although it is best to choose one which will have some meaning to you if you look at the class later.

The Java code which represents this class is shown below. Every aspect of the program will be covered later, but at this stage it is important to appreciate how to move to an implementation from a list of the data we want to store for each object in the class and the operations we want to carry out.

```
public class Library {                    //start of the class
    String author;
    String title;
    String location;
    String publisher;

    public void displayDetails() {        //start of the displayDetails method
    System.out.print("Title : " + title);
    System.out.println("   Author : " + author);
    System.out.print("Publisher : " + publisher);
```

```
System.out.println("    Stored at : " + location);
}                                   //end of the displayDetails method
// put the main method here
}                                   //end of the Library class
```

The first word **public** controls how visible this class is to other classes. This is discussed in detail in chapter 8. You can have more than one class in a file, but only one of them can be **public** (not including inner classes). The name of the file must be the same as the name of the **public** class, in this case *Library.java*. Inner classes, which are discussed in chapter 9, are classes which are wholly contained within another class. A file containing a **public** class can also contain **public** inner classes.

The word **class** precedes the name of the class, *Library*.

The opening brace marks the start of the class. It is paired with the corresponding closing brace at the very end of the code.

The four items of data that we want to store for each object in the class are listed. They are all strings, that is text. This defines the instance variables of the class, that is the information which is stored for each object in the class. The next stage is to define the class's single method.

The method is called *displayDetails*. It is preceded by two words: **public** controls the visibility of this method to other methods and classes; **void** means that this method does not return any information.

The opening brace indicates the start of the method and is paired with the closing brace at the end of the method.

The method **System.out.print** displays the text in quotes on the screen followed by the value of the instance variable after the + sign. The method **System.out.println** does the same except that it moves to a new line after printing the text. If you want to see how to read a string from the keyboard this is covered in chapter 16.

The text following the // characters is a comment which has no effect on the way the application runs.

The class *Library*, including its instance variables and its single method, has been defined. The class, however, is simply a definition of the behaviour of objects which belong to this class. To run our application we need to add another method to the application and create an object, that is an instance of the *Library* class. The method that we need to create is called **main**. Every application must have a **main** method.

The main method

When an application starts running, the **main** method is executed first. In the **main** method we are going to create a *Library* object, give its instance variables some data and use the *displayDetails* method to show this information on your screen. The method is inserted just before the final closing brace marking the end of the *Library* class. The Java code for the **main** method is shown below:

```
public static void main(String args[ ]) {          //start of the main method
    Library myBook = new Library( );
```

```
        myBook.author = "P. O'Brien";
        myBook.title = "The Wine Dark Sea";
        myBook.location = "POB66539";
        myBook.publisher = "Pan";
        myBook.displayDetails( );
    }                                          //end of the main method
```

When the application is run it displays the following message:

        Title : P. O'Brien   Author : The Wine Dark Sea
        Publisher : Pan   Stored at : POB66539

What's new

Every application has a **main** method which always starts in the same way.
The second line of the **main** method, shown below creates a new object called *myBook*
which is a member of the *Library* class.

    *Library myBook = **new** Library( );*

The first question that people ask when they see this line is "why do I need to have
the class name *Library* on the left side and the right side of the statement?". The left
side of the line indicates that *myBook* is a member of the *Library* class. The right side
of the line creates the object and runs a special method which has the same name as the
class. This is called a constructor method. Whenever a new object is created, a
constructor method is always run. In this case we have not written a constructor
method, so Java uses a default method which does nothing except initialise variables.

To assign a value to an instance variable the name of the object is specified, followed
by a period and then the name of the instance variable:

    myBook.author = "P. O'Brien";

The object name is *myBook* and we are assigning to its instance variable called
author the text *P. O'Brien*. The other instance variables are assigned in the same way.

A similar notation is used to execute the *displayDetails* method:

    myBook.displayDetails( );

The object name is followed by a period and the name of the method. Note that the
method name is followed by open and close brackets. If information is to be passed to
the method, it is done within these brackets.

You can create as many objects of a class as you wish. To create another object
called *yourBook*:

    *Library yourBook = **new** Library( );*

You can assign its instance variables and use its method in the same way, for
example:

yourBook.title = "Essential Java 2";

Running the application

The process for creating and running this application is the same as for the previous example. Remember that the name of the file containing the *Library* **public** class must be *Library.java*. To compile the application type:

javac Library.java

To run the application type:

java Library

One of the difficulties of learning to program in Java is that there is a lot to learn before you can fully understand even simple applications, compared to IDEs such as Visual Basic or even Visual C++. At this stage it is important to appreciate the concepts of object orientation in the previous example. We look in more detail at the Java language itself in the next chapter.

Using classes and objects

At this stage you should have an application that you have successfully created, compiled and run. It is important to understand the differences between classes and objects since this is fundamental to creating object-oriented applications. A class, such as *Library*, is a template which defines data and methods which operate on that data. An object, such as *myBook*, is a particular member of that class and has its own values for all of the instance variables defined for the class. For example, the *title* instance variable for the *myBook* object is *The Wine Dark Sea*, while the *title* instance variable for the *yourBook* object is *Essential Java 2*.

In the next chapters we look at the syntax of the Java language in detail and how we can create and use other classes and objects.

Naming conventions

You do not have to follow these naming conventions, but they are widely used by Java programmers throughout the world and do help you to read your own, as well as other people's, code more easily:

- Class names always begin with an upper case letter, for example *Library*.
- Constructor methods (covered in chapter 5) must begin with an upper case letter, since they have the same name as the class, for example *Library( )*.
- All non-constructor methods begin with a lower case letter, for example, **main**.

- Names which are made up of more than one word have the start of the second and subsequent words indicated by an upper case letter, for example *myLongVariableName.*

The Java Language

Introduction

In this chapter we are going to look at the Java language in more detail, in particular the different types of data you can use in Java and how you can manipulate it.

Applications and applets

Java can be used to write programs which run directly on computers via the Java interpreter without using a Web browser. Programs which run like this are called *applications*.

One of the special features of Java is that you can write programs which can be run within the environment provided by a Web browser such as Netscape Communicator or Internet Explorer. These types of programs are called *applets*.

In this chapter all of the examples are applications. In chapter 6 we look at the differences between applications and applets and how you can write applets.

Comments

It is important to add some helpful comments to your applications. It is not easy to define exactly where comments should be placed. Most programmers put them at the start of classes and methods and wherever the code is not self-explanatory. Try to avoid an excess of comments which can be distracting.

There are two ways of specifying comments:

// Everything after the two slashes on this line is a comment

/ Comments which go on for more than one line are delimited*
*by the slash/star and star/slash pair as shown */*

Terminating Java statements

Java statements are terminated by a semicolon at the end of the statement. It is easy to forget this and is one of the most common sources of error for new Java programmers.

Data types

One of the key design decisions that you must make when designing an application is to decide what data you need to represent. If, for example, you were saving information on a person, this would include their name, address, sex, salary and so on. Before you use this data in an application you need to decide what type it is and to state that in your application. Java offers a wide range of types as shown in table 3.1:

Table 3.1 *The primitive Java data types.*

Type	Description	Number of bytes
byte	integer	1
short	integer	2
int	integer	4
long	integer	8
float	floating point	4
double	floating point	8
boolean	boolean	1
char	character	2

The integer data types

Integers are whole number quantities and should be used to represent any data item which cannot be fractional, for example the number of rooms in a house, the number of people in a room and the number of television channels.

There are four integer data types: **byte**, **short**, **int** and **long**. They are all signed, that is they can represent both negative and positive numbers. The difference between them is that they are allocated different amounts of space and therefore can represent different ranges of integers. The larger the number of bytes the larger the range of numbers which can be represented:

- **byte** from -128 to 127.
- **short** from -32,768 to 32,767.
- **int** from -2,147,483,648 to 2,147,483,647.
- **long** from -9,223,372,036,854,775,808 to 9,223,372,036,854,775,807.

Most programmers use **int** as the default integer type unless they want to represent a quantity which is particularly small or large. If, for example, you wish to store the size of a typical disk drive in bytes you should use the **long** data type. The age of a person can just be represented by the **byte** data type.

The floating point data types

There are two floating point data types: **float** and **double**. The difference between them is that the **double** data type is stored in 8 bytes rather than 4 bytes. This increases the range of values and also the accuracy with which values can be stored. The positive ranges of values for **float** and **double** variables are:

- **float** from 1.4×10^{-45} to 3.4×10^{38}.
- **double** from 4.9×10^{-324} to 1.8×10^{308}.

The floating point data types should be used to represent quantities which inherently cannot be represented by integers, for example, the time taken to run 100m, a person's height and the average of a number of values. The **double** data type is useful when working with large numbers and when a high degree of accuracy is required. Any operation which requires a lot of complex high accuracy calculation, for example, in meteorology should use the **double** data type. The more calculations which are performed, the greater is the effect of rounding errors in the calculations.

The boolean data type

Booleans are used to represent items which can inherently only be one of two states, for example, a person's gender, yes/no, true/false. A boolean quantity can only be either **true** or **false**.

The char data type

The **char** data type takes up 2 bytes of space and represents a Unicode character which includes all of the familiar A→Z, a→z, 0→9 characters and punctuation marks as well as the vast majority of written characters used throughout the world, for example é and ç.

Table 3.2 *Common escape sequences.*

Code	Description
\n	New line.
\t	Tab.
\b	Backspace.
\r	Carriage return.
\\	Backslash.
\"	" character.

There are some special characters for which Java provides a simple way of writing, using escape sequences. The most commonly-used ones are listed in table 3.2.

The String data type

The **String**. data type is not included in the list of basic data types because **String** is a class. **String** always starts with a capital letter for this reason. A **String** is an instance of the **String** class You can however create and use **String** objects in a similar way to the primitive data types.

Names in Java

When you have decided what type your data is to be, you have to assign it a name. There are a few rules that define what names you can use:

- A name must start with a letter, an underscore (_) or a dollar sign($).
- Subsequent characters can be any of the above plus the digits 0→9.
- The name must not be a Java keyword.

Letters include any character with a Unicode character number above 00C0 which includes accented characters and glyphs, not just letters in the range a→z and A→Z.

These rules apply not only to the names of data items, but also to class, interface and method names.

Declaring data

To declare what type a data item is, specify the data type followed by the name of the variable, for example:

> *byte age;*
> *int count, c, numberOfPeople;*
> *float average, result, height;*

You can list one or more variables, separating them by commas and ending the declaration with a semicolon at the end of the line.

You can also assign initial values to variables when you declare them:

> *double xDimension = 23.51, yDimension = 45.87, zDimension = 65.98;*
> *char newLine = '\n', firstLetter = 'A';*
> *String welcome = "Welcome to the show";*

When assigning a value to a **char** the item must be enclosed in single quotes. Note that \n is a single character which corresponds to a new line. String data must be enclosed in double quotes. A **String** which only contains a single character is not the same as a **char** data item.

Arithmetic in Java

Java has the five usual arithmetic operators, shown in table 3.3.

Table 3.3 *The arithmetic operators.*

Operator	Meaning
+	Addition.
-	Subtraction.
/	Division.
*	Multiplication.
%	Modulus.

The same operator is used for both integer and floating point division. In integer division the result is never rounded up, for example *14/5* is *2* not *3*.

The modulus operator, *%*, gives the remainder after division, for example *14%5* is *4*, since the remainder of *14/5* is *4*.

Mixing data types

You can assign one variable to another using the equality operator, *=,* as you can in most programming languages, but what happens if the variables are of different types? If you perform a mathematical operation which mixes an **int** and a **float** variable, the **int** variable is converted to **float** before any calculations are carried out. Similarly if a **float** and a **double** variable are used, the **float** variable is converted to **double**. The wider the range of values that a data type can represent, the stronger it is, so a **double** is stronger than a **float** which is stronger than an **int**. Java converts a weaker type to a stronger type implicitly.

The application shown below converts kilometres to miles

```
public class KmToMile{
    public static void main(String args[ ]) {
        double kilometre = 3.2, mile;
        mile = kilometre * 5 / 8 ;
        System.out.println(kilometre + " kilometres is " + mile + " miles" );
    }
}
```

It displays the message:

3.2 kilometres is 2.0 miles

In this example, the **int** 5 is multiplied by a **double** value, *kilometre*, therefore it is converted to a **double** before this part of the calculation is carried out. The result is a **double** quantity which is divided by 8, an **int**. This **int** is converted to a **double** and the division is carried out to give a **double** result which is assigned to *mile*, another **double** quantity.

Consider what would happen if one line in the calculation was slightly altered:

mile = 5 / 8 * kilometre;

In this example, both 5 and 8 are **int**, therefore integer division is carried out to give a result of zero. This is converted to a **double** and multiplied by the **double** *kilometre*. It always gives a value of zero. If possible try to avoid arithmetic calculations which mix different data types, since it can cause problems. It would be better to use the following Java code:

mile = 5.0 / 8.0 * kilometre;

In the examples we have seen, the weaker types have been converted automatically to the stronger types. If you attempt to convert a stronger type to a weaker type this will cause an error:

float gallons = 4.5;
double litres;
gallons = litres * 0.22;

There are two problems here. The variable *gallons* is a **float**, but 4.5 is implicitly a **double** quantity, not a **float**. This is a common error in Java. Since a stronger type cannot be assigned to a weaker type this will cause an error. In the calculation, both *litres* and 0.22 are **double**, therefore the result is **double**, but this cannot be assigned to *gallons* since this is a **float** which is a weaker data type. Fortunately there is an easy solution to this problem by explicitly casting a value.

Casting

If you want to convert explicitly from one type to another, you can specify the type that you want the variable to be converted to by placing that type in brackets in front of the variable name, for example:

float gallons = (float) 4.5;
double litres;
gallons = (float)litres * (float)0.22;

This converts 4.5 into a **float** variable to assign it to *gallons*, and converts both *litres* and 0.22 into **float** for the calculation. Note that *litres* remains a **double** quantity if it is used elsewhere. This is called casting.

Assignment operators

We have already seen the assignment operator. In addition there are a few variations which are useful. If you want to assign the same value to more than one variable you can use expressions like the one shown below:

firstCount = secondCount = thirdCount = 0;

All of the variables are assigned the value zero.
There is also a shorthand way of writing expressions such as:

firstCount = firstCount + 7;
newValue = newValue / interval;

In the first line, *firstCount* is increased by 7. In the second line *newValue* is divided by *interval*. In both cases, the left-hand side is assigned to its current value after it has been operated on by a constant or a variable. A shorthand way of rewriting these two lines is:

firstCount += 7;
newValue /= interval;

As you would expect, you can use the subtraction and multiplication operators in the same way, as shown in table 3.4.

Table 3.4 *Shortcut operators.*

Operation	Meaning
c += d	c = c + d
c -= d	c = c - d
c /= d	c = c / d
c *= d	c = c * d
c++	c = c + 1
c--	c = c - 1

There is a special case of this type of operation, when an integer value is incremented or decremented by one:

firstCount = firstCount + 1;
firstCount += 1;
firstCount++;

All three of these lines perform the same operation. You can also use:

++firstCount;

If you want to decrease a variable by one, you can use either of these notations:

firstCount--;
--firstCount;

It is more common to add the operators after the variable name rather than before.

Why does Java provide these different ways of specifying the same operations? First, the notation is easy to use and most Java programmers feel that it provides a concise way of specifying these common operations. The second reason is that the code generated by the compiler may be different. If, for example, the ++ operator is specified, this is a signal to the compiler to use the increment instruction in the assembler rather than the addition instruction. Since the increment instruction may execute several times faster than the add instruction, the program will run faster. In practice, these days a good optimising compiler can determine the most efficient instructions to use, but the notation has been used and liked by many C++ programmers and so it is reasonable to stick with it.

Using strings in Java

In Java a string is a sequence of characters, and an instance of the class **String**, which has a set of methods for manipulating strings. You can concatenate strings using the + operator.

Strings can be defined just as if they were one of the basic types such as **float**, for example:

```
public class UsingStrings {
    public static void main(String args[ ]) {
        String best, worst, myPreferences;
        best = " Java ";
        worst = " COBOL ";
        myPreferences = "I prefer";
        myPreferences += best + "to";
        myPreferences += worst;
        System.out.println(myPreferences);
    } //end of the main method
} //end of the UsingStrings class
```

This application contains a single class called *UsingStrings*. It has one method called **main**. All applications must have a **main** method, which is where the application starts to run. Three **String** objects are created. The **String** *myPreferences* is built up to contain the text *I prefer Java to COBOL*. The **System.out.println** method displays this message on your screen.

It is important at this stage to try these applications for yourself. The most common problem is to make a mistake with the capitalisation of words. Java is case sensitive and, for example, *system* is not the same as *System*.

Operator precedence

When a sequence of mathematical operations is carried out, the order in which this is done can be very important, for example:

c = 9 + 6 / 3;

If the addition is carried out first the expression becomes 15/3 = 5. If the division is done first, it becomes 9+2 = 11. In this case, the division would be done first, since the division operator has a higher precedence than the addition operator. The operators, in order of precedence, are listed in table 3.5. If you are in doubt, or want to make it clear to another programmer who looks at your code later what the precedence is, it is a good idea to use brackets, since operations in brackets are always carried out first, for example:

average = (value1 + value2 + value3) / 3;

Table 3.5 *Operator precedence.*

Operator	Meaning
( ) [ ] .	Brackets. The . operator accesses methods and variables.
++ -- ! ~	Increment, decrement, not, complement.
new	Creates a new instance of a class.
* / %	Multiplication, division, modulus.
+ -	Addition, subtraction.
<< >>	Left shift, right shift.
< > <= >=	Less than, greater than.
== !=	Equal to, not equal to.
&	Bitwise AND.
^	Bitwise XOR.
|	Bitwise OR.
&&	Logical AND.
||	Logical OR.
= += -= *= /= %= ^= &= |= <<= >>=	These eleven operators all different forms of assignment.

When operators have the same precedence, the leftmost one is carried out first.

Displaying information on your screen

As we have seen, when you wish to display information on the screen in an application you use statements of the form:

System.out.println("Hello");

The **System** class has three fields which are using for input and output:

- **out** the standard output stream.
- **err** the standard error stream.
- **in** the standard input stream.

The standard output stream, **out**, and the error stream **err** are objects of the **PrintStream** class. This class has a comprehensive set of methods for displaying not only a **String**, but also all of the basic Java data types. You can also display more than one data type using **println** for example:

```
public class PrintlnClass {
    public static void main(String args[ ]) {
    int population = 45000000;
    float age = (float)23.4;
    String language = "Amharic";
    System.out.println("The language of Ethiopia is " + language);
    System.out.println("The population is " + population);
    System.out.println("The average age is " + age);
    }
}
```

This application has a single class and a **main** method. It defines an **int** variable called *population* and gives it a value of 45000000. A **float** variable called *age* is defined and assigned an initial value of 23.4. Note that 23.4 is implicitly **double**, but is explicitly cast to a **float** variable. Failing to do this is a common error. This application displays the text:

```
The language of Ethiopia is Amharic
The population is 45000000
The average age is 23.4
```

The **println** method adds a carriage return and line feed after displaying the specified information, so that the next item printed starts on a new line. If you want to print text on the same line use the **print** method in exactly the same way

The error stream, **err**, usually sends output to the same place as the standard output stream, **out**, on most systems.

The standard input stream, **in**, is a member of the **InputStream** class. Reading information from the keyboard is more complex than information and is covered in chapter 16.

4
Branching and Looping

Introduction

All programming languages allow you to write programs which do different things depending on the value of data. This gives computer programs the impression of intelligence – they are able to respond to changing data inputs. Java is no exception and allows you to write conditional statements using **if…else** statements

All of the programs we have looked at consist of lines of code that are run one after another, without any looping or conditional statements. All programming languages need to be able to repeat some parts of the program more than once. Java has three types of loop: **for**, **while** and **do**.

The If...else statement

In common with most programming languages the **if** statement provides a way for your programs to make decisions. The basic form of the **if** statement is:

if (condition) statement;

If the condition is met, the following statement is executed. If it is not met, the statement is ignored.

The condition takes the form of a test between two values. You can test for equality, non-equality, or if one value is larger or smaller than the other. Java has the usual set of operators that are found in most programming languages, as listed in table 4.1.

Table 4.1 *The comparison operators.*

Operator	Meaning
==	Equal.
!=	Not equal.
<	Less than.
>	Greater than.
<=	Less than or equal to.
>=	Greater than or equal to.

One common mistake when using **if** statements is to confuse the assignment operator = with the comparison operator = =. If you are unused to writing Java code this can be a hard mistake to spot the first few times.

To see the **if** statement in action we are going to look at a class called *FastEnough*.

```
public class FastEnough {
    int speed, memory;
        public static void main(String args[ ]) {
        FastEnough myComputer = new FastEnough( );
        myComputer.speed = 150;
        myComputer.checkSpeed( );
    }
    public void checkSpeed( ) {
        if (speed < 200) System.out.println(speed + " MHz is too slow");
    }
}
```

This class has two **int** instance variables called *speed* and *memory* representing the speed and memory size of a computer. The *memory* variable is used in the *checkMemoryAndSpeed* and *checkMemory* methods which are added later. Initially the *FastEnough* class has only two methods:

- The **main** method creates a *FastEnough* object and assigns a value to the *speed* of the computer.
- The *checkSpeed* method displays a message if the *speed* instance variable is less than 200 MHz.

When the application is run the **main** method is executed. This creates an instance of the *FastEnough* class called *myComputer*. Since *myComputer* is an object of class *FastEnough* it has copies of the *speed* and *memory* instance variables and can use the *checkSpeed* method of the *FastEnough* class.

The instance variable *speed* is assigned a value of 150 for the *myComputer* object. The notation used to reference an instance variable is to specify the name of the object(*myComputer*), the '.' character and then the name of the instance variable(*speed*).

The *checkSpeed* method for the *myComputer* object is called. A similar notation is used - the name of the object(*myComputer*), the '.' character and then the name of the method(*checkSpeed*) followed by the opening and closing brackets.

In the *checkSpeed* method, the **if** statement checks to see if the *speed* (in this case 150) is less than 200 and if it is prints the message *150 MHz is too slow*.

The **if** statement can be extended by adding an **else** clause. This has the basic form:

> **if** *(condition) statement1;* **else** *statement2;*

If the condition is met, *statement1* is executed, if it is not *statement2* is executed. Let's see this in action in an improved *checkSpeed* method:

```
public void checkSpeed( ) {
    if (speed < 200) System.out.println(speed + " MHz is too slow");
    else System.out.println(speed + " MHz is fast enough");
}
```

If the *speed* is 150 the same message *150 MHz is too slow* is displayed, if the *speed* is changed to 300, the message *300 MHz is fast enough* is displayed.

You can have as many **else** clauses as you wish, for example if the *checkSpeed* method is extended further:

```
public void checkSpeed( ) {
    if (speed < 200) System.out.println(speed + " MHz is too slow");
    else if (speed < 300) System.out.println(speed + " MHz is fast enough");
    else if (speed < 400) System.out.println(speed + " MHz is very fast");
    else if (speed <=450) System.out.println(speed + " MHz is the best");
    else System.out.println("Does your PC really run at " + speed + " MHz ?");
}
```

Only one message is displayed, depending on the speed of your computer. If your computer speed is, for example, 200 MHz, this is less than 300, so the message is *200 MHz is fast enough*. 200 is also less than 400 and less than 450, but these messages are not displayed. When one condition is met, the following statement is executed and the remainder of the **if**...**else** statement is ignored. If your computer speed is over 450 MHz a message questioning this is displayed. If none of the previous conditions are met, this unconditional statement is executed.

Logical operators

Often in an **if**...**else** statement you need to test more one condition. For example, you may wish to check not only the processor speed but also the amount of memory. The basic form of these statements is:

> **if** *((condition) logical operator (condition)) statement;*

You can have as many conditions separated by logical operators as you wish. Note the use of the brackets which is mandatory. A new method can be added to the *FastEnough* class which checks both the *speed* and *memory* variables:

```
public void checkMemoryAndSpeed( ) {
    if ((speed < 200) || (memory < 32)) System.out.println("Upgrade");
}
```

To demonstrate this method the *memory* instance variable for the *myComputer* class must be assigned a value and the method called by adding two lines to the **main** method:

```
myComputer.memory = 16;
myComputer.checkMemoryAndSpeed( );
```

The logical operator used in the *checkMemoryAndSpeed* method is the inclusive OR operator and is represented by two vertical lines as shown. If either, or both of the conditions is met the following statement is executed. In this example, if either the processor speed is less than 200 or the memory size is less than 32, or both, the message to upgrade is displayed.

The most common logical operators are shown in table 4.2.

Table 4.2 *The logical operators.*

Operator	Meaning
&&	AND, true if all conditions are met
||	Inclusive OR, true if any of the conditions are met.
^	Exclusive XOR., true if only one condition is met.
!	NOT, changes a true to false or a false to true.

The NOT operator ! is different from the other operators in that it requires only a single expression. If the expression evaluates to **true** this operator changes it to **false** and vice versa. The two expressions below have the same effect, although the first one is much clearer:

```
if (age >= 18) System.out.println("You can vote");
if (!(age < 18)) System.out.println("You can vote");
```

The switch statement

As the number of **else** clauses becomes greater it can be confusing. The **switch...case** construct provides a shorthand way of writing certain **if...else** statements, for example we could add a method called *checkMemory* to the *FastEnough* class which checks the memory size:

```
public void checkMemory( ) {
    String m;
```

```
        if (memory == 16) m = "far too little";
        else if (memory == 32) m = "just enough";
        else if (memory == 64) m = "sufficient memory";
        else m = "ample memory";
        System.out.println(memory + " MB is " + m);
}
```

Depending on the size of memory the **String** *m* is assigned the appropriate text. A different message is displayed depending on the memory size. If, for example, the memory size is 64 the message *64 MB is sufficient memory* is displayed.

This method can be called from the **main** method:

```
    myComputer.checkMemory( );
```

Exactly the same result can be achieved using a **switch** construct. The basic form is:

```
switch(variable) {
        case(value)    :    statements;
        case(value)    :    statements;
        default    :    statements;        //the default clause is optional
}
```

You can have as many **case** clauses as you wish. A modified form of the *checkMemory* method which uses **switch…case** statements is shown below:

```
public void checkMemory( ) {
        String m;
        switch (memory) {
            case(16)  :    m = "far too little";
                            break;
            case(32)  :    m = "just enough";
                            break;
            case(64)  :    m = "sufficient memory";
                            break;
            default    :    m = "ample memory";
        }
        System.out.println(memory + " MB is " + m);
}
```

If the value of the **int** variable *memory* is 16 the corresponding assignment statement is executed, followed by the **break** statement. The **break** statement ensures that the remainder of this **switch…case** statement is ignored. If you do not include **break** statements, the program executes until a condition is met and then the corresponding statement and all the following statements are executed.

If none of the specified conditions are met, the optional **default** statement is executed if it has been included.

There are a few limitations on the use of this statement. You can only test for four primitive types: **byte**, **char**, **int** and **short**. You cannot test for any condition apart from equality. Despite these limitations this is a useful statement that should be used in preference to multiple **if**...**else** statements wherever possible.

Block statements

A useful feature of Java is that a set of statements can be grouped to behave like a single statement by enclosing them within a { } pair, for example:

```
public class YouCanDrive {
    public static void main(String args[ ]) {
        int age = 17;
        if (age == 17) {
        System.out.println("You can drive a car");
        System.out.println("You can get married");
        System.out.println("but you can't vote");
        }
    }
}
```

If *age* is 17, then all three lines following the **if** statement are executed. Anywhere you can use a single statement you can use a group of statements within the { } pair.

Looping

Loops allow the same block of code to be repeated many times. There are three types of loop in Java. They are:

- **for** loops.
- **while** loops.
- **do**...**while** loops.

The for loop

One of the most common things that programmers want to do in a loop is to increment or decrement a value: **for** loops provide a way of doing this. The **for** loop has three components followed by the loop body.

```
for (count = 0; count < 10; count++) {
    System.out.println("count is " + count);
}
```

- The first part, *count* = 0, initialises the loop. If you have a loop counter, such as *count*, you can give it an initial value.

- The second part, *count < 10*, is the test condition. The body of the loop enclosed in braces will execute while this condition is met.
- The third part, *count++*, is an expression that is evaluated every time the body of the loop executes. While this is usually used to increment or decrement a loop counter, other expressions, for example *count += 3* can be used instead.

In the example, above the braces enclosing the body of the loop could have been omitted, since if they are not found, the body of the loop is expected to be only one line long.

Let's look at an application which uses loops. Recently 4,000 mink were released from a farm in Norfolk, England, the application shown below calculates how many mink there will be in 10 years, assuming there are as many male as female mink, they produce eight offspring every year, the new mink are ready to breed after a year and that no mink ever dies!

```java
public class Mink {
    int years, population;
    public static void main( String args[ ]) {
        Mink norfolk = new Mink( );
        norfolk.years = 10;
        norfolk.population = 4000;
        norfolk.howManyMink( );
    }
    public void howManyMink( ) {
        for (int c=1; c <= years; c++) {
            population += population/2 * 4;
            System.out.print("After " + c + " years ");
            System.out.println("there will be " + population + " mink");
        }
    }
}
```

The *Mink* class has two **int** instance variables:

- *years*, the number of years over which the population is to be calculated.
- *population*, the initial number of mink.

This class has two methods. The **main** method creates an instance of the *Mink* class, that is a *Mink* object, called *norfolk*, and assigns values to the variables *years* and *population* for that object.

The *howManyMink* method is called from the **main** method. This method calculates the number of mink, in this case after 10 years if the initial population of mink is 4000.

In the **for** loop, the initial value of the integer *c* is 1, every time the program goes around the loop it is increased and a test made to see if this loop counter is less than or equal to the number of years for which we want to carry out the calculations. When this condition is no longer met the loop ends.

Note that *c* is declared within the **for** statement and only exists while the loop is being executed. You could have declared *c* outside of the loop in the usual way, but if it is not going to be used elsewhere it is a less efficient use of memory.

The **for** statement is followed by an opening { and three lines before a closing } is found. All three of these statements are executed since they are within the { } pair. If these braces are omitted, only the line immediately following the **for** statement is executed.

If you run this application you will see the alarming message that there will be 236,196,000 mink in Norfolk in ten years time.

The while loop

We could have written the *howManyMink* method using a **while** loop, but it would have been rather more clumsy. The **while** loop has two parts: the body of the loop and a preceding condition. For example:

```
public void howManyMink( ) {
    int c = 1;
    while (c <= years) {
        population += population/2 * 4;
        System.out.print("After " + c + " years ");
        System.out.println("there will be " + population + " mink");
        c++;
    }
}
```

In this method, the test condition is *c <= years*, when this condition is met the loop is executed. The loop counter *c* is defined in the normal way and explicitly incremented at the end of the loop. The behaviour is exactly the same as the previous *howManyMink* method

You can include multiple test conditions in the **while** clause in the same way that you can have more than one test condition in an **if**...**else** statement.

The do...while loop

do...**while** loops are similar to **while** loops and in most cases they can be substituted for each other. The code below performs in a similar way to the previous example:

```
public void howManyMink( ) {
    int c = 1;
    do {
        population += population/2 * 4;
        System.out.print("After " + c + " years ");
        System.out.println("there will be " + population + " mink");
        c++;
```

```
} while (c <= years);
}
```

The body of the loop is preceded by **do** and an opening brace. The **while** condition follows the closing brace is at the end of the block.

In this case this method does exactly the same as the previous method which uses a loop with the **while** clause at the start. In some cases however there are differences between the two types of loops. A **do...while** loop is always executed at least once, since the test is at the end. A **while** loop which tests at the start may not be executed even once if the test fails.

The break statement

If you want to leave a loop before it ends, that is before the test condition is satisfied, you can use the **break** statement to exit from the current loop. The method shown below calculates when the mink population will exceed one million. The **do...while** loop is endless, since there is no test condition, just a **true** boolean. The only way in which the loop can end is when the population exceeds 1,000,000. When this occurs the **break** statement is executed and the loop is exited. The statement after the loop displays the message *Population will exceed 1 million after 6 years*.

```
public void moreThanOneMillion(int years, int population) {
    int c = 1;
    do {
        population += population/2 * 4;
        if (population > 1000000) break;
        c++;
    } while (true);
    System.out.println("Population will exceed 1 million after " + c + " years");
}
```

If you wish, you can add a label to the start of the loop and specify this label in the **break** statement as shown:

```
public void moreThanOneMillion(int years, int population) {
    int c = 1;
popLoop:
    do {
        population += population/2 * 4;
        if (population > 1000000) break popLoop;
        c++;
    } while (true);
    System.out.println("Population will exceed 1 million after " + c + " years");
}
```

This example quits the loop whose start is indicated by the *popLoop* label. If the loop is not nested within another, there is no difference between a labelled and an unlabelled **break** statement. If, however the loop is nested and one of the outer loops is labelled, the **break** statement can not only jump out of the inner loop it is executing, but also the outer loops.

A variation on the **break** statement is the **continue** statement. When a **continue** statement is executed the program ignores the remainder of the loop and goes to the start of the loop again. You can also have labelled **continue** statements. It does not matter how many nested loops there are or if they are of different types.

Arrays

Arrays are lists or tables of items. You can have one-dimensional arrays, for example a list of people's names, or a list of prices, or you can have multi-dimensional arrays, for example a timetable which has different trains along the horizontal axis and destinations along the vertical axis. In each of the grid squares defined by a particular train and a destination is the time that the train will arrive at that point. Arrays in Java can have many dimensions. Every element in an array is of the same type.

To declare a one-dimensional array you can use either of the following notations:

int ages[ ];

or:

int[ ] ages;

Just pick one of these and stick with it for consistency.

Next you have to create an array object:

*ages = **new** int[5];*

This creates a list of 5 integer items. The first is referred to as *ages[0]* and the last as *ages[4]*.

You can combine the stages of type declaration and instantiation in the single line:

*int[ ] ages = **new** int[5];*

The array elements are initialized (0 for numbers, **false** for booleans, null for strings and \0 for characters), however you can specify the initial values of the array elements:

int[ ] ages = {23, 45, 87, 17, 9};

This defines a five element array of type **int** and assigns *ages[0]* the number 23, *ages[1]* the number 45, and so on.

You can initialise a **String** array in a similar way:

***String[ ]** languages = {"Java", "C++", "Object Pascal"};*

Note that each element is enclosed in quotes.

If you want to change an array element you do so by specifying its name and the element that you want to change:

languages[2] = "Visual Basic";

You can create multi-dimensional arrays, although strictly speaking this is really an array of arrays:

   int table[ ][ ] = *new int[10][10];*

You address each element in a similar way, for example:

   table[4][6] = 90;

5
Creating and Using Classes and Objects

Introduction

We have looked at many of the key components of the Java language. In this chapter we are going to look in more detail at how to use the object-oriented aspects of Java to create and use classes and objects. In particular, we are going to look at how information is passed between methods and how constructor methods are used.

The Account class

The next application that we are going to develop has a single class called *Account* which keeps a record of bank account details. This class has five instance variables:

- *name* - a **String** representing the name of the customer.
- *address* - a **String** representing the address of the customer.
- *accountNumber* - a **String** giving a unique identifier for the account.
- *balance* - a **double** giving the amount of money in the account.

It also has five methods:

- *displayDetails* displays the account details.
- *inCredit* returns a **true** value if the account balance is zero or positive and **false** if the account is overdrawn.
- *credit* adds a specified amount to the balance.
- *debit* subtracts a specified amount from the balance.
- **main** creates an instance of the *Account* class and assigns values to its instance variables.

The definition of the instance variables is shown below:

```
public class Account {
    String name;
    String address;
    String accountNumber;
    double balance;
```

Every object we create which is an instance of the *Account* class will have its own set of these instance variables.

The displayDetails method

The first method we are going to add to this class is *displayDetails*, which prints the account details:

```
public void displayDetails( ) {
    System.out.println("Name : " + name);
    System.out.println("Address : " + address);
    System.out.println("Account number : " + accountNumber);
    System.out.println("Account balance : " + balance);
}
```

The access modifier for this method is **public**. Access modifiers control the degree of access to classes, methods and variables. There are three explicit access modifiers:

- **public** - access is allowed by all methods in all packages.
- **protected** - access is allowed by all methods in the class or in any subclasses.
- **private** - access is allowed only by methods within the class itself.

In addition, if an access modifier is not explicitly given, a default access modifier called *package* is used which gives access by subclasses and classes in the same package. A package is a collection of Java classes which have a related functionality. Java has many standard packages for example **java.awt** which is a collection of classes for creating user interfaces and displaying graphics. The classes in a package are made available to an application by an **import** statement as described in chapter 6.

The access modifiers are described in more detail in chapter 8.

It is good practice to reduce the degree of access to the minimum; it cuts down on the number of possible interactions and makes it easier to spot errors when they do occur.

The method is also described as **void**. This specifies the type of information that a method returns. A **void** method does not return any information. An **int** method returns an **int** data item and so on, by using the reserved word **return** followed by a literal or identifier of the correct type.

The inCredit method

The *inCredit* method, shown below, is also **public**, but returns a **boolean** value, that is it returns either **true** or **false** to the calling method.

```
public boolean inCredit( ) {
    if (balance < 0.00) return false; else return true;
}
```

This method checks to see if the account is overdrawn or in credit. The value returned is that specified in the **return** statement. If a method is specified as **boolean**, it must return a **boolean** value. Similarly a **float** method must return a **float** value. Methods can return any of the basic data types or an object of any type.

The credit and debit methods

The *credit* and *debit* methods are **public** and do not return any value since they are both **void**, but data is passed to them. A **double** value which is called *amount* (any name could be used) is passed to these methods and used to alter the balance.

```
public void credit(double amount) {
    balance = balance + amount;
}
public void debit(double amount) {
    balance = balance - amount;
}
```

When either of these methods is called, a **double** value (either a **double** number or identifier) is placed within the brackets. This value is then passed to the method. Note that the **double** variable *amount* in the *credit* method is not the same **double** variable *amount* in the *debit* method. These are both local variables which only exist within the method in which are used.

The main method

We have now defined all of the instance variables of the class and defined all of the methods. To use this class we are going to create an instance of the class, that is an *Account* object, in the **main** method, assign some values to the instance variables and use the methods:

```
public static void main (String args[ ]) {
    Account sam = new Account( );        // creates an instance of Account
    sam.name = "Sam Taylor";
    sam.address = "37 Church Lane, St. Neots, Cornwall, TR26 4RD";
    sam.accountNumber = "1448-985-881";
    sam.balance = -187.87;
```

```
        sam.credit(100.00);
        sam.debit(30.00);
        sam.displayDetails( );
        if (sam.inCredit( )) System.out.println("In credit");
        else System.out.println("Overdrawn");
}
```

The statement:

*Account sam = **new** Account( );   // creates an instance of Account*

creates an instance of the *Account* class called *sam*. To assign a value to one of the instance variables the following notation is used:

objectName.instanceVariable = value;

for example:

sam.name = "Sam Taylor";

This statement assigns the instance variable, *name*, for the *sam* object to *Sam Taylor* To use one of the methods a very similar notation is used:

objectName.methodName(data);

for example:

sam.credit(100.00);

This statement executes the *credit* method and passes the value 100.00 to the method where it is added to the balance. If no information is to be passed to the method, the brackets after the method name must still be used, as shown below:

sam.displayDetails( );

The value which is returned by methods which are not declared **void** can be used in the calling method, for example:

*if (sam.inCredit( )) **System**.out.println("In credit");*
*else **System**.out.println("Overdrawn");*

The method *inCredit* returns a **boolean** value. If this is **true** the message *In credit* is displayed, otherwise *Overdrawn* is displayed.

You can create as many objects of type *Account* as you wish. They will all have different values for the instance variables (they are called instance variables because every instance, or object you create has its own set of variables). The full application shown below, creates two *Account* objects called *sam* and *ann*, assigns values to their instance variables and uses the methods:

```
public class Account {
    String name;
    String address;
    String accountNumber;
```

```
    double balance;
    public static void main (String args[ ]) {
        Account sam = new Account( );
        sam.name = "Sam Taylor";
        sam.address = "37 Church Lane, St. Neots, Cornwall, TR26 4RD";
        sam.accountNumber = "1448-985-881";
        sam.balance = -187.87;
        Account ann = new Account( );
        ann.name = "Ann Cauldercote";
        ann.address = "19 Kents Hill, Olney, MK34 7YT";
        ann.accountNumber = "9987-734-276";
        ann.balance = 972.39;
        sam.credit(100.00);
        sam.debit(30.00);
        sam.displayDetails( );
        if (sam.inCredit( )) System.out.println("In credit");
        else System.out.println("Overdrawn");
        ann.displayDetails( );
        if (ann.inCredit( )) System.out.println("In credit");
        else System.out.println("Overdrawn");
    }
    public void displayDetails( ) {
        System.out.println("Name : " + name);
        System.out.println("Address : " + address);
        System.out.println("Account number : " + accountNumber);
        System.out.println("Account balance : " + balance);
    }
    public void credit(double amount) {
        balance = balance + amount;
    }
    public void debit(double amount) {
        balance = balance - amount;
    }
    public boolean inCredit( ) {
        if (balance < 0.00) return false; else return true;
    }
}
```

When you run this application it displays the following text:

Name : Sam Taylor
Address : 37 Church Lane, St. Neots, Cornwall, TR26 4RD
Account Number : 1448-985-881
Account balance : -117.87
Overdrawn

Name : Ann Cauldercote
Address : 19 Kents Hill, Olney, MK34 7YT
Account Number : 9987-734-276
Account balance : 972.39
In credit

Using constructors

The application we have created works as required, but it can be greatly improved. The most long winded part of the application is that we create an instance of the *Account* class and then have to allocate initial values to each of its instance variables. This is a very common thing to do when programming in Java and there is a streamlined way of doing it using a constructor method. A constructor method has the same name as the class itself and is executed when an object is instantiated. Constructors are therefore the only methods which always start with an uppercase letter, since classes should always start with an uppercase letter. The generalised form of instantiating an object is:

*classname objectName = **new** constructor(data items);*

for example, to instantiate an *Account* object:

*Account sam = **new** Account( );*

Since we have not actually written a constructor for this class, a default constructor simply initialises the values of instance variables to the default initial values. It would improve this application if we created a constructor for the *Account* class and passed it the required initial values of the instance variables. The constructor which does this is shown below:

public *Account(**String** nam, **String** add, **String** acc, **double** bal) {*
    name = nam;
    address = add;
    accountNumber = acc;
    balance = bal;
}

Note that the constructor has the same name as the class, *Account*. It cannot have any return type. It is passed four values which are assigned to the instance variables. To call this constructor for the *sam* object:

*Account sam = **new** Account("Sam Taylor",*
                             "37 Church Lane, St. Neots, Cornwall, TR26 4RD",
                             "1448-985-881",
                             -187.87);

Similarly for the *ann* object:

*Account ann = **new** Account("Ann Cauldercote",*
                                "19 Kents Hill, Olney, MK34 7YT",
                                "9987-734-276",
                                972.39);

These statements will instantiate the objects and also assign to the instance variables the specified initial values.

Encapsulating data

The introduction of a constructor method has improved our application, but perhaps you are wondering why we need to have some of the methods we have created, for example, the *credit* method (shown below) simply adds the specified figure to the balance.

```
public void credit(double amount) {
    balance = balance + amount;
}
```

Surely it would be easier simply to access the instance variable balance directly, for example for the *sam* object:

sam.balance = sam.balance + amount;

It is generally not a good idea to allow direct access to the instance variables of a class. It is better programming practice to reduce the visibility of instance variables to other classes and to provide accessor methods which access these instance variables for you. It makes it easier to find bugs when they occur, since you know that an instance variable can only be changed by using a method rather than modified directly.

Let's see how to modify the application we have written so that we have two classes, the *Account* class which contains the instance variable definitions and the methods and a second class called *NewAccount* which contains the **main** method (where the application starts running) and creates an instance of the *Account* class. We are going to make the following changes to the *Account* class:

- Make all of the instance variables **private**, so that they can only be accessed by methods in the *Account* class.
- Add accessor methods which return the values of the instance variables.
- Remove the **main** method (and place it into the *NewAccount* class).
- Make the *NewAccount* class the **public** class, since it is to contain the **main** method. You can only have one public class in a file. The name of the file must be the same as the name of this class.

The definition of the instance variables in the *Account* class is shown below:

```
class Account {
    private String name;
    private String address;
```

```
private String accountNumber;
private double balance;
...
```

The constructor method is unchanged, as are the *displayDetails*, *credit*, *debit* and *inCredit* methods. There are two sets of accessor methods which must be added, to set the values of the instance variables and to get them, for example to set the *name* instance variable:

```
public void setName(String customerName) {
    name = customerName;
}
```

This method changes the current value of the *name* instance variable to the **String** specified. For the *sam* object it is called in this way:

```
sam.setName("Samuel Taylor");        //change from Sam Taylor
```

There are corresponding methods for setting and getting all of the other instance variables, for example *getAddress( )* and *setAddress( )*.

This technique may seem to add complexity but it allows you much greater control over the use of your data. It is widely used throughout the standard set of Java classes to provide a controlled way of setting and getting the instance variables in a class. Note that it is no longer possible to access the instance variables directly, for example, the line of code:

```
sam.name = "Samuel Taylor";
```

is no longer permitted in any class except the *Account* class and will produce a compiler error (since the instance variable *name* is defined in the *Account* class and is **private** it is only accessible within that class). To change the *name* variable the accessor method *setName* must be used:

```
sam.setName("Samuel Taylor");
```

A completed version of the two classes and some examples of using the new accessor methods is shown below:

```
public class NewAccount {
    public static void main (String args[ ]) {
        Account sam = new Account("Sam Taylor",
                        "37 Church Lane, St. Neots, Cornwall, TR26 4RD",
                        "1448-985-881",
                        -187.87);
        sam.displayDetails( );
        if (sam.inCredit( )) System.out.println("In credit");
        else System.out.println("Overdrawn");
        sam.setName("Samuel Taylor");        // change name
        System.out.println("Confirmation of new name : " + sam.getName( ));
        sam.setAddress("17 High Street, Derby, DE5 6TY");  // change address
```

```
                sam.setBalance(32387.67);          // change the balance
                sam.displayDetails( );             //display all details again
        }
}
class Account {
        private String name;
        private String address;
        private String accountNumber;
        private double balance;
        public Account(String nam, String add, String acc, double bal) {
                name = nam;
                address = add;
                accountNumber = acc;
                balance = bal;
        }
        public void displayDetails( ) {
                System.out.println("Name : " + name);
                System.out.println("Address : " + address);
                System.out.println("Account number : " + accountNumber);
                System.out.println("Account balance : " + balance);
        }
        public void setName(String customerName) {
                name = customerName;
        }
        public void setAddress(String customerAddress) {
                address = customerAddress;
        }
        public void setAccountNumber(String customerNumber) {
                accountNumber = customerNumber;
        }
        public void setBalance(double customerBalance) {
                balance = customerBalance;
        }
        public String getName( ) {
                return(name);
        }
        public String getAddress( ) {
                return(address);
        }
        public String getAccountNumber( ) {
                return(accountNumber);
        }
        public double getBalance( ) {
                return(balance);
        }
```

```
    public void credit(double amount) {
        balance = balance + amount;
    }
    public void debit(double amount) {
        balance = balance - amount;
    }
    public boolean inCredit( ) {
        if (balance < 0.00)return false; else return true;
    }
}
```

This application produces the following output:

Name : Sam Taylor
Address : 37 Church Lane, St. Neots, Cornwall, TR26 4RD
Account number 1448-985-881
Account balance : -187.87
Overdrawn
Confirmation of new name : Samuel Taylor
Name : Samuel Taylor
Address : 17 High Street, Derby, DE5 6TY
Account number 1448-985-881
Account balance : 32387.67

Calling methods

When you have created an object you can call a method by specifying the object name and then the name of the method. If we add a new method to the *Account* class called *creditReport* we can call it as shown below:

sam.creditReport( );

The *creditReport* method is shown below:

```
public void creditReport( ) {
    String m;
    displayDetails( );
    if (inCredit( )) m = "in credit";
    else if (getBalance( ) > -100) m = "overdrawn - send notification";
    else if (getBalance( ) > -1000) m = "overdrawn - send warning letter";
    else m = "Overdrawn - send suspend account notification";
    System.out.println("Account " + m);
}
```

This method displays the bank account details followed by a variety of messages depending on the balance of the account. It calls three other methods of the *Account* class: *displayDetails*, *inCredit* and *getBalance* without specifying which object they refer to. The object whose instance variables are operated on in the *creditReport* method is called *sam*. This is implicitly passed to the *displayDetails*, *inCredit* and *getBalance* methods which therefore do not need to have the object explicitly specified when they are called.

In summary, when one method calls another method in the same class it is not necessary to specify the object name.

Command line arguments for applications

Sometimes when you are running an application you may want to pass some information to it from the command line, for example:

java PrintMyName John

This runs an application called *PrintMyName* and prints the message:

Hello John

In this example the text *John* is a command line argument. It is better to enclose the argument in quotes, that is:

java PrintMyName "John"

If you omit the quotes and the argument string includes a space, the space will signify the end of the first argument and the next printable character is the start of the second argument.

When applications run, the first method to be executed is the **main** method. This is passed an array of strings, which contain any information which is passed to the application when it started.

```
public class PrintMyName {
    public static void main (String args[ ]) {
        System.out.println("Hello " + args[0]);
    }
}
```

The array element *args*[0] contains the **String** *John*.

If you want to pass two arguments you separate the items by a space, for example:

java PrintOurNames "John Cowell" "Sally Aldridge"

This application prints the two names which have been passed:

```
public class PrintOurNames {
    public static void main (String args[ ]) {
        System.out.println("Hello " + args[0]);
        System.out.println("Hello " + args[1]);
    }
}
```

If you do not know how many arguments have been passed you can find this from the **length** of the array:

```
public class PrintEveryonesNames{
    public static void main (String args[ ]) {
        for (int c = 0; c < args.length; c++)
            System.out.println("Hello " + args[c]);
    }
}
```

This application displays the name of everyone listed.

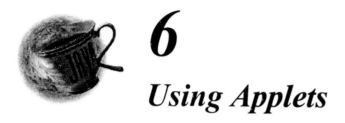

6

Using Applets

Introduction

One of the features which makes Java different from other languages is that you can write programs which can run within a browser on a Web page. HTML (Hyper Text Markup Language) is the language used to describe the content and layout of Web pages. HTML is excellent for displaying information with links to other Web pages, but if you want to create interactive applications which will run on the Web, Java is the most flexible and widely used way of doing this. Recently some alternative methods have become available, notably dynamic HTML and ActiveX, however Java is still the most powerful option available. Java programs which run within a browser environment are called applets.

The browser used in these examples is Netscape Communicator 4.5, which you can download from the Web, alternatively you can use Sun's applet viewer. The vast majority of applets will also work with Microsoft's Internet Explorer 4.01, however there are differences between some aspects of the Microsoft and the Sun implementations of Java, which are reflected in the Microsoft implementation of their browser.

In this chapter we are going to see how to create applets and embed them within Web pages.

Writing applets

To run your applets within a browser you need a Java aware browser, that is one capable of understanding Java applets, Unless you are using a very old browser this will not be a problem. It is advisable to use the latest versions available since both HTML and Java are developing fast and only the most recent browsers support all of the latest features. The latest browsers from companies such as Netscape and Microsoft are available free or at a very low cost and it is worthwhile updating.

A simple application which displays *My first application* looks like this:

```
public class HelloApplication {
    public static void main(String args[ ]) {
        System.out.println("My first application");
    }
}
```

An applet which displays the message *My first applet* looks very different:

```
import java.awt.*;
import java.applet.*;
public class HelloApplet extends Applet {
    public void paint (Graphics g){
        g.drawString("My first applet", 5, 30);
    }
}
```

Java has a pre-defined set of classes which carry out operations that are widely used and provide support for applications as diverse as database access and displaying images. Classes which have related functions are grouped together into packages. If you want to use a class which belongs to a package you need to import that package into your applet or application. The statements:

```
import java.awt.*;
import java.applet.*;
```

make available all of the classes which are defined in the **java.awt** package and the **java.applet** package. All applets extend the **Applet** class which is in the **java.applet** package. The **Applet** class extends (i.e. is a subclass of) the **Panel** class which provides an area on which an applet can display information. The concept of one class extending or inheriting from another is a key idea in all object languages and is described in detail in chapter 8. The **paint** method is called to display information on this area. This method is passed a **Graphics** object, called *g* in this example, which has a comprehensive set of methods for displaying text, basic shapes and images. The **Graphics** class is in the **java.awt** package which is imported.

The method in the **Graphics** class which displays text is called **drawString**. This is passed three parameters: the text to be displayed, enclosed in quotes, and the horizontal and vertical positions of the start of the text.

The applet is compiled in the same way as an application, but before we can run it we need to create an HTML file which refers to the applet. We can then run a browser and open the HTML file which in turn runs the Java applet.

The APPLET tag

HTML consists of a series of tags enclosed in < >, for example **<HEAD>**. The end of this section is denoted by **</HEAD>**.

If you want an HTML file to run a Java applet you must use the **APPLET** tag. In this example the **APPLET** tag has three parameters: the name of the Java class file; and the height and the width of the area available on the Web page for displaying output from the applet. The simplest possible HTML file for running the Java applet called *HelloApplet* is shown below:

```
<HTML>
<HEAD>
</HEAD>
<BODY>
    <APPLET
        code = HelloApplet.class
        width=350
        height=100>
    </APPLET>
</BODY>
</HTML>
```

In this example the Java class file must be in the same directory as the HTML file. When you open the HTML file it runs normally executing the HTML tags and displaying any information specified in the usual way, when it reaches the **APPLET** tag, it finds and runs the applet. When the applet is completed the remainder of the HTML is executed. The running applet is shown in figure 6.1.

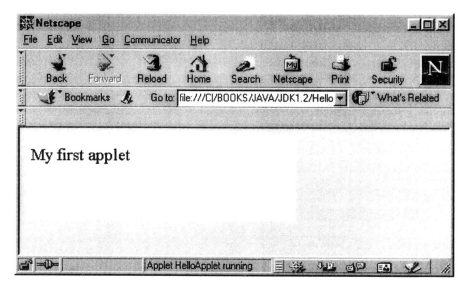

Fig. 6.1 Running an applet.

In chapter 7 we look at the **Graphics** class in detail.

Key methods of the Applet class

Since all applets are subclasses of the **Applet** class in the **java.applet** package, they inherit all of the methods of the **Applet** class. There are five methods which are especially useful in managing applets:

- **init( )**
- **start( )**
- **stop( )**
- **destroy( )**
- **paint( )**

If you do not add your own versions of these methods, the default versions of the methods, are called.

The init method

The **init** method is called whenever an applet is loaded by a browser. It is called before the **start** method and is an ideal place to initialize variables.

The method looks like this:

```
public void init( ) {
        //add your Java statements here
}
```

The start method

The **start** method is called after the initialization of the applet. While the **init** method is only called when the Web page is loaded, the **start** method is called every time that the page is loaded and restarted. If you go to another page and then return, the **start** method is called.

The method looks like this:

```
public void start( ) {
        //add your Java statements here
}
```

The stop method

The **stop** method is called whenever the browser leaves a page and goes to another page. If you are running an applet which is consuming a lot of system resources such as running an animation, you should stop it in this method to prevent it using up resources.

When the browser returns to the page the animation can be restarted in the **start** method.

The method looks like this:

```
public void stop( ) {
        //add your Java statements here
}
```

The destroy method

The **destroy** method is called just before an applet finishes, if, for example the browser is shut down. The **stop** method is called before this method. You can use this method to explicitly release system resources, however they are usually released automatically when the applet ends and therefore it is likely that you will use this method less than the other methods discussed here.

The method looks like this:

```
public void destroy( ) {
        //add your Java statements here
}
```

The paint method

The **paint** method is inherited from the **java.awt.Container** class and is used to draw text and graphics on the applets drawing area. This is covered in detail in chapter 7.

Command line arguments for applets

As we saw in chapter 5, you can pass arguments to an application when it starts running. We can do a similar thing with applets, but it requires co-operation between the Java applet and the HTML file. Within the **<APPLET> </APPLET>** pair, the name of the Java class file and the width and height of the applet drawing area are specified. To pass information to the applet, the names and values of the parameters are passed using **param name** and **value**. In this case there are two parameters or arguments being passed, the first is called *firstName* and is assigned the value *John Cowell*. The second is called *secondName* and is assigned the value *Sally Aldridge*.

The complete HTML file is shown below:

```
<HTML>
<HEAD>
</HEAD>
<BODY>
    <APPLET
```

```
        code = DisplayingNameApplet.class
        width=350
        height=100>
        <param name = firstName value = "John Cowell">
        <param name = secondName value = "Sally Aldridge">
     </APPLET>
  </BODY>
  </HTML>
```

We need to write some Java statements in our applet to receive these arguments. The best place to do this is in the **init** method, which is guaranteed to be called when the applets starts. Two **String** instance variables are declared, called *firstParam* and *secondParam*:

```
public class DisplayingNameApplet extends Applet {
    public String firstParam, secondParam;
```

In the **init** method, the two parameters are read using the **getParameter** method:

```
public void init( ) {
    firstParam = getParameter("firstName");
    secondParam = getParameter("secondName");
}
```

This method takes as a parameter the name of the parameter specified in the HTML file and returns the value of it. The two values read are assigned to the instance variables.

The **paint** method is automatically called when the applet runs, so commands to display information on the applet panel are guaranteed to be executed when the applet starts. In the **paint** method, *Hello* is displayed followed by the names which have been read. When the applet is run it should be similar to figure 6.2:

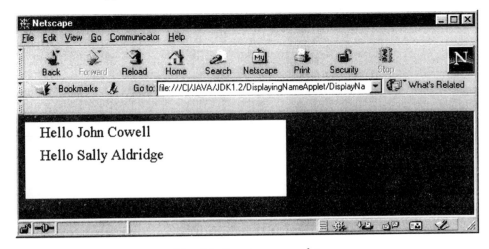

Fig. 6.2 Running an applet.

The whole applet is shown below:

```
import java.applet.*;
import java.awt.*;
public class DisplayingNameApplet extends Applet {
    public String firstParam, secondParam;
    public void init( ) {
        firstParam = getParameter("firstName");
        secondParam = getParameter("secondName");
    }
    public void paint(Graphics g){
        g.drawString("Hello " + firstParam, 20, 20);
        g.drawString("Hello " + secondParam, 20, 50);
    }
}
```

 *7*

The Graphics, Color and Font classes

Introduction

One of the great benefits of an object-oriented language is that libraries of classes can be created and used to add functionality to applications and applets. The Java Application Programming Interface (API) includes hundreds of classes. Since these classes have been thoroughly tested it is always better to use them rather than creating your own classes.

We are going to look at three classes:

- The **Graphics** class has many methods for displaying text and basic shapes such as squares and circles. It also allows you to display images.
- The **Font** class allows you to change the font in which text is displayed.
- The **Color** class allows you to change the colour of text, shapes and backgrounds.

The co-ordinate frame

All applets extend the **Applet** class, that is they are subclasses of the **Applet** class. The **Applet** class extends the **Panel** class and therefore all applets have a drawing area. The size of that drawing area is determined by the values of the **HEIGHT** and **WIDTH** attributes in the **APPLET** tag of the HTML file.

Anything drawn on a **Panel,** or other component which provides a drawing area, has a position which is specified by x and y co-ordinates. The origin (0, 0) is in the top left of the drawing area. Moving to the right is a positive x movement. Moving down the screen is a positive movement in the y direction as shown in figure 7.1.

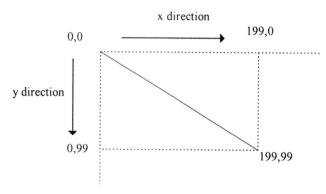

Fig. 7.1 The graphics co-ordinate system.

The drawing methods use x and y values to represent the start and end points of the object to be drawn, with the x value representing points across the screen and the y value representing points down the screen. To draw a line from the (0,0) position to (199,99) as shown in figure 7.1 you use the **drawLine** method, which is called from the **paint** method:

```
public void paint (Graphics g) {
    g.drawLine (0, 0, 199, 99);
}
```

Co-ordinates are specified as integer values, that is they must be whole positive numbers.

Importing classes

In Java, a package is a collection of classes which have a related function. The basic graphics and text drawing methods are implemented in the **Graphics** class, which is part of the **java.awt** package. To access any of the **Graphics** methods you must import the **Graphics** class by adding an **import** statement at the start of your file:

```
import java.awt.Graphics;
```

Similarly, to import the **Font** and **Color** classes:

```
import java.awt.Font;
import java.awt.Color;
```

Alternatively you can use an asterisk to specify that you wish to use any of the required classes and public items from the **java.awt** package:

```
import java.awt.*;
```

If you wish to use a class, you would usually create an instance of that class. Applets automatically create an instance of the **Graphics** class for use within your applets. The **Graphics** object created is passed as a parameter to the **paint** method which has the following format:

> **public void paint(Graphics g){**
>
>   ....
>
> **}**

Graphics drawing commands are placed in the **paint** method and these methods make use of the **Graphics** object which is passed to the method. The examples are particularly satisfying when learning how to use graphics, since you can immediately see if your applet has worked correctly.

The Graphics class

The **Graphics** class is abstract and contains over 50 methods that allow you to draw lines and basic shapes and to display and manipulate images. We are going to look at the most widely used of these.

Drawing lines

There is only one method for drawing lines:

> **void drawLine(int x1, int y1, int x2, int y2)**

The first two parameters are the x and y co-ordinates of the start of the line. The second two are the co-ordinates of the end of the line.

The applet below uses the **drawLine** method to draw the images shown in figure 7.2.

```
import java.awt.*;
import java.applet.*;
public class DrawingLines extends Applet {
    public void paint (Graphics g){
        int x = 0, change = 1;
        for (int y=150; y >= 0; y -= change) {
            g.drawLine(0, y, x, 0);
            x += change*2;
        }
    }
}
```

The left image was drawn with the integer variable *change* = 1, the right was drawn with a *change* value of 10.

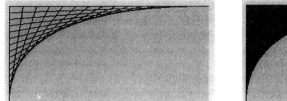

*Fig. 7.2 Using the **drawLine** method.*

Drawing rectangles

There are six **void** methods that display rectangles. The methods share some basic characteristics:

- **draw3DRect(int** x, **int** y, **int** width, **int** height, **boolean** raised)
- **drawRect(int** x, **int** y, **int** width, **int** height)
- **drawRoundRect(int** x, **int** y, **int** width, **int** height, **int** arcWidth, **int** arcHeight)
- **fill3DRect(int** x, **int** y, **int** width, **int** height, **boolean** raised)
- **fillRect(int** x, **int** y, **int** width, **int** height)
- **fillRoundRect(int** x, **int** y, **int** width, **int** height, **int** arcWidth, **int** arcHeight)

The last three methods produce filled versions of the first three shapes.

- The first four parameters are the same for all of the methods: the co-ordinates of the top left corner of the rectangle and its width and height.
- The **boolean** parameter gives the rectangle a raised or sunken appearance.
- The **drawRoundRect** and **fillRoundRect** methods have two additional parameters which control the width and height of the rounded corners.

The following line placed in an applet's **paint** method which is passed a **Graphics** object called *g*, produces the round cornered rectangle shown in figure 7.3:

*g.**drawRoundRect**(20, 20, 200, 100, 150, 80);*

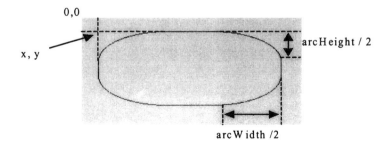

*Fig. 7.3 The **drawRoundRect** method.*

The **draw3DRect** and **fill3DRect** methods have an extra **boolean** parameter. If it is **true** the rectangle gives the impression that it is raised, if it is **false,** the impression that it is sunken.

Figure 7.4 shows all of the six methods. It was created using the applet below:

```
import java.applet.*;
import java.awt.*;
public class Rectangle extends Applet {
    public void paint(Graphics g) {
        int x = 20, y = 20, gap = 20, w = 100, h = 50;
        int arcW = 50, arcH = 50;
        boolean raised = true;
// display a 3D rectangle, plain rectangle and round cornered rectangle
        g.draw3DRect(x, y, w, h, raised);
        g.drawRect(x + w + gap, y, w, h);
        g.drawRoundRect(x + (w + gap)*2, y, w, h, arcW, arcH);
// display the filled versions on the line below
        g.fill3DRect(x, y + h + gap, w, h, raised);
        g.fillRect(x + w + gap, y + h + gap, w, h);
        g.fillRoundRect(x + (w + gap)*2,y + h + gap, w, h, arcW, arcH);
    }
}
```

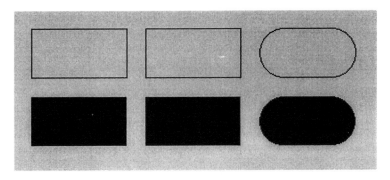

Fig. 7.4 Drawing 3D, plain and rounded rectangles.

The first impression is that there is no difference between the plain and 3D rectangles. In fact the only difference between them is that the 3D rectangles have a single row of pixels of a different colour added to two adjacent sizes of the rectangle and the effect is not noticeable unless you draw a number of adjacent rectangles so that the thickness of this line is increased.

Fig. 7.5 *Drawing 3D, raised, sunken, filled raised and filled sunken rectangles.*

Figure 7.5 shows all four possible 3D rectangles: raised, sunken, filled and raised, and filled and sunken. Each of the rectangles is in fact seven rectangles drawn within each other to emphasise the effect. The code used to draw these rectangles is shown below:

```
import java.applet.*;
import java.awt.*;
public class Rectangles3D extends Applet {
    public void paint(Graphics g) {
        int x = 20, y = 20, gap = 20, w = 80, h = 80;
        boolean raised = true;
        g.setColor(Color.yellow);     //draw the rectangles in yellow
//display raised, sunken, filled raised, filled sunken rectangles
        for (int c=0; c<7; c++) {
            g.draw3DRect(x + c, y + c, w-2*c, h-2*c, raised);
            g.draw3DRect(x + c + w + gap, y + c, w-2*c, h-2*c, !raised);
            g.fill3DRect(x+c+2*(w + gap), y + c, w-2*c, h-2*c, raised);
            g.fill3DRect(x+c+3*(w + gap), y + c, w-2*c, h-2*c, !raised);
        }
    }
}
```

The x and y attributes (that is the position of the top left corner of the rectangle) is increased by 1 for each rectangle drawn and both the height and width are decreased by 2. This enhances the effect. Note that colour of the rectangles has been made explicitly yellow, if you depend on the default settings for your system the 3D effect may not be as noticeable. We look at how to use the **Color** class later in this chapter.

Drawing circles and ovals

There are two **void** methods which are used for drawing ovals:

- **drawOval(int** x, **int** y, **int** width, **int** height)
- **fillOval(int** x, **int** y, **int** width, **int** height)

A circle is just a special case of an oval for which the width and height are the same. The applet shown in figure 7.6 draws the perhaps surprising group of ovals and illustrates a common misunderstanding of the **drawOval** and **fillOval** methods: the x and y co-ordinates specified as the first two parameters are not the centre of the oval, but the co-ordinates of the top left corner of a rectangle which encloses the oval drawn. The third and fourth parameters specify the width and height of that rectangle.

```
import java.applet.*;
import java.awt.*;
public class DrawingOvals extends Applet {
    public void paint(Graphics g) {
        int x = 20, y = 20, gap = 20, w = 100, h = 150;
        for (int c=0; c<15; c++)
            g.drawOval(x, y, w+10*c, h-10*c);
    }
}
```

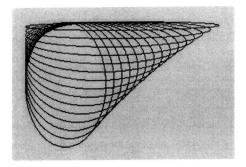

*Fig. 7.6 Using the **drawOval** method.*

Drawing arcs

An arcs is a sections of an oval. There are two **void** methods which are used for drawing them:

- **drawArc(int** x, **int** y, **int** width, **int** height, **int** startAngle, **int** arcAngle)
- **fillArc(int** x, **int** y, **int** width, **int** height, **int** startAngle, **int** arcAngle)

As for the **drawOval** and **fillOval** methods, the first four parameters specify the top left corner and the width and height of a rectangle which would fully enclose the oval of which the arc forms a part. The fifth parameter gives the starting position of the arc and the sixth and final parameter the number of degrees of the arc which is drawn.

The zero degrees position is the 3 o'clock position. The positive direction is anticlockwise.

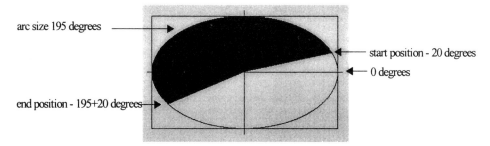

Fig. 7.7 Using the fillArc method.

The filled arc shown in figure 7.7 was created using the applet shown below:

```
import java.applet.*;
import java.awt.*;
public class DrawingArcs extends Applet {
    public void paint(Graphics g) {
        int x = 20, dx = 10, y = 20, dy = 10, w = 400, h = 200;
        //draw the enclosing rectangle
            g.drawRect(x, y, w, h);
        //draw the horizontal axis
            g.drawLine(x - dx, y + h/2, x+ w + dx, y + h/2);
        //draw the vertical axis
            g.drawLine(x + w/2, y - dy, x + w/2, y+ h + dy);
            g.drawOval(x, y, w, h);
            g.fillArc(x, y, w, h, 20, 195);
    }
}
```

The arc angle can be either positive or negative. A negative value draws an arc in a clockwise direction from the specified starting angle.

Drawing polygons

Polygons are shapes with three or more sides of different lengths. There are four **void** methods which are used for drawing them:

- **drawPolygon(int[ ] xPoints, int[ ] yPoints, int nPoints)**
- **drawPolygon(Polygon p)**
- **fillPolygon(int[ ] xPoints, int[ ] yPoints, int nPoints)**
- **fillPolygon(Polygon p)**

You specify a series of x, y co-ordinates and the **drawPolygon** methods connect these points together. The **fillPolygon** methods connect these co-ordinates and fill the area they create.

The difference between the two pairs of **fillPolygon** and **drawPolygon** methods is that one allows you to specify the co-ordinates as an array of x co-ordinates followed by an array of y co-ordinates and the number of points. The other requires you to create a **Polygon** object.

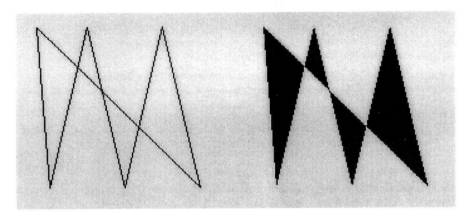

Fig. 7.8 Using the drawPolygon and fillPolygon method.

Figure 7.8 shows the **drawPolygon** and **fillPolygon** methods in action. Note that the first and last points are joined to give an enclosed area. The applet used to produce this figure is shown below:

```
import java.applet.*;
import java.awt.*;
public class DrawingPolygons extends Applet {
    public void paint(Graphics g) {
        int x[] = {20,30,60,90,120,150};
        int y[] = {20,200,20,200,20,200};
// co-ordinates are: 20,20  30,200  60,20  90,200  120,20  150,200
// x.length gives the number of elements in the array
        g.drawPolygon(x, y, x.length);
// draw the same shape filled and moved180 pixels to the right
        for (int c=0; c < x.length; c++)
            x[c] += 180;
        g.fillPolygon(x, y, x.length);
    }
}
```

If you wish to use the alternative **fillPolygon** and **drawPolygon** methods you can use the **paint** method shown below to replace the **paint** method in the previous example. Both methods produce exactly the same output. A **Polygon** object is created and pairs of co-ordinates are added using the **addPoint** method. To move all of the points along by 180 pixels, the **translate** method is used. This method takes two parameters, the first is the amount to add to the x co-ordinates, the second the amount to add to the y co-ordinates.

```
public void paint(Graphics g) {
    Polygon p = new Polygon( );
    p.addPoint(20,20);
    p.addPoint(30,200);
    p.addPoint(60,20);
    p.addPoint(90,200);
    p.addPoint(120,20);
    p.addPoint(150,200);
    g.drawPolygon(p);
// move all points 180 pixels to the right and 0 pixels down
    p.translate(180,0);
    g.fillPolygon(p);
}
```

The Color class

The **java.awt.Color** class encapsulates colours. Java uses the RGB model for representing colours. Colours in this model have four components: red green and blue components which allow any colour to be creating by varying the proportions of these primary colours and an alpha value which controls whether the colour is transparent or opaque. All colours are opaque unless you specify otherwise explicitly in the constructor for the colour you create. Each of the red, green and blue elements can be specified in the range of 0 to 255 (which can be represented in 8 bits or 1 byte). Since we have three colour elements, this gives us 3×8 bits, that is 24 bit colour which translates into approximately $2^{24} = 16.7$ million colours.

Table 7.1 Colours defined in the java.awt.Color class.

Colour	Red value	Green value	Blue value
Color.black	0	0	0
Color.blue	0	0	255
Color.cyan	0	255	255
Color.darkGray	64	64	64
Color.gray	128	128	128
Color.green	0	255	0
Color.lightGray	192	192	192
Color.magenta	255	0	255
Color.orange	255	200	0
Color.pink	255	175	175
Color.red	255	0	0
Color.white	255	255	255
Color.yellow	255	255	0

If your applet is likely to be viewed on a variety of computer screens, you cannot guarantee that every screen will be able to represent a wide range of colours. This could be a problem if you have created an image which uses colour to indicate different features and the screen used to view the image cannot differentiate between them. There are some predefined colours which it is likely that most screens will use. These are **Color** objects and are shown in table 7.1, which also shows the red, green and blue components. White, for example, is made up of the maximum amount of red, green and blue, while black has no red, green or blue.

Creating colours

The five most common constructors for the **Color** class are:

- **Color(float r, float g, float b, float a)**
- **Color(float r, float g, float b)**
- **Color(int r, int g, int b, int a)**
- **Color(int r, int g, int b)**
- **Color(int rgb)**

The parameters have the following meaning:

- The *r*, g and *b* parameters are either **float** values between 0.0 and 1.0 or **int** values between 0 and 255.
- The *a* parameter is also either a **float** or an **int** with the same range as for the *r*, g, and *b* parameters and specifies the degree of transparency. A colour with the maximum value is opaque (the default), the minimum value indicates transparency.
- The *rgb* parameter is a 24-bit integer value. Bits 0→7 represent the blue component, bits 8→15 represent green and bits 16→23 represent the amount of red.

To create a **Color** object you can either use the pre-defined colours or create your own, for example:

> **Color** *myYellowColour* = **Color.yellow;**
> **Color** *myReddishColour* = **new Color(255, 20, 50);**
> **Color** *myBlueishColour* = **new Color((float)0.1, (float)0.2, (float)(1.0));**

Before an object is drawn, you can specify the colour using the **setColor** method which takes a **Color** object as a parameter, for example:

> **Color** *myColor* = **new Color(20, 50, 120);**
> *g.***setColor***(myColor);*

A shorthand way of writing this is:

> *g.***setColor***(new Color(20, 50, 120));*

Any objects drawn will now have the new colour.

Displaying text and changing fonts

Text is displayed using the **drawString** method. The most common form of this method is:

> *drawString(String str, int x, int y)*

The first parameter is the text to be displayed. The second and third are the x and y co-ordinates of the start of the text.

If you use this method the text is displayed in a default font which is dependent on your system. If you wish to control the font explicitly you can use the **Font** class to create a **Font** object and then use the **setFont** method to ensure that all subsequent text is displayed using this font.

The most commonly-used constructor for the **Font** class requires three parameters:

> *Font(String name, int style, int size)*

- The name is the either a logical font name or a font face name. A logical name must be either **Dialog, DialogInput, Monospaced, Serif, SansSerif** or **Symbol**.
- The style must be either **Font.ITALIC, Font.PLAIN,** or **Font.BOLD**. The italic and bold styles can also be combined, that is, **Font.ITALIC + Font.BOLD**.
- The size is the point size of the font.

There is some confusing terminology associated with fonts. A common problem when using the **Font** class is to confuse the logical font name with the font face name (sometimes just called the font name). A font name refers to a particular font such as Helvetica bold or Courier italic. A logical name is a description of a font with particular characteristics, which is mapped onto the most appropriate font at run-time, for example on many systems a logical font name of Monospaced will map onto the Courier plain font which is a monospaced font, that is one in which each character takes up the same amount of space. Many fonts, such as Helvetica, vary the amount of space depending on the width of each character. Another confusion is the use of the font family name. This is the name of a collection of specific fonts, for example a family name such as Helvetica contains specific fonts such as Helvetica Bold. If you wish to specify a particular font which is certain to be available, specify the font name. If your system is designed to be more generic and to run on a variety of platforms with unknown fonts available, use the logical fonts.

Figure 7.9 shows text displayed with a variety of logical fonts.

This font is 14 point Serif PLAIN

This font is 18 point Monospaced ITALIC

This font is 22 point SansSerif ITALIC and BOLD

Fig. 7.9 *Displaying text using logical font names.*

The applet used to produce this output is shown below:

```
import java.applet.*;
import java.awt.*;
public class UsingFonts extends Applet {
    public void paint(Graphics g) {
        Font[ ] f = new Font[3];
        f[0] = new Font("Serif", Font.PLAIN, 14);
        f[1] = new Font("Monospaced", Font.ITALIC, 18);
        f[2] = new Font("SansSerif", Font.ITALIC+Font.BOLD, 22);
// f.length is the number of array elements
        for (int c = 0; c <f.length; c++){
            g.setFont(f[c]);
            String text = "This font is ";
            text += f[c].getSize( )+ " point " + f[c].getName( );
            int style = f[c].getStyle( );
            if (style == Font.BOLD) text += " BOLD"; else
                if (style == Font.ITALIC) text += " ITALIC"; else
                if (style == Font.PLAIN) text += " PLAIN"; else
                if (style == Font.ITALIC + Font.BOLD)
                    text += " ITALIC and BOLD";
            g.drawString(text,10,30 + c*30);
        }
    }
}
```

On your system you may have different fonts mapped onto the logical fonts, so you may not obtain exactly the same result if you try this applet.

The logical font names can be replaced by particular font names by substituting the three lines where the **Font** objects are instantiated with the three lines shown below:

```
f[0] = new Font("Times New Roman", Font.PLAIN, 14);
f[1] = new Font("Courier New", Font.ITALIC, 18);
f[2] = new Font("Arial Narrow", Font.ITALIC + Font.BOLD, 22);
```

This produces the output shown in figure 7.10:

This font is 14 point Times New Roman PLAIN

This font is 18 point Courier New ITALIC

This font is 22 point Arial Narrow ITALIC and BOLD

Fig. 7.10 Displaying text using font names.

The **Font** class has a useful set of methods for working with fonts as shown in table 7.2.

Table 7.2 Methods of the java.awt.Font class.

Method	Description
String getFamily( )	Returns the family name of the font, for example Helvetica could be returned for the font face Helvetica Bold
String getFontName( )	Returns the font face name, for example Helvetica Bold.
String getName( )	Returns the logical name of the font.
int getSize( )	Returns the size in points of the font.
int getStyle( )	Returns the style, which must be one of the following: **Font.PLAIN, BOLD, ITALIC,** or **ITALIC + BOLD.**
boolean isBold( )	Returns **true** if the font is bold.
boolean isItalic( )	Returns **true** if the font is italic.
boolean isPlain( )	Returns **true** if the font is neither bold nor italic.
String toString( )	Returns a **String** representation of the **Font** object.

Displaying images

The **Image** class is the **abstract** superclass of all classes which represent images. Since **Image** is abstract we cannot directly create an **Image** object, we have to use a method which returns an **Image** object. If you want to use an image there are two stages:

- Create an **Image** object and read the image from a file or URL using the **getImage** method.
- Display the image using the **drawImage** method.

To read the image you can use the **getImage** methods of the **Applet** class. There are two forms of this method:

- **getImage(URL)** takes a single parameter, a **URL** object, which is the absolute URL that gives the location and name of the image.

- **getImage(URL, String)** - The **URL** object in this method is an absolute URL which gives only the base address of the image file. The **String** gives the image location relative to the URL.

Both of these methods return an **Image** object.

The URL may specify a location on the Web or a local file address. You can explicitly specify the location, but if you reorganise the location of the applet on your system you will have to change the applet. The best way around this problem is to use the **getCodeBase** and **getDocumentBase** methods of the **Applet** class:

- **getCodeBase( )** returns the URL of the applet itself.
- **getDocumentBase( )** returns the URL of the Web page in which the applet is embedded.

If you use these methods to specify the location of your image files and maintain the same relative position between your images and either your applet or HTML files you will not have a problem with the applet being unable to find the image files.

When an image file has been read into an **Image** object, the **Image** object can be displayed using one of the **drawImage** methods in the **Graphics** class. There are numerous other **drawImage** methods available in this class, but the most commonly-used ones are shown below:

- **drawImage(Image** i, **int** x, **int** y, **ImageObserver)**
- **drawImage(Image** i, **int** x, **int** y, **int** width, **int** height, **ImageObserver)**
- **drawImage(Image** i, **int** x, **int** y, **Color, ImageObserver)**
- **drawImage(Image** i, **int** x, **int** y, **int** width, **int** height, **Color, ImageObserver)**

All of these methods share the same first three parameters:

- The **Image** parameter is the image object to be displayed.
- The *x* and *y* parameters are the position of the top left corner of the image.
- The *width* and *height* specify the size of the image.
- The **Color** parameter is the background colour to paint under any portions of the image which are not opaque.
- The **ImageObserver** parameter is the name of the object which is informed of the progress of the image as it is being loaded.

To see how this works in practice, the next applet opens an image and displays it in a variety of different aspect ratios.

```
import java.awt.*;
import java.applet.*;
public class DisplayingImages extends Applet {
    Image zebra;
    public void init( ) {
        setBackground(Color.white);
        zebra = getImage(getCodeBase( ), "Zebra.gif");
    }
    public void paint(Graphics g) {
```

```
        g.drawImage(zebra, 0, 0, 200, 200, this);
        g.drawImage(zebra, 250, 0, 100, 200, this);
        g.drawImage(zebra, 400, 0, 200, 100, this);
   }
}
```

The output from this applet is shown in figure 7.11:

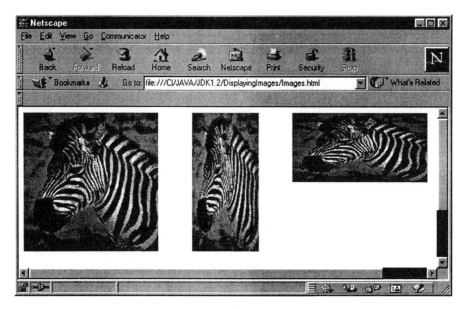

***Fig. 7.11** Displaying images.*

The **init** method is guaranteed to be run when the applet starts. The image is in file *Zebra.gif*. The **getCodeBase** method returns the location of the HTML document which initiated the applet. The image is stored in the same directory. The **getImage** method reads the image into the **Image** object called *zebra*. The **paint** method draws the image in a variety of positions and shapes using the **drawImage** method. The **ImageObserver** is **this**, the current object.

Browsers handle the display of images differently, for example Netscape Communicator only displays GIF and JPG format image files, Internet Explorer also displays other formats. Communicator seems to display images faster than Explorer. There are similar variations with the numerous other browsers which are available. Internet Explorer does not always display GIF images correctly if they differ from their actual size.

The safest option is to use GIF or JPG format for your image files and to ensure that you display the files in their default width and height using the **getWidth** and **getHeight** methods of the **Graphics** class, which return the actual width and height of the image, for example to display the *zebra* image with its actual size:

   *g.**drawImage**(zebra, 100, 100, zebra.**getWidth(this)**, zebra.**getHeight(this)**, **this**);*

8
Inheritance and Polymorphism

Introduction

One of the advantages of designing an object-oriented system is that you can re-use existing classes. If these classes have been fully tested you can use them to build new applications without re-testing them. Since this approach reduces the amount of new untested code, applications can be created quickly and are likely to have fewer errors. Java 2 has an extensive class library, many Java classes are available from other companies, and of course you can create your own classes to help you build complex applications quickly with the minimum of errors.

One of the problems with using class libraries is that you can often find a class which does most of the things you want but not everything. Fortunately there is a solution to this problem. Inheritance allows you to take all of the behaviour of a class and to extend it to a subclass. The subclass inherits all of the capabilities of the superclass and in addition has capabilities of its own. You can extend a superclass to give many different subclasses. These subclasses in turn can be extended to produce additional subclasses.

The syntax of Java which you use to specify that one class inherits from another is straightforward, but the way in which this facility is used is very powerful. In this chapter we are going to implement an application which uses inheritance.

A hierarchy of computer components

The best way to appreciate the power of inheritance is to look an example where it is used. The application we are going to develop is for organising information which a computer supplier could use. All of the components such as memory, disks, motherboards, processors and screens have some data items in common, such as a unique code, which identifies the piece of equipment, and a price. The components may also share some methods for example to calculate a discount on the price. Every type of component will also have some elements which are unique, for example a motherboard will use a particular chipset (for example BX) with a particular bus speed (100 MHz for the BX chipset), a processor will have a speed, memory will have a type (for example SDRAM). These features make this an ideal application for using inheritance.

The components which we want to record on our system are:

- Memory which has a unique product identifier, so that a particular type of memory can be identified. It has a cost, a size, and a type, which can be SDRAM, EDO or fast page.
- Motherboard, the board into which the memory, processor, graphics card and modem are plugged. It has a product identifier, a cost, a chipset type such as LX, TX or BX, and a bus speed.
- Disk which has a product identifier, cost, size and format such as SCSI or EIDE.
- Monitor which has a product identifier, cost, size, maximum horizontal and vertical resolution, and refresh rate.

Each of these items can be represented in a separate class (*Memory, MBoard, Disk* and *Monitor*). All of them have a product identifier and a cost in common, so we can place these data items into a superclass (*PCPart*) from which the other classes inherit.

We are going to implement a few methods for these classes to show how inheritance works. Sometimes a discount is offered to customers, so we need a method which will calculate a discount on the standard cost (*discount*). The only other method that we need is to display details of the object (*displayDetails*). This will be different for each class since the information stored for each class is different, for example the class which stores details of the motherboard has a chipset type which no other class uses.

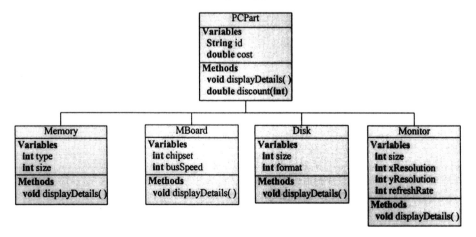

Fig. 8.1 The PC component hierarchy.

We can draw this class hierarchy as shown in figure 8.1.

The name of the class is shown at the top of each box, followed by the variables and then the methods of the class.

PCPart is the superclass of the other classes. Since, for example the *Memory* class is a subclass of the *PCPart* class, a *Memory* object not only has the *type* and *size* instance variables, but also the *id* and *cost* instance variables which it inherits from the *PCPart* class.

First we are going to implement the *PCPart* class, which is the superclass from which the other classes inherit:

```java
public abstract class PCPart {
    String id;          //product identifier
    double cost;        //cost of product
    public void displayDetails( ) {
        System.out.print("Id number is   " + id);
        System.out.println(" Cost is : " + cost);
    }
    public double discount(int percentageDiscount) {
        double theDiscount;
        theDiscount = cost * percentageDiscount/100.0;
        return theDiscount;
    }
}
```

This class has been defined in the same way as all the other classes we have seen so far. It has two instance variables:

- The **String** variable *id* which is a unique identifier which all products have.
- The **double** variable *cost* which is the cost of the product.

This class has two methods:

- The *displayDetails* method shows the values of the instance variables.
- The *discount* method is passed a percentage discount and calculates the reduction (or increase!) in the cost.

Note that the *PCPart* class is defined as **abstract**. An **abstract** class is one which cannot be instantiated, that is you cannot create any *PCPart* objects. This is because the *PCPart* class does not correspond to any real-world objects, it is just a convenient way of grouping together some instance variables and methods which other classes can inherit. If all of the classes in our application did not inherit from the *PCPart* class, we would have to duplicate the definition of the instance variables, *id* and *cost*, and the methods, *displayDetails* and *discount*, in every class, which would increase the size of the code and might lead to errors. If we omitted the word **abstract**, *PCPart* would be a concrete class and it would be possible to instantiate it. What use is a class if it cannot be instantiated? Other classes which are not **abstract** can inherit from this **abstract** class and can be instantiated. You can also inherit from a class which is not **abstract** as we shall see later in this chapter.

Defining the Memory subclass

We have defined the *PCPart* superclass, the next stage is to define the *Memory* subclass:

```
class Memory extends PCPart {
    int type;            //type of memory either SDRAM, EDO or FASTPAGE
    int size;            //memory size in MB
    static final int SDRAM = 0;  //SDRAM,EDO and FASTPAGE memory types
    static final int EDO = 1;
    static final int FASTPAGE = 2;
    public Memory(String ident, double price, int memType, int memSize){
        id = ident;
        cost = price;
        type = memType;
        size = memSize;
    }
    public void displayDetails( ) {
        super.displayDetails( );
        String text = "Memory type : ";
        if (type == SDRAM) text += "168 pin SDRAM";
        if (type == EDO) text += "72 pin EDO";
        if (type == FASTPAGE) text += "72 pin fast page";
        System.out.println(text + " " + size + " MB");
    }
}
```

There are some new features in this class. The *Memory* class **extends** the *PCPart* class. This means that *Memory* is a subclass of *PCPart* and inherits all of its methods and variables.

Two new instance variables are defined:

- The **int** *type* variable is the type of memory. This variable should only be assigned one of the **static final int** variables defined for the class, either *SDRAM, EDO* or *FASTPAGE* which represent the types of memory available.
- The **int** *size* variable is the size of the memory.

The three **static final int** variables are *SDRAM, EDO* and *FASTPAGE,* which correspond to the types of memory available. There is only one copy of a **static** variable that objects can refer to. Irrespective of how many objects you create they all share the same **static** variables. Variables which are declared as **static** are called class variables. If a variable is declared as **final** when it is defined, it cannot be changed. The effect of this is that the **static final** variables *SDRAM, EDO* and *FASTPAGE* are constant values which every instance of the class can use but not change.

The notation which is used to refer to class variables is the class name, the '.' character and the class variable name. If, for example, *m* is an instance of the *Memory* class we can define the memory type by statements such as:

    m.type = Memory.SDRAM;

rather than:

    m.type = 0;

The use of **static final** variables makes programs easier to read and maintain. Note that if you are referring to a class variable in a method which is in the same class (or a subclass) of the class in which the class variable is defined you do not have to specify the class name before the class variable name. In this application, since the class variable *SDRAM* is defined in *PCPart* and all of the concrete classes are subclasses of *PCPart* we can omit the class name. For example, if *m* is an instance of the *Memory* class instantiated in the application's **main** method we can write:

    m.type = SDRAM;

The *Memory* class has two methods:

- A constructor method *Memory* (all constructors have the same name as the class) is used to assign initial values to all of the instance variables of the class, not only *type* and *size*, but the *id* and *cost* instance variables inherited from *PCPart*.
- The *displayDetails* method displays details of the component. There is also a method called *displayDetails* in the superclass *PCPart*. This is an example of polymorphism.

Polymorphism

The *Memory* class has a method called *displayDetails*. There is a method of the same name with the same parameter list in the *PCPart* class, so how does Java know which method you are referring to? When you refer to a method Java looks to see if a method of that name with the specified parameter list is defined in its class, if it is, it uses it. If it does not find the method, it looks in the superclass to see if the method is defined there, if it is not it looks in the superclass of the superclass, and so on, until it finds the method or an error is reported. This is called polymorphism. The *displayDetails* method in the *Memory* class is said to override the *displayDetails* method in the *PCPart* class.

If you wish to explicitly use the superclass method, even if there is a method with the same name and parameter list in the class itself, you should precede the name of the method with **super**. In the *displayDetails* method in the *Memory* class, the *displayDetails* method of the superclass (*PCPart*) method is explicitly run by the line:

    super.*displayDetails( );*

The *Memory* class version of the *displayDetails* method includes this line since the *PCPart* class version of this method displays the identification number and cost. An alternative way of writing this method in *Memory* which would produce the same output is:

```java
public void displayDetails( ) {
    System.out.print("Id number is  " + id);
    System.out.println(" Cost is : " + cost);
    String text = "Memory type : ";
    if (type == SDRAM) text += "168 pin SDRAM";
    else if (type == EDO) text += "72 pin EDO";
    else if (type == FASTPAGE) text += "72 pin fast page";
    System.out.println(text + " " + size + " MB");
}
```

If we add a **main** method to the *PCPart* class we can see the application in action:

```java
public static void main(String args[ ]) {
    int reduction = 5;              //percentage reduction
    Memory m = new Memory("MEM884", 56, Memory.SDRAM, 128);
    m.displayDetails( );
    System.out.println(reduction + "% discount is " + m.discount(reduction));
}
```

Note that *m*, which is a *Memory* object, can use the *discount* method which is defined in *PCPart*, the superclass of *Memory*. The application produces this output:

```
Id number is MEM884  Cost is : 56.0
Memory type : 168 pin SDRAM 128 MB
5% discount is 2.8
```

The MBoard class

We can extend the application by adding a class called *MBoard*, which represents motherboards. This is a subclass of *PCPart*, that is *MBoard* **extends** *PCPart*. This class has two new instance variables, *chipset* and *busSpeed*, which are the defining features of motherboards for PCs.

Three **static final** integers represent the three most common types of chipset, LX, BX and TX.

The class is shown below:

```java
class MBoard extends PCPart{
    int chipset;                     //chipset LX, BX or TX
    int busSpeed;                    //speed of the motherboard bus
    static final int LX = 0;         //the three types listed are types chipsets
    static final int BX = 1;
    static final int TX = 2;
    public MBoard( ) {               //null constructor
    }
    public MBoard(String identifier, double price, int chips, int speed){
        id = identifier;
```

```
        cost = price;
        chipset = chips;
        busSpeed = speed;
    }
    public void displayDetails( ) {
        super.displayDetails( );
        String text = "Motherboard chipset used : ";
        if (chipset == BX) text += "BX";
        else if (chipset == LX) text += "LX";
        else if (chipset == TX) text += "TX";
        System.out.println(text + "  Bus speed : " + busSpeed);
    }
}
```

This class has two new methods, a constructor and *displayDetails*. Java is not confused by the fact that there are now three methods called *displayDetails* in this system. If we amend the **main** method in the *PCPart* class we can see this class in action:

```
public static void main(String args[ ]) {
    int reduction = 12;            //percentage reduction
    MBoard mb = new MBoard("LX349", 60.0, MBoard.LX, 100);
    mb.displayDetails( );
    System.out.println(reduction + "% discount is " + mb.discount(reduction));
}
```

This produces the text:

Id number is LX349 Cost is : 60.0
Motherboard chipset used : LX Bus speed : 100
12% discount is 7.2

The *Disk* and *Monitor* classes are implemented in the same way as the *MBoard* and *Memory* classes and are not shown here.

Extending a subclass

Sometimes companies will sell a motherboard with a processor already fitted, this could be an Intel Pentium II processor or one of the AMD or Cyrix clones. If we wanted to define a class we would need all of the characteristics of the *MBoard* class and some additional ones which define the processor. We can do this by creating a class called *MBoardAndProc* which extends the *MBoard* class.

The *MBoardAndProc* class will inherit all of the variables and methods of the *MBoard* class and also all of the methods of the *PCPart* class. A class inherits not only from its immediate superclass, but also from all of its superclasses:

- *PCPart* is a superclass of *MBoard* and also *MBoardAndProc*.

- *MBoard* is a subclass of *PCPart* and a superclass of *MBoardAndProc*.
- *MBoardAndProc* is a subclass of both *PCPart* and *MBoard*.

This relationship is shown in figure 8.2:

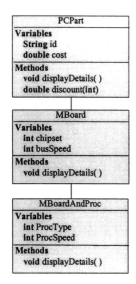

Fig. 8.2 Extending the MBoard class.

The *MBoardAndProc* class has all of the methods and variables of the *PCPart* and *MBoard* class and in addition two instance variables representing the processor speed and type, *procSpeed* and *ProcType*. The type of processor can be either Pentium II, AMD or Cyrix, therefore three **final static int** class variables are defined called, *PENTIUM, AMDK6* and *CYRIX*. The *MBoardAndProc* class is shown below:

```
class MBoardAndProc extends MBoard {
    int procType;        //processor type PENTIUM, AMDK6 or CYRIX
    int procSpeed;       //processor speed
    static final int PENTIUM = 0;    //there are three types of processor
    static final int AMDK6 = 1;
    static final int CYRIX = 2;
    public MBoardAndProc(String identifier,
                         double price,
                         int chips,
                         int speed,
                         int type,
                         int proSpeed){
        id = identifier;
        cost = price;
        chipset = chips;
        busSpeed = speed;
        procType = type;
        procSpeed = proSpeed;
```

```
    }
    public void displayDetails( ) {
        super.displayDetails( );
        String text = "Processor type : ";
        if (procType == PENTIUM)text += "Pentium II";
        else if (procType == AMDK6)text += "AMD K6";
        else if (procType == CYRIX)text += "Cyrix mark III";
        System.out.println(text + " speed : " + procSpeed);
    }
}
```

In the *displayDetails* method for this class, the method of the same name in the *MBoard* class is called, which in turn refers explicitly to the *displayDetails* method in the *PCPart* class, by using the **super** prefix.

We can change the **main** method again to create an instance of this class as shown below:

```
public static void main(String args[ ]) {
    int reduction = 12;          //percentage reduction
    MBoardAndProc mbp = new MBoardAndProc("LXP45",
                                          150.0,
                                          MBoard.BX,
                                          100,
                                          MBoardAndProc.PENTIUM,
                                          450);
    mbp.displayDetails ( );
    System.out.println(reduction + "% discount is " + mbp.discount(reduction));
}
```

Objects belonging to the *MBoardAndProc* class can also use the *discount* method which is inherited from the *PCPart* class. This **main** method produces the following output.

Id number is LXP45   Cost is : 150.0
Motherboard chipset used : BX   Bus Speed : 100
Processor type : Pentium II   speed : 450
12% discount is 18.0

Class and instance variables

In the last section we looked briefly at class and instance variables. The use of these types of variables is important and is also a common problem area for many programmers, so we are going to revisit their use.

The *Mercedes* class defined below has some instance variables which are used to store the features of different models in the *Mercedes* range. In the **main** method two objects, *s320* and *e430,* are instantiated.

```
public class Mercedes {
    String manufacturer;
    int model;
    double price;
    int engineSize;
    boolean ABS;
    boolean airConditioning;
    boolean CD;

public static void main(String args[ ] ) {
    Mercedes s320 = new Mercedes( );
    Mercedes e430 = new Mercedes( );
    }
}
```

Since all of the variables defined are instance variables, that is their definitions are not preceded by the word **static**, a copy of each variable exists for each instance or object, for example *s320.manufacturer* is a different variable from *e430.manufacturer*. They may both contain the same **String** *Mercedes*, but changing the value of *s320.manufacturer* does not affect the string stored in *e430.manufacturer*. Since these variables will always have the same value it would make sense for them to actually be the same, that is for *s320.manufacturer* and *e430.manufacturer* to be the same variable. We can do this by adding the word **static** before the definition of the *manufacturer* variable:

static String *manufacturer;*

There is now only one copy of this variable per class not one per instance, therefore it would be helpful to assign a value of this class variable where it is defined:

static String *manufacturer = "Mercedes";*

Similarly since all Mercedes have air conditioning and ABS brakes (but not CD players) the **boolean** variables which represent these features can be made **static**:

static boolean *ABS = **true**;*
static boolean *airConditioning = **true**;*

The instance variable which represents the vehicle model, called *model* has been defined as an **int**, this initially seems surprising since the model name is a **String** such as *E430* or *S600*. If a **String** were saved it would occupy more space and it is generally good practice to avoid using strings where possible, since it can lead to errors. If this information was stored in a database and a simple spelling mistake had been made, typing *S660* instead of *S600*, a search for *S600* would fail to identify this vehicle. An alternative method is to define some integer constant values for each of the possible types of model:

static final int *e200 = 0, e240 = 1, e280 = 2, e320 = 3;*
static final int *s280 = 4, s320 = 5, s420 = 6, s500 = 7, s600 = 8;*

These integers are defined as **static**, that is they are class variables and only one exists for the class irrespective of how many objects of that class are created. They are also defined as **final**, which means that their value cannot be changed after this initial definition. They are effectively constants.

A revised version of the *Mercedes* class with the new variable definitions and an example of how the class and instance variables are used is shown below:

```
public class Mercedes {
    static String manufacturer = "Mercedes";
    int model;
    double price;
    int engineSize;
    static boolean ABS = true;
    static boolean airConditioning = true;
    boolean CD;
    static final int e200 = 0, e240 = 1, e280 = 2, e320 = 3;
    static final int s280 = 4, s320 = 5, s420 = 6, s500 = 7, s600 = 8;
    public static void main(String args[ ]) {
        Mercedes s320 = new Mercedes( );
        s320.model = Mercedes.s320;
        s320.price = 28000;
        s320.engineSize = 2996;              //in cc's
        s320.CD = false;
    }
}
```

Static methods

Methods, as well as variables, can be **static**. In fact the first method we met, **main**, is a **static** method. When you call a method which is not **static** the name of the object calling that method is implicitly passed to it, for example the *priceChange* method which we can add to the *Mercedes* class, is shown below. It is a non-**static** method.

```
public void priceChange(double change) {
    System.out.print("old price is " + price);
    price += price*change/100.0 ;
    System.out.println(" new price is :" + price);
}
```

If it is called with the statement:

```
s320.priceChange(5);
```

The name of the object, *s320*, is implicitly passed to the method, which displays the old price, calculates the new price, modifies the instance variable *price* and displays its new value.

If we want to change the value of a class variable, that is a variable which is defined as **static,** we need a **static** method (Java allows you to change a class variable in a method which is not **static,** but it is more usual to use a **static** method).

The **static** method shown below changes the value of the **static** variable *manufacturer*:

```
public static void manufacturerChange(String takeover) {
    System.out.print("old manufacturer is " + manufacturer);
    manufacturer = takeover;
    System.out.println(" new manufacturer is " + manufacturer);
}
```

It can be called by:

Mercedes.manufacturerChange("Nissan");

to display the message:

old manufacturer is Mercedes new manufacturer is Nissan

There are some important differences. When the *manufacturerChange* method is called, the class name is specified rather than an object name, since the method is **static** and applies to the whole class not just an individual object. It is not passed the name of any particular object. The method definition itself contains the word **static.** You cannot change any instance variables in a **static** method since when the method is called it is not for any particular object. You can only change class variables, that is **static** variables, in a **static** method.

Overloading methods

Java can use polymorphism to differentiate between methods in superclasses and subclasses which have the same name and the same parameter lists. A check is made in the object's class for the method, if it is not found the superclass is checked, if it is not found its superclass of the superclass is checked and so on.

It is also possible to have methods with the same name but different parameter lists in the same class. Java checks first the name and then the list of parameters to find a match. You can have as many methods with the same name in a class as you wish, provided that they take different parameters. This sounds like an interesting but not especially useful aspect of the language, however it is extensively used throughout the standard Java classes supplied in the packages and is a very useful feature of the language. We have already been using this aspect of the language implicitly when displaying text using a variety of **println** methods. The statements:

```
System.out.println("This is text");
System.out.println(23.5);          //this displays a double
System.out.println(true);          //this displays a boolean
```

call three different methods, which have the same name but which take different parameters, the first takes a **String**, the second a **double** and the third a **boolean**. Since these parameters are of different types they require different treatment and a different method is needed for each. The methods are said to be overloaded. The class shown below has three different overloaded methods called *hello*. They are differentiated by having different parameter lists.

```
public class Welcome {
    public static void main(String args[ ]) {
        Welcome w = new Welcome( );
        w.hello( );
        w.hello("Beverley");
        w.hello("Beverley", "Ford");
    }
    public void hello( ) {
        System.out.println("hello stranger");
    }
    public void hello(String name) {
        System.out.println("hello " + name);
    }
    public void hello(String firstName, String surname) {
        System.out.println("hello " + firstName + " " + surname);
    }
}
```

This application prints the messages:

hello stranger
hello Beverley
hello Beverley Ford

Constructors are methods which have the same name as the class and are called whenever an instance of a class is created. If you do not write your own constructors Java uses a default constructor which does nothing except initialize variables to their default values. You can overload constructors in exactly the same way as you can overload other methods.

Access control

Java allows you to control access to methods, that is the degree of visibility of methods to other methods which are defined with the same class, within a subclass or within the same package. The less access that you allow to your methods and variables the easier it is to find out where a problem occurs when a variable has a value you did not expect. There are three explicit access controllers which can be used with methods:

- **public** - access is allowed by all methods in all packages.
- **protected** - access is allowed by all methods in the class or in any subclasses.

- **private** - access is allowed only by methods within the class itself.

In addition, if an access controller is not explicitly given, access is called *package* which gives access by subclasses and classes in the same package.

A class called *ClassOne* contains methods with each of the four possible access controllers. Table 8.1 shows whether each of the four methods can be accessed by other methods in:

- *ClassOne* itself.
- *ClassTwo*, which is a subclass of *ClassOne*.
- *ClassThree*, which is not a subclass of *ClassOne* but is in the same package.
- *ClassFour*, which is not a subclass of *ClassOne* and is not in the same package.

Table 8.1 *Access controllers.*

	ClassOne	ClassTwo	ClassThree	ClassFour
public	✓	✓	✓	✓
package	✓	✓	✓	✗
protected	✓	✓	✗	✗
private	✓	✗	✗	✗

- The **public** method in *ClassOne* can be accessed by methods in any of the classes.
- The *package* method in *ClassOne* cannot be accessed by methods in *ClassFour* which is not a subclass of *ClassOne* and is not in the same package.
- The **protected** method in *ClassOne* can only be accessed by other methods in *ClassOne* and methods in *ClassTwo*, which is a subclass of *ClassOne*.
- The **private** method in *ClassOne* can only be accessed by other methods in the same class.

The access controller precedes the name of the method when it is defined, for example:

> **public void** *myPublicMethod( ) {*

You can also control the degree of visibility of instance and class variables in a similar way, for example:

> **private Button** *exit = new Button( );*
> **public int** *total;*
> **protected String** *name;*
> **float** *value;*

A outer class, that is a class which is not declared within another class can have the default *package* or **public** access, although there can only be one **public** outer class in a file (the file must have the same name as the **public** class).

Inner classes are defined wholly within another class. They are covered in the next chapter. Inner classes may be **private**, *package*, **protected** or **public**. It is possible to have a **public** outer class and a **public** inner class in the same file, although usually an inner class is created because it is intimately bound up with the operation of the outer class and therefore should be made **private**.

Interfaces

An interface consists of a series of definitions of abstract methods – methods without a body, for example:

```
public interface CarDetails {
    void priceChange(double p);
}
```

If you want a class to inherit an interface, you use the **implements** keyword rather than **extends**:

*class Mercedes **implements** CarDetails*

Any class which implements the *CarDetails* interface must override the *priceChange* method, therefore the interface ensures that the class must contain its own version of this method. An interface can contain as many methods as you wish.

Java does not support multiple inheritance, that is, a class cannot inherit from two superclasses, but you can extend a class and implement one or more interfaces.

*class Mercedes **extends** LuxuryCars **implements** CarDetails*

9

Mouse and Keyboard Events

Introduction

When you click on the mouse or move it or press a key, a series of events occur. Java has defined some classes which allow you to detect that an event has occurred and to take some action in response to it. You can choose which events you want to listen for and which you want to ignore.

If you have worked with events in JDK1.0 you will find that the classes and methods you must use are completely different. Your old applications will still work, but the classes and methods they use for the event handling have been deprecated, that is they are still available in this version but may not be supported in the future. By flagging a class or method as deprecated Sun are giving you notice not to use it and if possible to change existing applications to the new way of doing things.

The MouseEvent class

There are two types of mouse event, those related to the movement of the mouse, and those which deal with pressing the mouse buttons or moving the mouse over a component. These events are defined as **static int** values in the **java.awt.event.MouseEvent** class.

The two mouse motion events are:

- **MOUSE_MOVED**
- **MOUSE_DRAGGED**

These events occur as a continuous stream whenever the mouse is moved or dragged. To catch these two events and respond to them you must use either the **MouseListener** interface or the **MouseAdapter** class.

There are five other mouse events:

- **MOUSE_PRESSED** - a mouse button is pressed.
- **MOUSE_RELEASED** - a mouse button is released.
- **MOUSE_CLICKED** - a mouse button is clicked, that is pressed and released.
- **MOUSE_ENTERED**, the mouse cursor enters a component.
- **MOUSE_EXITED**, the mouse cursor leaves a component.

When a mouse button is clicked the sequence of events is **MOUSE_PRESSED**, **MOUSE_RELEASED** and **MOUSE_CLICKED**. To catch these five events you must use the **MouseMotionListener** interface or the **MouseMotionAdapter** class.

The **MouseEvent** class also defines some useful methods which provide information about a mouse event as shown in table 9.1:

Table 9.1 *The key methods of the MouseEvent class.*

Method	Description
int getClickCount( )	Returns the number of clicks associated with the event. A single click gives a value of one a double click a value of two.
Point getPoint( )	Returns the x, y position where the event occurred as a **Point** object.
int getX( )	Returns the x position where the event occurred.
int getY( )	Returns the y position where the event occurred.
void translatePoint(int x, int y)	Moves the x and y co-ordinates by the amount specified in the parameters.

There are also two particularly useful methods which are inherited from the **java.awt.AWTEvent** class, which is the root event class for all AWT events:

Table 9.2 *Methods the MouseEvent class inherits from the AWTEvent class.*

Method	Description
int getID( )	Returns an integer which indicates the mouse event which has occurred.
String toString( )	Returns a string which gives full details of the mouse event.

Handling mouse events is often an area which new Java programmers find difficult, but there are well-defined steps which you need to follow when using the **MouseListener** or the **MouseMotionListener** interfaces. First we are going to look at the **MouseListener** interface.

The MouseListener interface

There are three stages to handling mouse events:

- Create a class which implements the **MouseListener** interface.
- Attach the mouse listener to a particular component.
- Override all of the methods defined in the **MouseListener** interface in your class to catch the mouse events.

The applet we are going to look at next displays a message showing which mouse event has occurred and the mouse position where it occurred. The running applet is shown in figure 9.1:

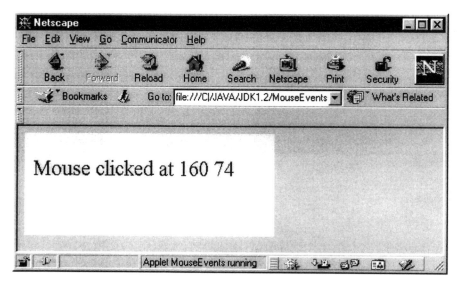

Fig. 9.1 Displaying mouse events.

To create this applet we first need to import three packages:

> *import java.applet.*;*
> *import java.awt.*;*
> *import java.awt.event.*;*

Since the *MouseEvents* class which we are creating is an applet it extends the **Applet** class; since we also want to handle the mouse events we need to implement the **MouseListener** interface:

> *public class MouseEvents extends Applet implements MouseListener {*

The second stage is to attach a mouse listener to a particular component. All applets extend the **Panel** class, which defines the area in which the applet runs. To add a mouse listener to this panel, the **addMouseListener** method is used in the constructor for the *MouseEvents* class:

```
public MouseEvents( ) {
    addMouseListener(this);
}
```

The parameter **this** refers to the current component, in this case the applet panel.

There are five methods in the **MouseListener** interface which are shown in table 9.3. They are all **void**, that is they do not return any information. When a class implements an interface it must include its own forms of all the methods defined in the interface, even if some of the methods you define are empty.

Table 9.3 *The methods of the MouseListener interface.*

Method	Description
void mouseClicked(MouseEvent)	Invoked when any mouse button is clicked on a component.
void mouseEntered(MouseEvent)	Invoked when the mouse cursor moves over a component.
void mouseExited(MouseEvent)	Invoked when the mouse cursor is no longer over a component.
void mousePressed(MouseEvent)	Invoked when any mouse button is pressed.
void mouseReleased(MouseEvent)	Invoked when any mouse button is released.

When one of these events occurs the corresponding method is called, for example when a mouse button is clicked, the **mouseClicked** method is called:

```
public void mouseClicked(MouseEvent e) {
    display(e.getID( ),e.getX( ),e.getY( ));
}
```

This method, in common with all of the **MouseListener** interface methods, is passed a **MouseEvent** object which contains information relating to the event, such as the identity of the event, which is returned by the **getID** method, and the x and y position where the mouse event occurred given by the **getX** and **getY** methods.

The methods **mousePressed**, **mouseReleased**, **mouseEntered** and **mouseExited** contain exactly the same line of Java as the **mouseClicked** method.

The *display* method was written to avoid duplicating Java code in each of the five methods which handle the mouse events. This method puts information into a **String** instance variable, called *m*, about the event which has occurred and the position where it has occurred. This method also calls the **repaint** method which displays the **String**:

```
private void display(int evt, int x, int y) {
    if (evt == MouseEvent.MOUSE_CLICKED) m = "Mouse clicked";
    else if (evt == MouseEvent.MOUSE_ENTERED) m = "Mouse entered";
    else if (evt == MouseEvent.MOUSE_EXITED) m = "Mouse exited";
    else if (evt == MouseEvent.MOUSE_PRESSED) m = "Mouse pressed";
    if (evt == MouseEvent.MOUSE_RELEASED) m = "Mouse released";
```

```
        m += " at " + x + " " + y;
        repaint( );
    }
```

The complete application is shown below:

```java
import java.applet.*;
import java.awt.*;
import java.awt.event.*;
public class MouseEvents extends Applet implements MouseListener {
    String m;
    public MouseEvents( ) {
        addMouseListener(this);
    }
    public void mouseClicked(MouseEvent e) {
        display(e.getID( ),e.getX( ),e.getY( ));
    }
    public void mousePressed(MouseEvent e) {
        display(e.getID( ), e.getX( ),e.getY( ));
    }
    public void mouseReleased(MouseEvent e) {
        display(e.getID( ), e.getX( ),e.getY( ));
    }
    public void mouseEntered(MouseEvent e) {
        display(e.getID( ),e.getX( ),e.getY( ));
    }
    public void mouseExited(MouseEvent e) {
        display(e.getID( ),e.getX( ),e.getY( ));
    }
    private void display(int evt, int x, int y) {
        if (evt == MouseEvent.MOUSE_CLICKED) m = "Mouse clicked";
        else if (evt == MouseEvent.MOUSE_ENTERED) m = "Mouse entered";
        else if (evt == MouseEvent.MOUSE_EXITED) m = "Mouse exited";
        else if (evt == MouseEvent.MOUSE_PRESSED) m = "Mouse pressed";
        if (evt == MouseEvent.MOUSE_RELEASED) m = "Mouse released";
        m += " at " + x + " " + y;
        repaint( );
    }
    public void paint(Graphics g) {
        g.setFont(new Font("Serif", Font.PLAIN, 30));
        g.drawString(m, 50, 50);
    }
}
```

Note that this applet imports **java.awt.event.*** in addition to the packages **java.applet.*** and **java.awt.***.

An alternative way of implementing this application is to use the **toString** method which returns a description of the event, for example in the **mouseClicked** method:

```
public void mouseClicked(MouseEvent e) {
    m = e.toString( );
    repaint( );
}
```

The **repaint** method is called to display the string *m*, and the *display* method is no longer required. To see the output shown in figure 9.2 you will have to reduce the font size from 30 as used in the previous applet to 15 otherwise it may not fit onto your screen.

```
java.awt.event.MouseEvent[MOUSE_CLICKED,(311,69),mods=16,clickCount=1] on panel0
```

Fig. 9.2 Using the toString method.

The **toString** method gives the name of the class where the mouse event is defined, the name of the event itself, the co-ordinates of the mouse position, the state of any modifier keys, such as shift and ctrl, the click count, which is the number of clicks associated with the event, and finally the component where the event occurs.

If you double-click the mouse the click count value is 2. This value is returned by the **getClickCount** method.

Which button was pressed?

If you want to know which mouse button was pressed and if a modifier key such as shift, ctrl or alt was also pressed, the information is contained within the **MouseEvent** object and can be obtained using the **getModifiers** method. This method returns an **int**. To find if a modifier key is pressed when for example a mouse clicked event occurs, you can use the **isAltDown**, **isShiftDown** and **isControlDown** methods which return a boolean which is **true** if the corresponding key is pressed.

There are no methods for determining which mouse button was pressed, however there are three masks inherited from the **InputEvent** class which can be used. These masks are called **InputEvent.BUTTON1_MASK**, **BUTTON2_MASK** and **BUTTON3_MASK**. If the "logical and" of the modifier value and a button mask is non-zero then that button was pressed. The "logical and" operator is &.

The previous applet has been modified to see these methods and masks in action. The application displays a message indicating if a single or double-click has occurred, which button was pressed and which (if any) of the modifier keys were pressed.

Double click Button1 CONTROL key is down

Fig. 9.3 Interpreting the modifier value.

The running application is shown in figure 9.3.

Note that this applet only deals with events from buttons one and three. There is a bug in Java 2, which means that button two modifiers are not handled correctly. If you extend the applet shown to display button two events and the state of the modifier keys, unexpected results occur. The **getModifiers** method returns a bitmap, with different bits being set to indicate which button has been clicked and the state of the shift, ctrl and alt keys; the same bit is used to indicate that button two has been pressed and that the alt key is pressed. This error is likely to be fixed in later releases of the JDK.

The code used to produce this application is shown below:

```
import java.applet.*;
import java.awt.*;
import java.awt.event.*;
public class MouseEventModifiers extends Applet implements MouseListener {
    String m;
    public MouseEventModifiers() {
        addMouseListener(this);
    }
    public void mouseClicked(MouseEvent e) {
        if (e.getClickCount() == 1) m = "Single click";
        else if (e.getClickCount() == 2) m = "Double click";
        int mod = e.getModifiers();
        if ((mod & InputEvent.BUTTON1_MASK) !=0) m += " Button1 ";
        else if ((mod & InputEvent.BUTTON3_MASK) !=0 ) m += " Button3 ";
        if (e.isAltDown()) m += " ALT key is down ";
        if (e.isControlDown()) m += " CONTROL key is down ";
        if (e.isShiftDown()) m += " SHIFT key is down ";
        repaint();
    }
    public void mousePressed(MouseEvent e) {
    }
    public void mouseReleased(MouseEvent e) {
    }
    public void mouseEntered(MouseEvent e) {
    }
    public void mouseExited(MouseEvent e) {
    }
    public void paint(Graphics g) {
        g.setFont(new Font("Serif", Font.PLAIN, 18));
        g.drawString(m, 10, 80);
```

```
        }
    }
```

Whenever a mouse click event occurs the **mouseClicked** event is invoked. If the **getClickCount** method returns the value 1, the text *Single click* is assigned to the **String** *m*, if the mouse is double-clicked the **getClickCount** method returns 2 and the text *Double click* is assigned to *m*.

The **getModifiers** method is called. The "logical and" operator is indicated by the & character. The "logical and" of the modifier and each of the three button masks is found. If a non-zero value is produced then that is the mouse button which was pressed.

The state of the alt, shift and control buttons at the time the mouse button was pressed is found using the **isAltDown**, **isControlDown** and **isShiftDown** methods and the message **String** *m* is changed to indicate which modifier button (if any) was pressed.

Finally the **repaint** method is called to display the **String** *m*.

One important thing to notice about this application is that even though we only wanted to use the **mouseClicked** method we had to create empty **mousePressed**, **mouseReleased**, **mouseEntered** and **mouseExited** methods, since the **MouseEventModifiers** class we have created implements the **MouseListener** interface. Any class which implements an interface must override all of the methods of the interface whether they are used or not.

Java provides a way of improving this application so that we do not need to create a group of empty classes by using the **MouseAdapter** class rather than the **MouseListener** interface.

The MouseAdapter class

The application we have created works well, but is inconvenient to include empty methods which are not required in the application. These methods are required since Java only supports single inheritance, that is a class can only extend one class and all applets must extend the **Applet** class. To catch the mouse events an applet must implement the **MouseListener** interface. If a class uses an interface all of the methods of that interface must be implemented even if they are empty methods. The **MouseAdapter** class is an **abstract** class which implements the **MouseListener** interface. This class has a set of methods which are identical to those in the **MouseListener** interface. Since Java does not allow multiple inheritance the **MouseAdapter** class is usually used to extend an inner class within a class which needs to handle mouse events. The applet shown below is functionally identical to the previous applet but uses and inner class:

```
import java.applet.*;
import java.awt.*;
import java.awt.event.*;
public class InnerClasses extends Applet {
    String m;
```

```
    public InnerClasses( ) {
        MyListener m = new MyListener( );
        addMouseListener(m);
    }
    //start an inner class called MyListener
    public final class MyListener extends MouseAdapter {
        public void mouseClicked(MouseEvent e) {
            if (e.getClickCount( ) == 1) m = "Single click";
            else if (e.getClickCount( ) == 2) m = "Double click";
            int mod = e.getModifiers( );
            if ((mod & InputEvent.BUTTON1_MASK) !=0) m +=" Button1 ";
            else if ((mod & InputEvent.BUTTON2_MASK) !=0) m +=" Button2 ";
            else if ((mod & InputEvent.BUTTON3_MASK) !=0) m +=" Button3 ";
            if (e.isAltDown( )) m += " ALT key is down ";
            if (e.isControlDown( )) m += " CONTROL key is down ";
            if (e.isShiftDown( )) m += " SHIFT key is down ";
            repaint( );
        }
    } //end of MyListener class
    public void paint(Graphics g) {
        g.setFont(new Font("Serif", Font.PLAIN, 18));
        g.drawString(m, 10, 80);
    }
} //end of InnerClasses class
```

There are some important differences between this applet and the previous one:

- The *InnerClasses* class extends the **Applet** class but does not implement the **MouseListener** interface.
- The inner class called *MyListener* extends the **MouseAdapter** class.
- Only methods from the **MouseAdapter** class which are needed are created, in this case only the **mouseClicked** method. The empty methods such as **mousePressed** are not created.
- An instance of the inner class *MyListener* is created. and the **addMouseListener** method is used to listen to events which happen on the panel of the applet.

If you only wish to handle a few of the mouse events it is probably best to create an inner class which extends the **MouseAdapter** class so that you do not have to create empty methods. In the rare cases where you have a class which does not extend any other class you can extend the **MouseAdapter** class directly without the need for an inner class.

If you wish to handle most or all of the mouse events it is best to implement the **MouseListener** interface.

The MouseMotionListener interface

The **MouseMotionListener** interface receives mouse events related to mouse motion and dragging. There are only two methods in this class which catch these two mouse events as shown in table 9.4:

*Table 9.4 The methods of the **MouseMotionListener** interface.*

Method	Description
void mouseDragged(MouseEvent)	Invoked when any mouse button is pressed and the mouse moved on a component.
void mouseMoved(MouseEvent)	Invoked when the mouse is moved on a component.

In the next application we are going to use both of the methods of the **MouseMotionListener** interface to create an applet which draws a line that follows the movement of the mouse when it is dragged. When the mouse is first pressed, this marks the start of the line. As it is dragged a stream of events are produced which are handled by the **mouseDragged** method to draw a line from the previous to the new position. When the mouse button is released this marks the end of the line. The mouse can be moved to a new position. When the mouse button is pressed again this marks the start of another line. The apparently continuous smooth lines are really a series of very short straight lines, one of which is drawn every time a mouse button is pressed and the mouse moved. The application in action is shown in figure 9.4.

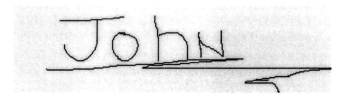

Fig. 9.4 Using the Scribble applet.

The complete code for this applet is shown below. Since we are using both of the methods of the **MouseMotionListener** interface we can implement this interface rather than creating an inner class which extends the **MouseMotionAdapter** class. In the same way that the **MouseAdapter** class is a concrete subclass of the **MouseListener** interface, the **MouseMotionAdapter** class is a concrete subclass of the **MouseMotionListener** interface. The **MouseMotionAdapter** class is normally used to extend an inner class. An instance of this inner class is created in the outer class, in a similar way to the use of the **MouseAdapter** class in the previous example:

```
import java.applet.*;
import java.awt.*;
import java.awt.event.*;
public class Scribble extends Applet implements MouseMotionListener {
```

```
      Point start, finish;
      boolean first = true;
      public Scribble( ) {
            setBackground(Color.yellow);
            addMouseMotionListener(this);
      }
      public void mouseDragged(MouseEvent evt) {
            start = finish;
            finish = new Point(evt.getX( ),evt.getY( ));
//don't draw a line if it's the first point
            if (!first) repaint( ); else first = false;
      }
      public void mouseMoved( MouseEvent evt) {
//when the next mouseDragged event occurs start a new line
//not connected to the last line
            first = true;
      }
      public void update(Graphics g) {
            paint(g);
      }
      public void paint(Graphics g) {
            g.drawLine(start.x, start.y, finish.x, finish.y);
      }
}
```

The *Scribble* class has three instance variables: two **Point** objects, *start* and *finish* which store the co-ordinates of the start and end position of the line to be drawn, and a **boolean** called *first*. When the applet starts, the constructor for the *Scribble* class is invoked, it changes the background colour and assigns the **MouseMotionListener** to the panel which provides the default drawing area for an applet. When the first drag event occurs the **mouseDragged** method is executed. This makes the end point of the previous line the start point of the new line. The co-ordinates of the current point are found using the **getX** and **getY** methods for the **MouseEvent** object *evt*. If this is the first mouse drag event which has occurred the boolean *first* will be **true**, if this is the case do not draw the line but make this boolean **false**, so that the next time this event occurs the line is drawn.

When the mouse button is not pressed and the mouse is moved, mouse move events occur and the **mouseMoved** method is called. This assigns the **boolean** *first* to **true**, which ensures that the next time the mouse is dragged it marks the start of a new and unconnected line. If this line is omitted, when the mouse button is pressed and the mouse dragged, the end of the previous line would be connected to the start of the new line.

A new **update** method is used which does nothing except call the **paint** method which draws a line between the start and end co-ordinates as indicated by the two **Point** objects *start* and *finish*. If the default **update** method was used the panel would be erased every time that **paint** was called which would result in a very short moving line when the mouse was dragged.

The KeyEvent class

When a keystroke occurs in a component a key event happens. There are three events which can occur when a key is pressed. These events are defined in the **java.awt.event.KeyEvent** class:

- **KEY_PRESSED** occurs when a key is pressed down.
- **KEY_RELEASED** occurs when a pressed down key is released.
- **KEY_TYPED** occurs when a character is entered; this may be a simple **KEY_PRESSED** event followed by a **KEY_RELEASED** event, however if a character requires more than one key, for example *shift+a*, only one **KEY_TYPED** event occurs, but two **KEY_PRESSED** and two **KEY_RELEASED** events.

The **KEY_TYPED** event is a high-level event which is platform and keyboard independent. If you wish to detect character input this event should be used. The difficulty with this event is that it does occur when keys are pressed which do not produce printable characters, for example F1.

The **KEY_PRESSED** and **KEY_RELEASED** events are lower level events which are dependent on the platform and keyboard layout. They are the only way to handle input from keys which do not produce printable input.

The **KeyEvent** class defines an extensive set of virtual key codes to report which key has been typed. Some of the most commonly-used are shown in table 9.5.

Table 9.5 KeyEvent class constants.

Constant	Key represented
VK_DOWN	Down arrow.
VK_HOME	Home key (start of line).
VK_LEFT	Left arrow key.
VK_PAGE_DOWN	Page down.
VK_PAGE_UP	Page up.
VK_RIGHT	Right arrow key.
VK_UP	Up arrow.
VK_F1 → **VK_F12**	One of the twelve function keys.
VK_UNDEFINED	No defined key has been pressed.
VK_0 → **VK_9**	One of the numeric characters.
VK_A → **VK_Z**	One of the letters; there is no distinction between lower and upper case letters.

The only keys which are defined by the Java language are **VK_ENTER, VK_TAB**, and **VK_BACK_SPACE**; all of the other constants may be subject to change in future releases of the JDK. The virtual key codes do not identify a physical key on the keyboard, for example the key which produces **VK_Q** on the US Windows keyboard produces **VK_A** on the French Windows keyboard.

The **KeyEvent** class has some useful methods for finding out what sequence of keys has been pressed, the most commonly-used methods are shown in table 9.6:

Table 9.6 *The key methods of the KeyEvent class.*

Method	Description
int getKeyCode( )	Returns an **int** code for the key associated with this event.
char getKeyChar( )	Returns the character displayed, for example *shift* followed by *a* returns the character *A*.
String getKeyText(int)	Returns a **String** which describes the key code passed to it, for example *F1* or *Home*.
boolean isActionKey( )	Returns **true** if the key is an action key such as the up arrow key.
void setKeyCode(int)	Changes the key code associated with this event to the specified value.
void setKeyChar(char)	Sets the character associated with this event to the specified value.

In the next applet we are going to use some of these methods, in particular to show the difference between the **getKeyCode**, **getKeyChar** and **getKeyText** methods, but first we need to look at the **KeyAdapter** class and the **KeyListener** interface which have some methods which are invoked when a keyboard event occurs.

The KeyAdapter class

The **KeyListener** interface has methods which can receive keyboard events. The **KeyAdapter** class is a class which implements **KeyListener** and has exactly the same set of methods. The relationship between these two classes is similar to that between the **MouseAdapter** class and the **MouseListener** interface and the **MouseMotionAdapter** class and the **MouseMotionListener** interface.

The **KeyListener** interface has three void methods which receive one of the three keyboard events.

Table 9.7 *The methods of the KeyListener interface.*

Method	Description
void keyPressed(KeyEvent)	Invoked when a key is pressed.
void keyReleased(KeyEvent)	Invoked when a pressed key is released.
void keyTyped(KeyEvent)	Invoked when a printable key is typed.

All three of these methods are passed a **KeyEvent** object as a parameter. In the next applet we are going to create an inner class which extends the **KeyAdapter** class. This applet is shown in figure 9.5.

A	a	Not an Action key
Shift	Not printable	Not an Action key
A	A	Not an Action key
Caps Lock	Not printable	Action key
A	A	Not an Action key
Up	Not printable	Action key
Home	Not printable	Action key
Shift	Not printable	Not an Action key
4	$	Not an Action key
Quote	#	Not an Action key
Unknown keyCode: 0xdd	]	Not an Action key

Fig. 9.5 *Logging keyboard events.*

There are three columns of information displayed. The first column is produced by the **getKeyText** method and gives a textual representation of the key which has been pressed, such as **Home** and **Up** (for the up arrow key). The second column uses the **getKeyChar** method to find which printable character key has been pressed, if a non-printable key has been pressed the text *Not printable* is displayed.

Sun's documentation says that an unprintable character will return **KeyEvent.CHAR_UNDEFINED** from the **getKeyChar** method, however the value of this field has not been correctly defined and therefore to see if the returned character is printable a test is made against a locally defined **final static char** called *UNDEFINED*. This bug is likely to be fixed in service releases versions of Java 2.

Finally in the third column the **isAction** method is called to find out if an action key has been pressed and displays the message *Action key* or *Not an Action key*. The sequence of keys used to produce the output shown in figure 9.5 was *a, shift a, caps lock, up arrow, Home, shift, 4, #,].*

When the lower case *a* is pressed the **getKeyText** method is passed the key code of the key which has been pressed and returns an uppercase A - this method does not differentiate between upper and lower case *a*. The **getKeyChar** method returns a lower case *a* which is displayed in the second column which is not an action key. The **getKeyChar** is able to differentiate between upper and lower case letters.

The *shift a* pair which is displayed as upper case *A* are viewed as two separate key pressed events and the **keyPressed** method is called twice. The **getKeyText** method displays the text *Shift* when the shift key is pressed, this is not a printable key and so the message *Not printable* is displayed The shift key It is not an action key. Note that many non-printable keys are not action keys. When the *a* key is pressed, the **getKeyText** method displays an upper case *A*. The **getKeyChar** method displays an upper case *A* which is not an action key.

The *Up* and *Home* keys are not printable action keys.

When I try to type a *$* sign which is *shift+4* on my keyboard the pressing of the *shift* key is reported as before. Pressing the *4* key returns the text *4* from the **getKeyText** method and as expected the *$* sign from the **getKeyChar** method.

More surprising is that when I press the *#* key, the **getKeyText** method returns the text of *Quote*, while **getKeyChar** displays the correct character.

Pressing the key which produces a closed square bracket *]* on my keyboard produces the response *Unknown keyCode 0xdd*. The hexadecimal number is the value returned by the **getKeyCode** method and passed to the **getKeyText** method. The **getKeyChar** method displays the correct character.

The applet used to produce the output is shown below. If you run this applet on your system you may get different results if your computer is configured in a different way.

```java
import java.applet.*;
import java.awt.*;
import java.awt.event.*;
public class KeyboardEvents extends Applet {
    int y = 20;
    String keyText, printable, action;
    public KeyboardEvents()     {
        setBackground(Color.yellow);
        setFont(new Font("Serif", Font.PLAIN, 18));
        MyListener m = new MyListener();
        addKeyListener(m);
    }
    public final class MyListener extends KeyAdapter {
        static final char UNDEFINED = (char)0;
        public void keyPressed(KeyEvent e) {
            keyText = e.getKeyText(e.getKeyCode());
            if (e.getKeyChar() == UNDEFINED)
                printable = "Not printable";
                else printable = String.valueOf(e.getKeyChar());
            if (e.isActionKey()) action ="Action key";
            else action = "Not an Action key";
            repaint();
        }
    } // end of the MyListener class
    public void update(Graphics g) {
        paint(g);
    }
    public void paint(Graphics g){
        g.drawString(keyText, 30, y);     //describes the key code
        g.drawString(printable, 250, y);  //displays the char or "non printable"
        g.drawString(action, 370, y);     //states if it is an action key
        y += 20;
```

```
        }
    }
}
```

The organisation of this applet is very similar to the applets we have used earlier for handling mouse events. The constructor method creates an instance of a listener class (which is an inner class in this case) and assigns it to listen to events which occur on the applet panel. *MyListener* is an inner class which extends the **KeyAdapter** class. It contains one method, **keyPressed** which is invoked when a key pressed event occurs. This method is passed a **KeyEvent** object. The **getKeyCode** method returns an integer value which represents the key pressed, this is passed to the **getKeyText** method which returns a **String** describing the key which is assigned to the instance variable **keyPressed**. The instance **String** variable *printable* is assigned the character returned by the **getKeyChar** method or the text *Not printable*. Finally the **String** instance variable *action* is assigned text indicating if the key is an action key.

The **repaint** method is called via the **update** method. The **update** method does nothing except call **paint** and so ensures that the applet panel is not cleared every time **paint** is invoked.

The **paint** method displays the three strings and increases the value of the integer instance variable *y*, which specifies the y co-ordinate of the text which is displayed. This ensures that the information on different key depressions is reported on different lines.

The KeyListener interface

The previous application can be modified so that the text is displayed in response to key typed events, that is from the **keyTyped** method. There are some important changes to the output as shown in figure 9.6. To produce this display the key sequence *shift+h, I, return*, was used.

Unknown keyCode: 0x0	H	Not an Action key
Unknown keyCode: 0x0	i	Not an Action key
Unknown keyCode: 0x0	□	Not an Action key

Fig. 9.6 Using the keyTyped method.

The **getKeyCode** method always returns **VK_UNDEFINED** which causes the **getKeyText** method to display the text *Unknown keyCode: 0x0*. The **getKeyChar** method displays the characters *H* and *i* correctly (successfully combining *shift+h* to produce an upper case *H*). No printable character is an action key. Pressing the return key does cause a key typed event but the square representing this character is not meaningful. The character produced is dependent on your system.

The applet used to produce this is shown below. It is similar to the previous applet except that the **KeyListener** interface is implemented, rather than creating an inner class which extends the **KeyAdapter** class. Since we are implementing an interface all of the methods of that interface must be over-ridden even if it is only with empty methods as is the case with the **keyPressed** and the **keyReleased** methods.

```java
import java.applet.*;
import java.awt.*;
import java.awt.event.*;
public class KeyTypedEvents extends Applet implements KeyListener {
int y = 20;
String keyText, printable, action;
    public KeyTypedEvents( )    {
        setBackground(Color.yellow);
        addKeyListener(this);
    }
    public void keyTyped(KeyEvent e) {
        keyText = e.getKeyText(e.getKeyCode( ));
        if (e.getKeyChar( ) == KeyEvent.CHAR_UNDEFINED)
            printable = " Not printable";
            else printable = " " + e.getKeyChar( );
        if (e.isActionKey( )) action ="Action key";
        else action = "Not an Action key";
        repaint( );
    }
    public void keyPressed(KeyEvent e){
    }
    public void keyReleased(KeyEvent e){
    }
    public void update(Graphics g) {
        paint(g);
    }
    public void paint(Graphics g){
        setFont(new Font("Serif", Font.PLAIN, 18));
        g.drawString(keyText, 30, y);       //describes the key code
        g.drawString(printable, 250, y);    //displays the char or "non printable"
        g.drawString(action, 370, y);       //states if it is an action key
        y += 20;
    }
}
```

10

The AWT Components

Introduction

The majority of applications written today use a graphical user interface (GUI) to display and input information. These user interfaces may appear slightly different depending on the platform you are working on, a PC, a Mac, or a Sun workstation, but the basic components from which they are built are very similar.

Java provides a set of classes in the **java.awt** package which represent all of the basic components such as buttons and list boxes. It also provides a set of classes for handling the events which occur when for example you click on a button or select an item from a list box. Many of the features which you would expect to find in a platform-specific integrated development environment (IDE) such as Visual C++ are available in Java using the Abstract Window Toolkit (AWT) classes.

Event-driven programming

We have already seen how actions such as moving the mouse or pressing a key on the keyboard produce events which can be detected and acted upon. In a similar way when you create a user interface with the AWT components, events occur when you use these components, perhaps typing some text, selecting an item from a list or clicking on a check box. The **java.awt** package allows you to create and display these components, while the **java.awt.event** package provides a set of classes which allow you to respond to their events.

The AWT classes

There are two types of AWT component. One group acts as a container for other components, for example the **Applet** class extends the **Panel** class which extends the

Container class and therefore provides an area for other components to be displayed on or to draw on directly.

The components which are placed on the container components all derive from the **Component** class as shown in figure 10.1:

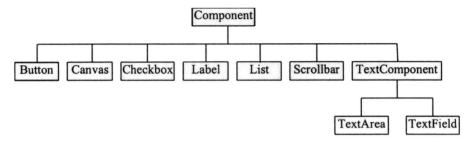

Fig. 10.1 The AWT components.

These container components are covered in chapter 12.

The Button class

The **Button** class has only two constructors:

- **Button( )** draws a button without any text on its face.
- **Button(String)** draws a button with the specified text on its face.

To display a button or any component use the **add** method, which is inherited from the **Component** class. Three buttons are shown in figure 10.2; note that the size of the button automatically changes to fit the text displayed on its face.

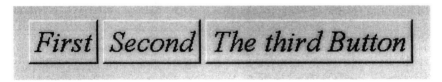

Fig. 10.2 Displaying buttons.

The code used to create this applet is shown below.

```
import java.applet.*;
import java.awt.*;
public class Buttons extends Applet {
    public Buttons() {
        setFont(new Font("Serif", Font.ITALIC, 30));
        Button firstButton = new Button("First");
        add(firstButton);
        add(new Button("Second"));
        add(new Button("The third Button"));
```

```
    }
}
```

The **add** method displays the buttons on the panel drawing area which is available since this is an applet and the **Applet** class inherits from the **Panel** class. The **add** method requires the name of the object which is to be displayed to be passed to it. This can be done in two ways. The button with *First* on its face is instantiated and a **Button** object called *firstButton* is created. This is passed to the **add** method. The second and third buttons are instantiated within the call to the **add** method itself. If your application has more than one button and you wish to distinguish between them, it is advisable to instantiate the buttons before displaying them with the **add** method so that you have an object name to refer to. It is not sufficient to instantiate a button to display it, you must use the **add** method.

*Table 10.1 The key methods of the **Button** class.*

Method	Description
void addActionListener(ActionListener)	Adds the action listener to receive events from the **Button** object.
String getActionCommand( )	Returns the name of the action event produced by the **Button** object.
String getLabel( )	Returns the **Button** object's label.
void removeActionListener(ActionListener)	Removes the action listener so that it no longer receives action events from this **Button** object.
void setLabel(String)	Changes the **Button** object's label to the specified **String**.

Handling events

The handling of events for the AWT classes is very similar to the technique used for handling mouse and keyboard events. The **ActionListener** interface extends the **EventListener** interface (as do the **MouseListener**, **MouseMotionListener** and **KeyListener** interfaces). A class which uses the events produced by the AWT components must implement the **ActionListener** interface. This class inherits a substantial number of methods from the **EventListener** class but has only has one method of its own, called **actionPerformed**, which is passed an **ActionEvent** object containing details of the event which has occurred. The **addActionListener** method is used to attach the AWT object to the listener. All of the AWT classes which produce visual components have their own version of the **addActionListener** method.

The following application adds listeners to two buttons and displays a different message depending on which was pressed. The running applet is shown in figure 10.3.

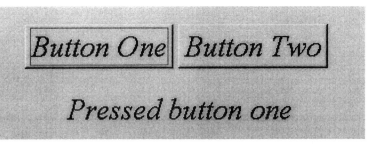

Fig. 10.3 *Which button was pressed?*

The class used to create this applet extends the **Applet** class (as do all applets) and implements the **ActionListener** interface. Two **Button** objects are declared as instance variables and instantiated in the constructor method for the class The **addActionListener** method is used to listen for events from both buttons. The **actionPerformed** method is called whenever a button event occurs. It is passed an **ActionEvent** object which provides full details of the event which has occurred. The **getSource** method is used to find out which button has been pressed. The instance variable *message* is assigned different text depending on which button was pressed. The **repaint** method calls the **paint** method, which displays the text. The complete applet code is shown below:

```
import java.applet.*;
import java.awt.*;
import java.awt.event.*;
public class UsingButtons extends Applet implements ActionListener {
    private Button buttonOne = new Button("Button One");
    private Button buttonTwo = new Button("Button Two");
    private String message;
    public UsingButtons( ) {
        add(buttonOne);
        add(buttonTwo);
        setFont(new Font("Serif", Font.ITALIC, 30));
        buttonOne.addActionListener(this);
        buttonTwo.addActionListener(this);
    }
    public void actionPerformed(ActionEvent e) {
        if (e.getSource( ) == buttonOne) message = "Pressed button one";
        else if (e.getSource( ) == buttonTwo) message = "Pressed button two";
        repaint( );
    }
    public void paint(Graphics g) {
        g.drawString(message, 50, 100);
    }
}
```

The Label class

The **Label** class is used to display text which can be changed by the application but not by the user, at run-time. There are three constructors for this class:

- **Label( )** creates a blank label with no text.
- **Label(String)** creates a label with the specified text.
- **Label(String, int)** creates a label with the specified text and alignment. The integer alignment value must be one of three possible values: **Label.CENTER**, **Label.LEFT** or **Label.RIGHT**.

The different alignment of three labels is shown in figure 10.4:

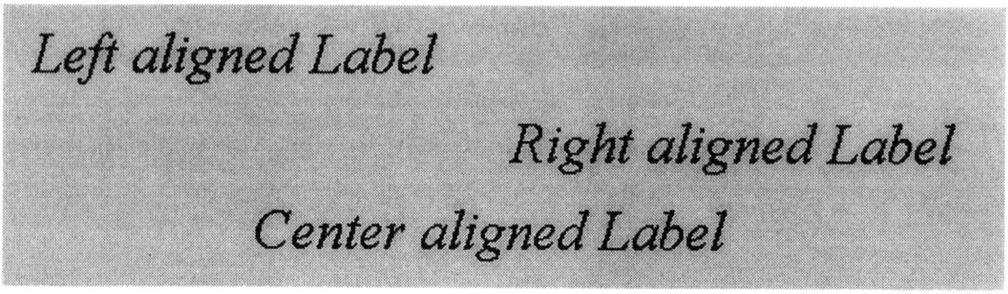

Left aligned Label

Right aligned Label

Center aligned Label

*Fig. 10.4 Changing **Label** alignment.*

The code used to create this applet is shown below:

```
import java.applet.*;
import java.awt.*;
public class UsingLabels extends Applet {
    public UsingLabels( ) {
        setLayout(new GridLayout(3,1)); //display labels in a 3 by 1 grid
        setFont(new Font("Serif", Font.ITALIC, 30));
        add(new Label("Left aligned Label", Label.LEFT));
        add(new Label("Right aligned Label", Label.RIGHT));
        add(new Label("Center aligned Label", Label.CENTER));
    }
}
```

There is one feature in this applet which we have not seen before. The **setLayout** method is used to specify how components are displayed. The default layout used by **Panel** components is **FlowLayout**. In this applet, it is changed to **GridLayout**. Until now when we have added components to the applet **Panel**, we have not said where these components are to be put, we have just relied on the default **FlowLayout**. Each component has been added one after the other from the left of the **Panel** to the right. When there is insufficient room for a component to fit into the remaining space on the line, it is shown at the start of the next line. The **GridLayout** works differently. The **Panel** is divided into a set of squares (in this case 3 vertical squares by one horizontal square). Each component which is added is placed in the next free grid square. The first grid square to be filled is in the top left corner, the next square used is on the right of that square, or the start of the next line if no more squares are free on the current line. If the applet above did not specify that the **GridLayout** was to be used, the three **Label** objects would simply have been displayed next to each other irrespective of their alignment. If **GridLayout** is used, each **Label** occupies the whole of the grid square in which it is placed (only one component may be placed in a square). If the default **FlowLayout** is used only sufficient space is allocated to each label to show the text it contains. The layout managers are important as they are used to control how components are displayed on the screen; they are covered in detail in chapter 11.

Table 10.2 *The key methods of the **Label** class.*

Method	Description
int getAlignment( )	Returns the alignment of the **Label** object's text.
String getText( )	Returns the text displayed by the **Label**.
void setAlignment(int)	Sets the alignment to one of the three possible values.
void setText(String)	Assigns the text of the **Label** to the specified **String**.

The Scrollbar class

The **Scrollbar** class implements the familiar scroll bar found in every GUI. It is a useful component which can be used to specify a value without the need to type a number or choose a value from a list. There are two types of **Scrollbar**, vertical and horizontal. The position of the bubble, or slider, determines the value returned by this component. Figure 10.5 shows a vertical **Scrollbar.**

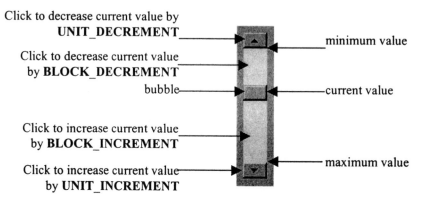

Fig. 10.5 *The Scrollbar class.*

There are several ways to control the position of the bubble and hence the value returned:

- Clicking on the space between the bubble and the arrow at the maximum value moves the bubble towards that arrow by an amount defined by

AdjustmentEvent.BLOCK_INCREMENT. Clicking on the space between the bubble and the minimum arrow decreases the value returned by **AdjustmentEvent.BLOCK_DECREMENT.**

- Clicking on the end arrow itself at the maximum value moves the bubble towards that arrow and increases the value returned by a smaller amount which is given by **AdjustmentEvent.UNIT_INCREMENT.** Similarly clicking on the arrow at the opposite end decreases the value by **AdjustmentEvent.UNIT_DECREMENT.** These two values are usually the same. Since you may not have a mouse, or may prefer to use a keyboard, there is a convention that pressing the **Page Up** and **Page Down** keys moves the bubble by **BLOCK_INCREMENT** and **BLOCK_DECREMENT** respectively.
- You can also move the bubble, and hence the value returned by dragging the bubble directly.

You can control the minimum and maximum values returned by the **Scrollbar.** There are three constructors for the **Scrollbar** class:

- **Scrollbar( )** creates a vertical **Scrollbar.**
- **Scrollbar(int** *orientation*) creates either a vertical or horizontal **Scrollbar.** The value of the *orientation* parameter of the **Scrollbar** can be either **Scrollbar.HORIZONTAL** or **Scrollbar.VERTICAL.**
- **Scrollbar(int** *orientation*, **int** *value*, **int** *visible*, **int** *minimum*, **int** *maximum*) creates a **Scrollbar** with the specified orientation. The *value* parameter gives the initial value returned by the **Scrollbar** and therefore determines its position. The *visible* parameter is the width of the bubble. The *minimum* and *maximum* values determine the values which are returned by the **Scrollbar** when the bubble is at the two ends of its movement.

Sun's documentation states that the maximum value returned by a **Scrollbar** is equal to the *maximum* parameter minus the width of the *value* parameter. If you write an applet and view it using Netscape Communicator 4.5 or the applet viewer you will find that this is the case, if however you run the same applet using Microsoft's Internet Explorer 4.01, you will find that the maximum value is equal to the *maximum* parameter, and the size of the *value* parameter is not taken into account.

Handling Scrollbar events

When the bubble is moved, one of the following five adjustments, defined in the **AdjustmentEvent** class, occurs as listed in table 10.3.

The **AdjustmentListener** interface can be used to detect these events; it only has one method called **adjustmentValueChanged** and receives an **AdjustmentEvent** object.

Table 10.3 *The adjustment types defined in the **AdjustmentEvent** class.*

Field	Description
TRACK	The bubble is dragged directly.
UNIT_INCREMENT	The left arrow of a horizontal **Scrollbar** or the bottom arrow of a vertical **Scrollbar** is clicked.
UNIT_DECREMENT	The right arrow of a horizontal **Scrollbar** or the top arrow of a vertical **Scrollbar** is clicked.
BLOCK_INCREMENT	The track between the bubble and the left arrow, or between the bubble and the bottom arrow is clicked.
BLOCK_DECREMENT	The track between the bubble and the right arrow, or between the bubble and the top arrow is clicked.

In the application shown in figure 10.6, as the bubble is moved the size of the displayed text changes and its size is also displayed.

Fig. 10.6 *Changing text size using a **Scrollbar** object.*

The applet code is shown below:

```
import java.applet.*;
import java.awt.*;
import java.awt.event.*;
public class UsingScrollbars extends Applet implements AdjustmentListener {
    private Scrollbar size;
    private int textSize = 10;
    public void init( ) {
        setLayout(new GridLayout(6, 1));
        size = new Scrollbar(Scrollbar.HORIZONTAL, textSize,10,textSize,60);
        add(size);
        size.addAdjustmentListener(this);
    }
    public void adjustmentValueChanged(AdjustmentEvent e) {
        if (e.getSource( ) == size) {
            textSize = e.getValue( );
            setFont(new Font("Serif", Font.ITALIC, textSize));
            repaint( );
```

```
        }
    }
    public void paint(Graphics g) {
        g.drawString("Text Size " + textSize, 50, 100);
    }
}
```

Note that the *maximum* parameter in the **Scrollbar** constructor is 60 and the *value* parameter (the width of the bubble) is 10. This will give a maximum value of 60-10=50 if you use Netscape Communicator or the applet viewer to run this applet. If you use Internet Explorer the maximum value is 60. In both cases the minimum value is 10.

This applet implements the **AdjustmentListener** interface. The horizontal **Scrollbar** has an initial value *textSize*, which is the same as the size of the text displayed by the **paint** method. The *visible* parameter is 10 and the minimum value returned by the **Scrollbar** is equal to the initial size of the text, that is 10. The maximum parameter is 60. The **Scrollbar** is displayed on the **Panel** using the **add** method and a listener for the adjustment events is created. When the bubble is moved one of the five adjustment events occurs and the **adjustmentValueChanged** method is called. A check is made to see if this event originated from the **Scrollbar** called *size*. If it did, the value returned by the **Scrollbar** using the **getValue** method is assigned to the *textSize* integer variable. The **repaint** method calls the **paint** method which displays the text message *Text Size* followed by the size of the text. The text is drawn with a size of *textSize* in position (50, 100).

The **Scrollbar** class has a comprehensive set of supporting methods, the most commonly-used ones are shown in table 10.4.

Table 10.4 *The key methods of the Scrollbar class.*

Method	Description
int getBlockIncrement( )	Returns the block increment (and decrement) value.
int getMaximum( )	Returns the maximum value.
int getOrientation( )	Returns the orientation, either horizontal or vertical.
int getUnitIncrement( )	Returns the unit increment (and decrement) value.
int getValue( )	Returns the current value.
void setBlockIncrement(int)	Sets the block increment value.
void setMaximum(int)	Sets the maximum value which can be returned.
void setMinimum(int)	Sets the minimum value which can be returned.
void setOrientation(int)	Specifies either vertical or horizontal orientation.
void setUnitIncrement(int)	Sets the unit increment (and decrement) value.
void setValue(int)	Sets the value of the **Scrollbar**.
void setValues(int, int, int, int)	Sets the value, visible, minimum and maximum values.

The Checkbox class

The **Checkbox** class embodies two popular GUI components, check boxes and radio buttons. Both of these components are useful when you have to choose between two options, for example male/female yes/no. They are commonly-used to present a list of options; to choose an option, you click on the check box or radio button to select it. The difference between these components is that check boxes are independent of each other: any number may be checked; radio buttons behave like a single group: only one of the group may be selected, selecting one radio button automatically de-selects all the others. In Java, **Checkbox** objects which are grouped under a **CheckboxGroup** object behave like radio buttons and have a difference appearance.

There are five constructors for the **Checkbox** class:

- **Checkbox( )**
- **Checkbox(String, boolean, CheckboxGroup)**
- **Checkbox(String, boolean)**
- **Checkbox(String, CheckboxGroup, boolean)**
- **Checkbox(String)**

The **String** parameter specifies a label which is placed adjacent to the **Checkbox**. The **boolean** parameter gives the initial state of the **Checkbox**. The **CheckboxGroup** parameter specifies the group (if any) to which the **Checkbox** belongs.

Three **CheckBox** components are shown in figure 10.7. The items which have been selected are displayed below the check boxes.

*Fig. 10.7 Using **Checkbox** objects.*

To respond to events for this class the **ItemListener** interface must be used. This has a single method called **itemStateChanged**, which is passed an **ItemEvent** object. This method is called whenever a change in state of the check box occurs. The complete applet used to produce the application shown in figure 10.7 is shown below:

```
import java.applet.*;
import java.awt.*;
import java.awt.event.*;
public class UsingCheckbox extends Applet implements ItemListener {
    private Checkbox modem, dvd, monitor17;
    private String text = "";
    public UsingCheckbox( ) {
        setFont(new Font("Serif", Font.PLAIN, 16));
        //instantiate, display and add listener for modem
```

```
        modem = new Checkbox("Modem", false);
        add(modem);
        modem.addItemListener(this);
        // instantiate, display and add listener for dvd
        dvd = new Checkbox("DVD", false);
        add(dvd);
        dvd.addItemListener(this);
        // instantiate, display and add listener for monitor17
        monitor17 = new Checkbox("17 inch monitor", false);
        add(monitor17);
        monitor17.addItemListener(this);
    }
    public void itemStateChanged(ItemEvent e) {
        text = "";
        if (modem.getState()) text += "modem ";
        if (dvd.getState()) {
            if (text == "" ) text += "DVD ";
            else text += "and DVD ";
        }
        if (monitor17.getState()) {
            if (text == "") text += "17in Monitor";
            else text += "and 17in Monitor";
        }
        repaint();
    }
    public void paint(Graphics g) {
        if (text == "") text = "nothing";
        g.drawString("You have chosen: " + text, 10, 50);
    }
}
```

The **addItemListener** method adds a listener to each of the three **Checkbox** objects. When one of these check boxes is clicked on, that is when it changes its state, the **itemStateChanged** method is called. This method uses the **getState** method to see the state of each of the three **Checkbox** objects and the **String** called *text* is assigned a different value depending on their state. The **repaint** method calls the **update** method which calls **paint** to displays *text*. In **paint**, a check is made to see if any item has been selected, if it has not, the message *You have chosen nothing* is displayed. In this application you can select as many of the **Checkbox** objects as you wish, sometimes however you may wish to limit the choice so that only one of the **Checkbox** objects can be selected. To do this they must be placed within a **CheckboxGroup** object.

Figure 10.8 shows a similar application to that shown in figure 10.7. The components shown are also **Checkbox** objects but have been grouped within a **CheckboxGroup**. This alters the appearance of the components which appear as round 'radio buttons' and it also alters their functionality. In this application the choices are mutually exclusive, that is only one may be selected. When one of these **Checkbox** objects is selected all of the others in the group are automatically deselected.

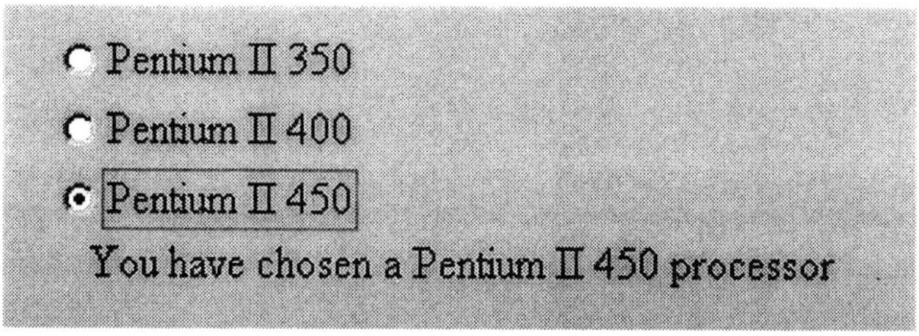

*Fig. 10.8 Using **Checkbox** objects with a **CheckboxGroup**.*

The complete listing for this application is shown below:

```
import java.applet.*;
import java.awt.*;
import java.awt.event.*;
public class UsingRadioButtons extends Applet implements ItemListener {
    private Checkbox pentium350, pentium400, pentium450;
    private String text = "Pentium II 450";
    public UsingRadioButtons() {
        setFont(new Font("Serif", Font.PLAIN, 16));
        setLayout(new GridLayout(10,1));
        CheckboxGroup g = new CheckboxGroup();
        // instantiate, display and add listener for pentium350
        pentium350 = new Checkbox("Pentium II 350", g, false);
        add(pentium350);
        pentium350.addItemListener(this);
        // instantiate, display and add listener for pentium400
        pentium400 = new Checkbox("Pentium II 400", g, false);
        add(pentium400);
        pentium400.addItemListener(this);
        // instantiate, display and add listener for pentium450
        pentium450 = new Checkbox("Pentium II 450", g, true);
        add(pentium450);
        pentium450.addItemListener(this);
    }
    public void itemStateChanged(ItemEvent e) {
        if (e.getSource() == pentium350) text = "Pentium II 350";
        else if (e.getSource() == pentium400) text = "Pentium II 400";
        else if (e.getSource() == pentium450) text = "Pentium II 450";
        repaint();
    }
    public void paint(Graphics g) {
        g.drawString("You have chosen a " + text + " processor", 10, 90);
```

```
      }
   }
```

The only significant difference between this application and the previous one is that a **CheckboxGroup** object, called *g*, is created and in the constructor for the **Checkbox** objects this **CheckboxGroup** is specified. The Java code in the **itemStateChanged** method is simplified since only one of the possible **CheckBox** objects can be selected. The most commonly-used methods for the **Checkbox** class are shown in table 10.5.

Table 10.5 *The key methods of the **Checkbox** class.*

Method	Description
void addItemListener(ItemListener)	Attaches a listener to the **Checkbox** object to receive item events.
CheckboxGroup getCheckboxGroup( )	Returns the **CheckboxGroup** for this **Checkbox** object.
String getLabel( )	Returns the text adjacent to the **Checkbox**.
boolean getState( )	Returns the checked/unchecked state of the **Checkbox**. If checked the state returned is **true**.
void removeItemListener(ItemListener)	Removes the item listener attached to this **Checkbox** object.
void setCheckboxGroup(CheckboxGroup)	Assigns the **Checkbox** object to this **CheckboxGroup**. If it is a member of another group it is removed from that group.
void setLabel(String)	Sets the text adjacent to the **Checkbox** to the specified string.
void setState(boolean)	Sets the checked/unchecked state of the **Checkbox** to the value specified.

The List class

The **List** class displays a list of items and allows you to select one or more of these items. If the size of the list is not big enough to include all the list items, a vertical scroll bar is automatically supplied as shown in figure 10.9. You can enable a **List** object to allow multiple selection of list items or limit the selection to a single item.

There are three constructors for the **List** class:

- **List( )** creates a **List** object without any items.

- **List(int, boolean)** creates a **List** object with the specified number of items visible (a scroll bar is automatically added if there are more items than this in the list). If the boolean is **true**, multiple selection of rows is allowed.
- **List(int)** creates a **List** with the specified number of rows.

When an item is selected, the event can be received by the **ItemListener**; specifically the **itemStateChanged** method is called. To handle this event you must implement both the **ItemListener** interface.

Figure 10.9 shows a **List** object containing a list of processor types. When an item is selected by you double-clicking on it, the text below the **List** is changed to display details of that item. Multiple selection of rows is not allowed in this application.

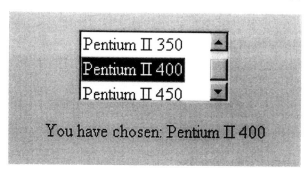

*Fig. 10.9 Selecting items from **List** objects.*

The Java application used to produce this applet is shown below:

```java
import java.applet.*;
import java.awt.*;
import java.awt.event.*;
public class UsingLists extends Applet implements ItemListener {
    private List l;
    private String text = "";
    public UsingLists( ) {
        setFont(new Font("Serif", Font.PLAIN, 16));
        //instantiate, display and add listener
        l = new List(3, false);
        l.add("Pentium II 300");
        l.add("Pentium II 350");
        l.add("Pentium II 400");
        l.add("Pentium II 450");
        add(l);
        l.addItemListener(this);
    }
    public void itemStateChanged(ItemEvent e) {
    //come here if a list item is selected
        text = l.getSelectedItem( );
```

```
        repaint( );
    }
    public void paint(Graphics g) {
        if (text == "") text = "nothing";
        g.drawString("You have chosen: " + text, 50, 100);
    }
}
```

The constructor for the **List** class used in this applet specifies that three items at a time may be displayed and that multiple selections are not allowed. The individual list items are entered into the **List** using the **add** method. An **ItemListener** is added to receive item selection events. The selected item is returned by the **getSelectedItem** method. This is assigned to the string *text*, the **repaint** method is called which calls **update** which calls **paint** to display this string message.

Multiple selection in List objects

Usually you only wish to select one item from a list, but in certain circumstances you may wish to select more than one item. The **List** class offers full support for multiple selection. In the application shown in figure 10.10, a **List** object is shown with two items displayed and a message below indicating which items have been selected. To select a single item, click on it as before. To select more than one item press the ctrl key at the same time as you click on an item.

The output of a Java applet and the applet itself are shown below:

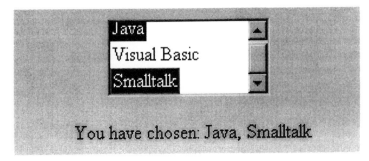

*Fig. 10.10 Selecting more than one item from a **List** object.*

```
import java.applet.*;
import java.awt.*;
import java.awt.event.*;
public class ListWithMultipleSelection extends Applet implements ItemListener {
    private List l;
    private String text[ ] = new String[10];
    public ListWithMultipleSelection( ) {
        setFont(new Font("Serif", Font.PLAIN, 16));
```

```
//instantiate, display and add listener
l = new List(3, true);
l.add("Java");
l.add("Visual Basic");
l.add("Smalltalk");
add(l);
l.addItemListener(this);
}
public void itemStateChanged(ItemEvent e) {
//come here if a list item is selected
    text = l.getSelectedItems( );
    repaint( );
}
public void paint(Graphics g) {
    String m = "You have chosen: ";
    if (text[0] == null) m += "nothing"; else {
        for (int c=0; c<text.length; c++) {
        //separate each item with a comma and space
        if (c != 0) m += ", ";
        m += text[c];
        }
    }
    g.drawString(m, 50, 100);
    }
}
```

The differences between this applet and the previous one is that *text* is defined as an array of strings. The first item selected is stored in the first element of this array and so on. In the **itemStateChanged** method the **getSelectedItems** method is used (note the letter 's' on the end of this method name). This method returns a **String** array containing the items selected. In the **paint** method a check is made to see if the first entry in the *text* array is null, if it is, no items have been selected and the text *you have chosen nothing* is displayed. If it is not null each of the selected items is added to the string *m*. The items added are separated by a comma and a space. The number of elements in the array is given by *text.length*.

The **List** class has a comprehensive set of methods for managing list items; the most commonly-used ones are shown in table 10.6. Note that there are methods with similar names for dealing with lists which allow and prohibit multiple selection of items, for example the **getSelectedIndex** method should be used where multiple selection is not allowed. The equivalent method for lists which allow multiple selection is **getSelectedIndexes**.

Table 10.6 *The key methods of the **List** class.*

Method	Description
void add(String)	Adds the specified **String** to the end of the list.
void add(String, int)	Adds the **String** in the specified position.
void deselect(int)	Deselects the specified item.
int getItemCount( )	Returns the number of items in the list.
String getItem(int)	Returns the item with the specified index.
String[ ] getItems( )	Returns a list of all the items in the list.
int getRows( )	Returns the number of visible lines in the list.
int getSelectedIndex( )	Returns the index of the selected item.
int[ ] getSelectedIndexes( )	Returns the indices of the selected items.
String getSelectedItem( )	Returns the currently selected item.
String[ ] getSelectedItems( )	Returns an array of all the selected items.
boolean isIndexSelected(int)	Returns **true** if the item with the specified index is selected.
boolean isMultipleMode( )	Returns **true** if multiple selections allowed.
void remove(int)	Removes the item with the specified index from the list.
void remove(String)	Removes the first occurrence of the item with the specified text.
void removeAll( )	Removes all the items from the list.
void replaceItem(String, int)	Replaces the **String** at the specified index with the new **String.**
void select(int)	Selects the item with the specified index.
void setMultipleMode(boolean)	If **true,** multiple selections are allowed.

The TextComponent class

This class is a superclass of the **TextField** and the **TextArea** classes and therefore defines some common functionality, in particular a set of methods for getting and setting the text in the component, selecting text and determining whether the text in the component can be edited. The most commonly-used of these methods are shown in table 10.7.

The best way to see how to use these methods is to look at the two subclasses **TextArea** and **TextField**. The **TextField** class is used for entering and editing a single line of text. The **TextArea** class has very similar functionality to the **TextField** class but can be used where more than one line if text is required.

***Table 10.7** The key methods of the **TextComponent** class.*

Method	Description
void addTextListener(TextListener)	Adds a text event listener to receive text events.
int getCaretPosition( )	Returns the caret position for text insertion
String getSelectedText( )	Returns the selected text.
int getSelectionEnd( )	Returns the end position of the selected text.
int getSelectionStart( )	Returns the start position of the selected text.
String getText( )	Returns the text in the component.
boolean isEditable( )	Returns **true** if the text in component can be edited.
void select(int, int)	Selects the text between the specified start and end positions.
void selectAll( )	Selects all of the text.
void setCaretPosition(int)	Sets the caret for the insertion of text to the specified position.
void setEditable(boolean)	If passed **true**, the text can be edited.
void setSelectionEnd(int)	Sets the end position of selected text.
void setSelectionStart(int)	Sets the start position of selected text.
void setText(String)	Changes the text to the **String** specified.

The TextArea class

TextArea components are able to display more than one line of text which can be edited. If all of the text cannot be viewed at one time, horizontal and vertical scroll bars are added as required, although you can explicitly add them if you wish. There are five constructors for this class:

- **TextArea( )** creates a new blank **TextArea** object.
- **TextArea(int** *rows*, **int** *columns*) creates a blank **TextArea** object with the specified number of rows and columns.
- **TextArea(String, int** *rows*, **int** *columns*, **int** *scroll*) creates a **TextArea** object containing the specified text, with the specified number of rows and columns. The final parameter is used to indicate if scrollbars are required: **SCROLLBARS_VERTICAL_ONLY**, **SCROLLBARS_HORIZONTAL_ONLY**, **SCROLLBARS_NONE**, or **SCROLLBARS_BOTH**.
- **TextArea(String, int** *rows*, **int** *columns*) creates a **TextArea** object containing the specified text and number of rows and columns.
- **TextArea(String)** creates a **TextArea** object with the specified text.

In the next application, shown running in figure 10.11, there is a single **TextArea** object which is editable. You can select text by dragging the mouse over the text, as expected the selected text appears highlighted. When you click on the *CUT* button the text is removed and put into a clipboard. When the *PASTE* button is clicked the text is inserted at the current position of the cursor.

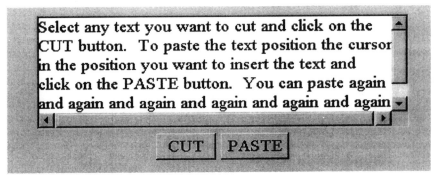

*Fig. 10.11 Using the **TextArea** class.*

The complete listing for this applet is shown below:

```
import java.applet.*;
import java.awt.*;
import java.awt.event.*;
public class UsingSelection extends Applet implements ActionListener {
    private TextArea myText = new TextArea(5,40);
    private Button cut = new Button(" CUT ");
    private Button paste = new Button("PASTE");
    private String clipBoard;
    public UsingSelection( )       {
        setFont(new Font("Serif", Font.PLAIN, 18));
        add(myText);
        add(cut);
        cut.addActionListener(this);
        add(paste);
        paste.addActionListener(this);
    }
    public void actionPerformed(ActionEvent e) {
        String newString;        //the text after cutting or pasting
        int cursorPosition;
        String s = myText.getText( );//the text in the TextArea component
        if (e.getSource( ) == cut) {
//cut the selected text
//put selected text into the clipBoard
            clipBoard = myText.getSelectedText( );
//get the text before the selected text
```

```
                newString = s.substring(0,myText.getSelectionStart( ));
//add the text after the selected text
                newString += s.substring(myText.getSelectionEnd( ), s.length( ));
//save the cursor position at the start of the selected text
                cursorPosition = myText.getSelectionStart( );
//the new text is the same as the old with the selected part removed
                myText.setText(newString);
//set the new cursor position
                myText.setCaretPosition(cursorPosition);
        }
        if (e.getSource( ) == paste) {
//paste the text
//get the text before the caret into newString
                newString = s.substring(0, myText.getCaretPosition( ));
//add the text in the clipBoard
                newString += clipBoard;
//add the text after the caret
                newString += s.substring(myText.getCaretPosition( ),s.length( ));
//the new cursor position is just after the pasted text
                cursorPosition = myText.getCaretPosition( ) + clipBoard.length( );
//the new text is the old text with the clipBoard text inserted
                myText.setText(newString);
//set the new cursor position
                myText.setCaretPosition(cursorPosition);
        }
    }
}
```

The clicking of the buttons causes action events which means that this application must implement the **ActionListener** interface. This interface only has one method called **actionPerformed** which is called whenever a button is clicked. A check is made in this method to see which of the two buttons has been clicked. When the *CUT* button is clicked:

- The selected text is copied into the **String** *clipBoard* using the **getSelectedText** method.
- The text which is before the selected text is copied to the **String** *newString*. The **substring** method of the **String** class is used to do this. The start position of this text is the first character in the string, the end position is given by the start of the selected text (given by the **getSelectionStart** method).
- The text after the selected text is added to *newString*. This text is also found using the **substring** method. The start of the substring is given by the end of the selected text (given by the **getSelectionEnd** method)
- The new cursor position is given by the start position of the selected text, this is saved in the *cursorPosition* variable.

- The text displayed in the **TextArea** is changed to *newString* using the **setText** method.
- The new cursor position is assigned to *cursorPosition* using **setCaretPosition** method.

When the text is to be pasted a similar set of operations takes place:

- The text before the current cursor position is copied to the string *newString*.
- The text in the *clipBoard* string is added (this text was placed there by the previous cut operation).
- The text after the cursor position is added.
- The new text is assigned to the **TextArea** object.
- The cursor is positioned at the end of the pasted text.

Table 10.8 The key methods of the TextArea class.

Method	Description
void insert(String, int)	Inserts the specified string in the specified position.
void replaceRange(String, int, int)	Replaces the text between the specified start and end position with the specified text.

The **actionPerformed** method of this applet can be substantially streamlined by using two methods shown in table 10.8. The greatly improved method is shown below:

```
public void actionPerformed(ActionEvent e) {
    if (e.getSource( ) == cut) {
    //copy the selected text to the clipBoard
        clipBoard = myText.getSelectedText( );
    //cut the text by replacing it with an empty string
        int start = myText.getSelectionStart( );
        int end = myText.getSelectionEnd( );
        myText.replaceRange("", start, end);
    //deselect any text
        myText.setSelectionEnd(myText.getSelectionStart( ));
    }
    if (e.getSource( ) == paste)
    //paste the text in the clipBoard into the current position
        myText.insert(clipBoard, myText.getCaretPosition( ));
}
```

Using the TextListener interface

The previous application added a listener to the buttons in the applet. In the next applet we are going to add a **TextListener** to two **TextArea** objects. The running applet is shown in figure 10.12. When text is typed in either of the two **TextArea** objects it appears in the other. It is not only the effect of the printable keys which is duplicated, the editing carried out in either of the objects is duplicated in the other. As the amount of text increases, scroll bars are automatically added to allow you to see all of the text. If the amount of text decreases so that either the horizontal or vertical scroll bars are not necessary, they are automatically removed.

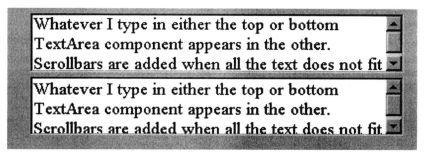

*Fig. 10.12 Using the **TextArea** class.*

The complete listing for this applet is shown below:

```
import java.applet.*;
import java.awt.*;
import java.awt.event.*;
public class UsingTextArea extends Applet implements TextListener {
    private TextArea top = new TextArea(2,40);
    private TextArea bottom = new TextArea(top.getRows( ),top.getColumns( ));
    public UsingTextArea( )      {
        setFont(new Font("Serif",Font.PLAIN,18));
        add(top);
        top.addTextListener(this);
        add(bottom);
        bottom.addTextListener(this);
    }
    public void textValueChanged(TextEvent t){
        if (t.getSource( ) == top) {
//the text in the top box has changed, disable the bottom box listener
//get the text in the top box and assign it to the bottom box
//and re-enable the listener for the bottom box
            bottom.removeTextListener(this);
            bottom.setText(top.getText( ));
            bottom.addTextListener(this);
```

```
    } else {                    //the text in the bottom box has changed
        top.removeTextListener(this);
        top.setText(bottom.getText( ));
        top.addTextListener(this);
    }
  }
}
```

When the text in either **TextArea** object changes, the **textValueChanged** method is called. When the text changes in either of the components, the listener for the other component is removed; the text in the two components is made the same; and finally the listener is added again.

The listener for the component where text is not being typed has to be disabled, since if, for example, a change was made to the text in top component, a **textValueChanged** event would occur for the top component. The copying of this text to the bottom component would cause a **textValueChanged** event in the bottom component. The new text in the bottom component would be copied to the top causing another **textValueChanged** event. The whole process would infinitely repeat itself causing the applet to crash.

The TextField class

TextField objects are able to contain only a single line of text which can be edited. **TextArea** objects can contain more than one line. There are four constructors for the **TextField** class:

- **TextField( )** creates a new blank **TextField** object.
- **TextField(int)** creates a **TextField** object with the specified number of columns.
- **TextField(String, int)** creates a **TextField** object with the specified text and number of columns.
- **TextField(String)** creates a **TextField** object with the specified text.

A useful feature of the **TextField** class not available to the **TextArea** class is that a **TextField** object can be used for receiving passwords. Normally whatever character is typed appears in the **TextField**, however if you use the **setEchoChar** method to assign an echo character, only that character is displayed whatever is typed. This is a useful feature if you do want your password to be displayed on the screen. The '*' character is normally used as the echo character. There are three methods which manage this feature as shown in table 10.9.

Table 10.9 The key methods of the TextField class.

Method	Description
boolean echoCharIsSet( )	Returns **true** if an echo character is set.
char getEchoChar( )	Returns the echo character.
void setEchoChar(char)	Sets the echo character.

The applet shown in figure 10.13 prompts for a name and a password to be input. The echo character is set to '*'. Whatever is typed into the password field the * character is echoed, however the actual characters typed are still available to the applet. In this example if the name is *John* and the password is *Essentials* the message *Welcome John* is displayed. The message *Password not recognized* is displayed for all other input.

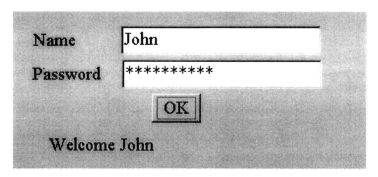

Fig. 10.13 Using the TextField class.

The complete code for this application is shown below:

```
import java.applet.*;
import java.awt.*;
import java.awt.event.*;
public class Passwords extends Applet implements ActionListener {
    private TextField name = new TextField(20);
    private TextField password = new TextField(20);
    private Button ok = new Button(" OK ");
    private String m="";
    public Passwords( )      {
        setFont(new Font("Serif",Font.PLAIN,18));
        add(new Label("Name      "));
        add(name);
        add(new Label("Password "));
        add(password);
        add(ok);
        ok.addActionListener(this);
//echo a * whatever is typed
        password.setEchoChar('*');
    }
    public void actionPerformed(ActionEvent e) {
        if (e.getSource( ) == ok) {
            if ((name.getText( ).compareTo("John") == 0) &&
                (password.getText( ).compareTo("Essentials") == 0))
                m = "Welcome John";
```

```
            else m = "Password not recognized";
        }
        repaint( );
    }
    public void paint(Graphics g) {
        g.drawString(m, 30, 130);
    }
}
```

The Canvas class

The final class we are going to look at in this chapter is the **Canvas** class. it provides a blank rectangular area on which you can draw. It cannot contain AWT components. To get any useful functionality you need to subclass the **Canvas** class and override its **paint** method to display text or graphics.

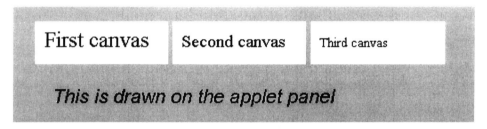

Fig. 10.14 Using the Canvas class.

In the applet shown in figure 10.14 an inner class called *Can*, which extends the **Canvas** class, is defined and three instances of it are created. Each instance provides its own drawing area:

The complete Java code is shown below:

```
import java.applet.*;
import java.awt.*;
public class UsingCanvas extends Applet {
    public UsingCanvas( ){
        setFont(new Font("SansSerif", Font.ITALIC, 22));
        add(new Can("First canvas",25));
        add(new Can("Second canvas",20));
        add(new Can("Third canvas",15));
    }
    public class Can extends Canvas {
    // extend the Can class and override the its paint class
        private String message = "";
        private int textSize = 20;
        public Can(String text, int size) {
```

```
            setFont(new Font("Serif", Font.PLAIN, textSize));
            message = text;
            textSize = size;
            setSize(150, 50);    //must specify size or 0,0 is used
            setBackground(Color.white);
        }
        public void paint(Graphics g) {
        // the paint method for the Can class
            g.drawString(message, 10, 30);
            }
        }//end of Can class
    public void paint(Graphics g) {
        // the paint method for the UsingCanvas class
        g.drawString("This is drawn on the applet panel", 40, 100);
    }
}
```

11

The Layout Managers

Introduction

If you have tried some of the applets in the previous chapter, you will have found that the applets functioned correctly, but that the layout of the components may have been different. On looking more closely at these applets you will see that the components are added from left to right and when the first row is full the next component to be added is placed in the row below. This is the default layout for **Panel** objects and is called **FlowLayout**. There are five layout managers defined for AWT components which we are going to look at in this chapter:

- **FlowLayout**
- **BorderLayout**
- **CardLayout**
- **GridLayout**
- **GridBagLayout**

These layout managers can be used when writing applets and applications, or in fact any program where AWT components are added to a container component such as a **Panel** or a **Frame**.

The Swing components have an additional layout manager called **BoxLayout** which we will look at in chapter 13.

The FlowLayout class

All applets extend the **Panel** class. The default layout for **Panel** objects is **FlowLayout**. There are three constructors for the **FlowLayout** class:

- **FlowLayout( )** creates a **FlowLayout** object with centred components and a horizontal and vertical gap of 5 units between components.

- **FlowLayout(int, int, int)** creates a **FlowLayout** object with the specified alignment, and horizontal and vertical gaps.
- **FlowLayout(int)** creates a **FlowLayout** object with the specified alignment.

The alignment must be one of the following:

- **CENTER**. The components in each row are centred.
- **LEADING**. The components are justified to the leading edge of the container component's orientation, that is the left edge in a left to right orientation.
- **LEFT**. The components are left justified.
- **RIGHT**. The components are right justified.
- **TRAILING**. The components are justified to the trailing edge of the container component's orientation, that is the right edge in a left to right orientation.

Containers which can use a layout manager have a **setLayout** method. In the case of **Panel** objects, the default layout manager is **FlowLayout** with an alignment of **CENTER**. The applet shown in figure 11.1 shows three buttons and the layout and alignment has been made explicit in the Java code.

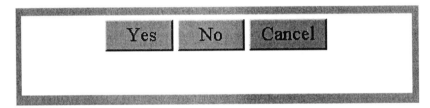

Fig. 11.1 Using *FlowLayout* with centre alignment and default gaps.

The code for this applet is shown below:

```
import java.applet.*;
import java.awt.*;
public class UsingFlowLayout extends Applet {
    public UsingFlowLayout( ) {
    setFont(new Font("Serif", Font.PLAIN, 20));
    setBackground(Color.white);
    setLayout(new FlowLayout(FlowLayout.CENTER));
    add(new Button(" Yes "));
    add(new Button(" No "));
    add(new Button(" Cancel "));
    }
}
```

There are two ways to vary the layout produced with this layout manager: the first is to change the alignment, the second is to vary the horizontal or vertical gap between the components. The applet shown in figure 11.2 has left alignment and horizontal and vertical gaps between the components of 20 rather than the default of 5.

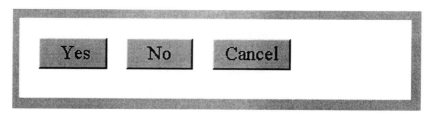

Fig. 11.2 *Using FlowLayout with left alignment and increased gaps.*

The code used to produce this applet is shown below:

```
import java.applet.*;
import java.awt.*;
public class UsingFlowLayout extends Applet {
    public UsingFlowLayout( ) {
    setFont(new Font("Serif", Font.PLAIN, 20));
    setBackground(Color.white);
    FlowLayout f = new FlowLayout( );
    setLayout(f);
    f.setHgap(20);
    f.setVgap(20);
    f.setAlignment(FlowLayout.LEFT);
    add(new Button(" Yes "));
    add(new Button(" No "));
    add(new Button(" Cancel "));
    }
}
```

There is a useful set of methods in the **FlowLayout** class for working with the alignment and spacing of components.

Table 11.1 *The key methods of the **FlowLayout** class.*

Method	Description
int getAlignment( )	Returns the alignment of the components.
int getHgap( )	Returns the horizontal gap between components.
int getVgap( )	Returns the vertical gap between components.
void setAlignment(int)	Sets the alignment of the components.
void setHgap(int)	Sets the horizontal gap between components.
void setVgap(int)	Sets the vertical gap between components.

The BorderLayout class

The **BorderLayout** class breaks up the available space on the container component into five regions, north, south, east, west and centre. When adding a component to a border layout you have to specify which region it will go into. There are two constructors for the **BorderLayout** class:

- **BorderLayout( )** creates a new **BorderLayout** with default horizontal and vertical gaps of zero.
- **BorderLayout(int** *horizontal,* **int** *vertical)* creates a new **BorderLayout** with the specified horizontal and vertical gaps between the components.

Five buttons displayed using a border layout are shown in figure 11.3. The figure on the left has the default horizontal and vertical gaps of zero, while the figure on the right has gaps of 30.

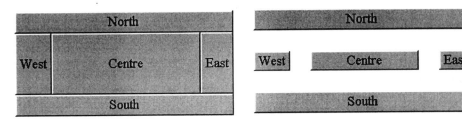

*Fig. 11.3 Using **BorderLayout** with different gap sizes.*

The applet used to produce the image on the right of figure 11.3 is shown below. To create the image on the left use the same applet with the **BorderLayout** constructor which does not take any parameters.

```
import java.applet.*;
import java.awt.*;
public class UsingBorderLayout extends Applet {
    public UsingBorderLayout(){
        setFont(new Font("Serif", Font.PLAIN, 20));
        setBackground(Color.white);
    //make the horizontal and vertical gaps 30
        setLayout(new BorderLayout(30,30) );
    //The order does not matter
        add(new Button("North"), BorderLayout.NORTH);
        add(new Button("East"), BorderLayout.EAST);
        add(new Button("Centre"), BorderLayout.CENTER);
        add(new Button("South"), BorderLayout.SOUTH);
        add(new Button("West"), BorderLayout.WEST);
    }
}
```

Note that when an AWT component is added to one of the five sectors, it occupies the whole sector. Adding another component to the same sector overwrites the previous one. If you fail to specify a sector the central sector is used.

In addition to explicitly stating the sector in which a component is placed you can use four relative positioning constants which are dependent on the component orientation (see the **java.awt.ComponentOrientation** class). This class encapsulates the language-specific ordering of text and can handle four different orderings for languages, Western European, Japanese and Chinese, middle Eastern languages such as Hebrew and for languages such as Mongolian. If the **ComponentOrientation** is used for Western European languages the relative constants **BEFORE_LAST_LINE**, **AFTER_LAST_LINE**, **BEFORE_LINE_BEGINS**, and **AFTER_LINE_ENDS** correspond to **NORTH**, **SOUTH**, **EAST** and **WEST**. The **ComponentOrientation** and associated classes are not yet fully completed and it is advisable at this stage in the development of Java not to use these relative positioning constants which are not supported by many browsers.

The **BorderLayout** class has methods of the same name and parameters as the **FlowLayout** class for working with the gap between components. These are listed in table 11.1.

The CardLayout class

The **CardLayout** class is different to the other layout managers, since each part of the **CardLayout** is a separate card only one of which can be viewed at a time. You can have as many cards in a **CardLayout** as you wish and there is a full set of methods for displaying a specified card.

In common with the other layout managers we have looked at so far, there are two constructors:

- **CardLayout( )** creates a new **CardLayout**.
- **CardLayout(int** *horizontal*, **int** *vertical*) creates a new **CardLayout** with the specified horizontal and vertical gaps.

The applet shown in figure 11.4 uses a **CardLayout** to display three cards. Each card has a single button, which is clicked to show the next card in the sequence.

Fig. 11.4 Using *CardLayout*.

To respond to these button events the **ActionListener** interface must be implemented. When a button click event occurs the **actionPerformed** method is called to display the next card in the sequence. If the current card is the last in the sequence the first is displayed. The complete Java code for this applet is shown below:

```
import java.applet.*;
import java.awt.*;
import java.awt.event.*;
public class UsingCardLayout extends Applet implements ActionListener {
```

```
CardLayout c = new CardLayout( );
public UsingCardLayout( ) {
    setFont(new Font("Serif", Font.PLAIN, 25));
    setLayout(c);
    Button first = new Button("Button one");
    add("cardOne", first);
    first.addActionListener(this);
    Button second = new Button("Button two");
    add("cardTwo", second);
    second.addActionListener(this);
    Button third = new Button("Button three");
    add("cardThree", third);
    third.addActionListener(this);
    c.show(this, "cardTwo");
}
public void actionPerformed(ActionEvent e) {
    c.next(this);
}
}
```

The **add** method used in this application differs slightly from that used for other layouts. The card is given a name, for example *cardOne*, which can be used to refer directly to that card.

The key methods which are used for controlling the card which is to be displayed are shown in table 11.2.

Table 11.2 *The key methods of the **CardLayout** class.*

Method	Description
void first(Container)	Displays the first card.
void last(Container)	Displays the last card.
void next(Container)	Displays the next card in the sequence.
void previous(Container)	Displays the previous card.
void show(Container, String)	Displays the card with the specified name.

The sequence of the cards is determined by the order in which they are created. The first panel created is the first in the sequence. New cards are added to the end of the list of cards.

If you wish to add a number of AWT components to a card, you can add another container component to that card, for example a **Panel** and add components to that **Panel**. The **Panel** can have its own type of layout.

The applet shown in figure 11.5 has applied the **CardLayout** to the applet panel and has two cards. The first card has a **Panel** added to it which has a **FlowLayout**. This **Panel** has three buttons. The second card also has a **Panel** containing three buttons but it is given a **BorderLayout**. The resulting two cards are shown in figure 11.5. Note that in the left image, which uses **FlowLayout**, since there is insufficient room for the button labelled *Right - cardOne* to fit on the same line as the first two buttons it is placed on the line below.

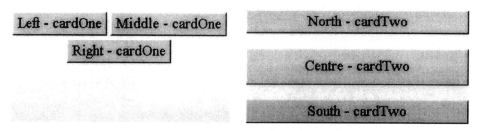

Fig. 11.5 Using cards with different layouts.

Whenever any of the buttons on either of the cards is clicked the other card is displayed. The Java applet which produced this is shown below:

```
import java.applet.*;
import java.awt.*;
import java.awt.event.*;
public class CombiningLayouts extends Applet implements ActionListener {
    CardLayout c = new CardLayout( );
    public CombiningLayouts( ) {
        setFont(new Font("Serif", Font.PLAIN, 15));
        setLayout(c);
    //create a Panel called P1 and give it FlowLayout
        Panel p1 = new Panel( );
        p1.setLayout(new FlowLayout( ));
        Button left = new Button("Left - cardOne");
        Button middle = new Button("Middle - cardOne");
        Button right = new Button("Right - cardOne");
    //add these three buttons to panel p1
        p1.add(left);
        p1.add(middle);
        p1.add(right);
    //add the Panel p1 to cardOne
        add("cardOne",p1);
    //create a second Panel called p2 and give it BorderLayout
        Panel p2 = new Panel( );
        p2.setLayout(new BorderLayout(20,20));
    //create three new buttons and add to the Panel p2
        Button north = new Button("North - cardTwo");
        Button south = new Button("South - cardTwo");
        Button centre = new Button("Centre - cardTwo");
        p2.add("North", north);     //adds a button to the North region
        p2.add("South", south);     //adds a button to the South region
        p2.add("Center", centre);   //adds a button to the Center region
```

```
        //add the panel to cardTwo
            add("cardTwo", p2);
        //add the listeners for each button
            left.addActionListener(this);
            middle.addActionListener(this);
            right.addActionListener(this);
            north.addActionListener(this);
            south.addActionListener(this);
            centre.addActionListener(this);
        }
        public void actionPerformed(ActionEvent e) {
            c.next(this);
        }
    }
```

Note the alternative **add** method which is used to add the buttons to the second **Panel** which use **BorderLayout**.

The GridLayout class

The **GridLayout** class divides the container area into a rectangular grid. Every new component you add goes into a single grid cell. The cells are filled from left to right and top to bottom. There are three constructors for this class:

- **GridLayout( )** creates a **GridLayout** with a single row.
- **GridLayout(int** *rows*, **int** *columns*) creates a **GridLayout** with the specified number of rows and columns.
- **GridLayout(int** *rows*, **int** *columns*, **int** *horizontal*, **int** *vertical*) creates a grid layout with the specified number of rows, columns, horizontal and vertical gap between components.

If the number of cells is not enough for every component, the number of rows remains constant and the number of columns increases.

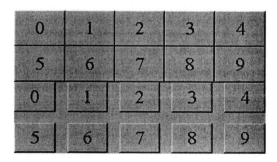

*Fig. 11.6 Using **GridLayout**.*

Figure 11.6 shows the applet which is divided initially into two equal sections using **GridLayout** (and specifying 2 rows and 1 column). A **Panel** is added to each of the two rows and 10 buttons are added to each **Panel**. The bottom group has a vertical and horizontal gap of 15 between components.

The applet code is shown below:

```
import java.applet.*;
import java.awt.*;
public class UsingGridLayout extends Applet {
    public UsingGridLayout( ){
        setFont(new Font("Serif", Font.PLAIN, 25));;
        //divide the applet panel into 2 rows
        setLayout(new GridLayout(2, 1));
        //instantiate a panel with GridLayout and no gaps
        Panel top = new Panel( );
        top.setLayout(new GridLayout(2, 5));
        //instantiate a panel with GridLayout and gaps of 15
        Panel bottom = new Panel( );
        bottom.setLayout(new GridLayout(2, 5, 15, 15));
        //add 10 buttons to each panel
        for (int c = 0; c <=9; c++) {
            top.add(new Button(String.valueOf(c)));
            bottom.add(new Button(String.valueOf(c)));
        }
        //add the Panels (with their buttons) to the applet panel
        add(top);
        add(bottom);
    }
}
```

*Table 11.3 The key methods of the **GridLayout** class.*

Method	Description
int getColumns( )	Returns the number of columns.
int getRows( )	Returns the number of rows in the grid.
void setColumns(int)	Sets the number of columns to the specified value.
void setRows(int)	Sets the number of rows to the specified value.

The GridBagLayout class

In the **GridBagLayout** class the display area is divided into an array of rectangular cells in the same way as for the **GridLayout** class; the difference is that components may occupy one or more adjacent cells. Every component which is added to a **GridBagLayout** has a **GridBagConstraints** object associated with it which controls aspects of how the component is laid out. The sequence that you have to follow when using the **GridBagLayout** class is as follows:

- Give the container component a **GridBagLayout**.
- Create an instance of the component to be added.
- Create an instance of the **GridBagConstraints** class.
- Define the values of the instance variables of the **GridBagConstraints** object.
- Associate the component with the **GridBagConstraints** object, using the **setConstraints** method of the **GridBagLayout** class.
- Add the component to the layout.

For every component added there must be an associated **GridBagConstraints** object. The **GridBagLayout** class is the most complex of the layout classes to use for this reason. The most commonly-used variables of the **GridBagConstraints** class are:

- **anchor.** If the component is smaller than the display area this variable specifies where it is placed. This field has one of the following possible values: **CENTER, NORTH, NORTHEAST, EAST, SOUTHEAST, SOUTH, SOUTHWEST, WEST,** or **NORTHWEST.** The default is **CENTER.**
- **fill.** If the component is smaller than its display area this variable determines how the extra space is used: **NONE,** the component is not resized. **BOTH,** the component entirely fills the display. **HORIZONTAL,** the component is made wide enough to fill the container. **VERTICAL,** the component is made tall enough to fill the container. The default is **NONE.**
- **gridheight.** The number of cells in a column for the display area. The default value is 1. Specify **REMAINDER** if it the component is the last in its column.
- **gridwidth.** The number of rows for the display area. The default is value is 1. Specify **REMAINDER** if the component is the last in its row.
- **gridx.** The horizontal position where the leftmost cell has a **gridx** value of 0. A value of **RELATIVE** (the default) adds the component to the right of the previously added component.
- **gridy.** The vertical position, where the topmost cell has a **gridy** value of 0. A value of **RELATIVE** (the default) adds the component directly below the previously added component.
- **weightx.** If the width of a layout is smaller than the width of the container, the **weightx** value determines how to distribute the remaining space. A component with a **weightx** of 2.0 will have twice the space allocated compared to a component with a **weightx** of 1.0.
- **weighty.** If the height of a layout is smaller than the height of the container, the **weighty** value determines how to distribute the remaining vertical space.

Figure 11.7 shows the **GridBagLayout** class in use.

Buttons *one* and *two* have the same **weightx** and **weighty** values and the default **gridwidth** and **gridheight** values (1), they are therefore the same size. Button *three* has a **gridwidth** value of GridBagConstraints.REMAINDER and therefore occupies the remaining width of the display area. Its height is the same as buttons *one* and *two*, since it has the same **gridheight** and **weighty** values.

Buttons *four* and *five* have the same default **gridheight** value as buttons *one*, *two* and *three* but in figure 11.7 are much taller. This is because they have a **weighty** value of 3.0 compared to 1.0.

Note that a **weighty** of 3.0 does not mean that the height will be three times that of a component with a **weighty** of 1.0. It does mean that any extra space left after the default height of the components has been considered will be divided in a 3:1 ratio.

Button *four* is twice the width of buttons *one* and *two* since it has a **gridwidth** value of 2 rather than 1.

Button *five* has a **gridwidth** value of **GridBagConstraints.REMAINDER** and therefore occupies the remaining width of the display area.

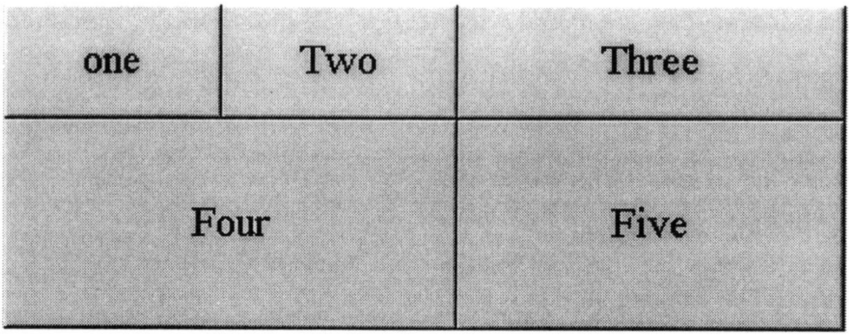

Fig. 11.7 The GridBagLayout class.

The complete code for this applet is given below:

```
import java.applet.*;
import java.awt.*;
public class UsingGridBagLayout extends Applet {
    public UsingGridBagLayout( ) {
    setFont(new Font("Serif", Font.PLAIN, 20));
    GridBagLayout g = new GridBagLayout( );
    setLayout(g);
    GridBagConstraints gc = new GridBagConstraints( );
// resize the components to fill the entire horizontal and vertical space.
    gc.fill = GridBagConstraints.BOTH;
    gc.weightx = 1.0;
    gc.weighty = 1.0;
    Button buttonOne = new Button("one");
// this gridwidth will make sure that buttonOne occupies the entire width
    g.setConstraints(buttonOne, gc);  //setConstraints for weighting to have effect
    add(buttonOne);
    Button buttonTwo = new Button("Two");
    g.setConstraints(buttonTwo, gc);
    add(buttonTwo);
    Button buttonThree = new Button("Three");
    gc.gridwidth = GridBagConstraints.REMAINDER;
```

```
        g.setConstraints(buttonThree, gc);
        add(buttonThree);
// The weighty value means that buttonFour will be taller than the previous row.
        gc.weighty = 3.0;
// The gridwidth  value means that buttonFour will be twice the width
// of buttons one and two which have the default gridwidth of 1.
        gc.gridwidth = 2;
        Button buttonFour = new Button("Four");
        g.setConstraints(buttonFour, gc); //setConstraints for weighting to have effect
        add(buttonFour);
//      The weightx value means buttonFive will be much wider than button Four
        gc.weightx = 2.0;
        gc.gridwidth = GridBagConstraints.REMAINDER;
        Button buttonFive = new Button("Five");
        g.setConstraints(buttonFive, gc); //setConstraints for weighting to have effect
        add(buttonFive);
        }
}
```

12

Windows, Dialogs and Menus

Introduction

All of the examples so far which use the AWT components have been applets. All applets extend the **Applet** class which extends the **Panel** class. The **Panel** class is one of Java's container classes which provides an area for you to place AWT components. If you wish you can also create additional drawing areas using, for example an instance of the **Dialog**, **Frame** or even another instance of the **Panel** class. Each of these container classes have a different appearance and functionality. However if you want to use the AWT components you are not limited to applets since applications can also use the container classes to provide an area on which to draw the components. In this chapter we are going to look at the subclasses of the **Container** class in the AWT package and how you can create both applets and applications which use these classes.

There are some additional subclasses of **Container** which are in the **javax.swing** package which are used for displaying the lightweight Swing components. This is covered in chapter 13.

The Container class

The **Container** class and its subclasses is shown in figure 12.1. It is an abstract superclass of all the classes which can hold components.

The **Window** class, although not an abstract class, is rarely used directly, and its subclasses are generally used instead. First we are going to look at how to create applications and applets which use the **Frame** class, which is the most commonly-used of these classes.

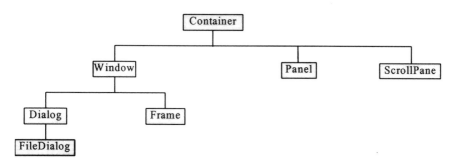

*Fig. 12.1 The **Container** class and its subclasses.*

The Frame class

A **Frame** object is a window with a title and a border. The default layout is **BorderLayout,** unlike the **Panel** found in applets which is **FlowLayout.** There are two constructors for the **Frame** class:

* **Frame( )** constructs a **Frame** object.
* **Frame(String)** constructs a **Frame** object with the specified title.

There are two common mistakes when using a **Frame:** a **Frame** is invisible until you execute its **setVisible** method; the default size is just sufficient to show a small part of the title bar but can be changed with the **setSize** method.

Creating an application which uses a frame

First we are going to create an application using the **Frame** class. Figure 12.2 shows an application consisting of a **Frame** containing a single button, which entirely fills the **Frame** (since the default layout for a **Frame** object is **BorderLayout**).

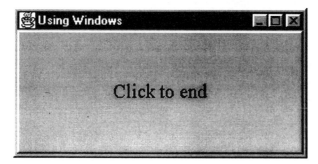

*Fig. 12.2 An application which uses the **Frame** class.*

The **Frame** has some functionality; it can be resized or minimised, but not closed, by clicking on the icons in the top right corner of the **Frame**. When the button is clicked it changes visually to a pressed state, but no action is taken. The code used to produce this application is shown below:

```
import java.awt.*;
public class UsingWindows extends Frame {
    private Button b = new Button("Click to end");
    public UsingWindows( ) {
        setTitle("Using Windows");
        setSize(300, 150);
        setBackground(Color.yellow);
        setFont(new Font("Serif", Font.PLAIN, 20));
        add(b);
        setVisible(true);
    }
    public static void main (String args[ ]) {
        UsingWindows u = new UsingWindows( );
    }
}
```

A common way of creating applications which use a **Frame** is to extend the **Frame** class as has been done in this application. An instance of the *UsingWindows* class is created in the **main** method. This class has one instance variable, a **Button** component. In the constructor, the title which appears at the top of the **Frame** is specified using the **setTitle** method. The size is specified using the **setSize** method. The background colour and the font are set. Finally the button is added to the **Frame** with the **add** method and the **Frame** is displayed using the **setVisible** method. Note that the button occupies the whole area of the **Frame**, since the default **BorderLayout** is in force and the background colour of yellow cannot therefore be seen.

The application as it stands is very unsatisfactory, we need to make some changes to handle the closing of the window when the **Button** is clicked. We are also going to change the layout to **FlowLayout** so that the **Button** does not occupy the whole of the **Frame** area.

To handle the button click event we need to change the *UsingWindows* class so that it implements the **ActionListener** interface as well as extending the **Frame** class. The **addActionListener** method of the **Button** object ensures that **Button** events are handled. When the **Button** is clicked, the **actionPerformed** method is called. In this method, the window is closed using the **dispose** method of the **Window** class and the application is terminated. The layout is changed to **FlowLayout**, so that the button does not occupy the whole of the **Frame** and the background yellow colour is seen. Note that **java.awt.event.*** is imported. The running application is shown in figure 12.3.

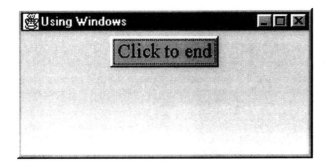

Fig. 12.3 *An application with a **Frame** using **FlowLayout**.*

The complete application is shown below.

```
import java.awt.*;
import java.awt.event.*;
public class UsingWindows extends Frame implements ActionListener {
    private Button b = new Button("Click to end");
    public static void main (String args[ ]) {
        UsingWindows u = new UsingWindows( );
    }
    public UsingWindows( ) {
        setTitle("Using Windows");
        setSize(300,150);
        setBackground(Color.yellow);
        setFont(new Font("Serif",Font.PLAIN,20));
        setLayout(new FlowLayout(FlowLayout.CENTER));
        add(b);
        b.addActionListener(this);
        setVisible(true);
    }
    public void actionPerformed(ActionEvent e) {
//come here when the button is clicked
        dispose( );          //close the window
        System.exit(0);      //end the application
    }
}
```

There is still one remaining problem with this application. When the close icon in the top right of the **Frame** is clicked nothing happens. To deal with this event we need to look at the **WindowListener** interface and the associated **WindowAdapter** class.

The WindowListener interface

When you want to handle the window events, you can either implement the **WindowListener** interface or extend the abstract **WindowAdapter** class. When there is a change in the window, for example when the close icon is pressed, one of seven methods is called and passed a **WindowEvent** object. The seven methods of the **WindowListener** interface and **WindowAdapter** class are listed in table 12.1.

Table 12.1 *The key methods of the* *WindowListener* *interface.*

Method	Description
void windowActivated(WindowEvent)	Called when a window is activated.
void windowClosed(WindowEvent)	A window is closed.
void windowClosing(WindowEvent)	A window is in the process of being closed. You can override the close event at this point.
void windowDeactivated(WindowEvent)	A window is deactivated.
void windowDeiconified(WindowEvent)	An icon is converted to a window.
void windowIconified(WindowEvent)	A window is minimised to an icon.
void windowOpened(WindowEvent)	A window is opened.

To improve the previous application so that the close icon terminates the application, an inner class called *Close* is created. This extends the **WindowAdapter** class and overrides one of its methods, **windowClosing**, which is called when the close icon is pressed. In the method the **Frame** is closed and the application terminated. In the constructor for the *UsingWindows* class an instance of this inner class is created and a window listener added to receive the window events.

The final application is given below:

```
import java.awt.*;
import java.awt.event.*;
public class UsingWindows extends Frame implements ActionListener {
    private Button b = new Button("Click to end");
    public static void main (String args[ ]) {
        UsingWindows u = new UsingWindows( );
    }
    public UsingWindows( ) {
        setTitle("Using Windows");
        setSize(300, 150);
        setBackground(Color.yellow);
        setFont(new Font("Serif", Font.PLAIN, 20));
        setLayout(new FlowLayout(FlowLayout.CENTER));
        add(b);
        b.addActionListener(this);
        setVisible(true);
```

```
            Close c = new Close( );
            addWindowListener(c);
    }
    public void actionPerformed(ActionEvent e) {
            dispose( );        //close the window
            System.exit(0);    //end the application
    }
    public class Close extends WindowAdapter {
            public void windowClosing(WindowEvent e) {
            //come here when the close icon is clicked
                    dispose( );        //close the window
                    System.exit(0);    //close the application
            }
    }//end of the Close class
}
```

You can create as many frames as you wish in your application.

Creating an applet which uses a frame

Applets can also use **Frame** objects however since all applets extend the **Applet** class, no applet can also extend the **Frame** class; Java does not support multiple inheritance, that is inheritance directly from more than one superclass. Therefore in the applet shown below in figure 12.4 the **Frame** object and the **Button** object are instance variables of the *UsingWindowsApplet* class. Apart from this change the application and the applet are very similar. Note that when the button or the close icon is clicked the window is closed, but the browser used to display the applet is not closed.

The appearance of the **Frame** will be slightly different depending on the browser used to run the applet. Figure 12.4 shows the window produced using Netscape Communicator 4.5 (on the left) and Microsoft Internet Explorer 4.01.

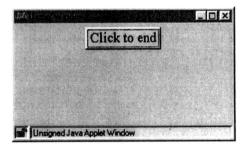

Fig. 12.4 The applet viewed with Netscape Communicator and Internet Explorer.

```
    import java.awt.event.*;
    import java.applet.*;
    public class UsingWindowsApplet extends Applet implements ActionListener {
```

```
    private Button b = new Button("Click to end");
    private Frame f = new Frame( );
    public UsingWindowsApplet( ) {
        f.setTitle("Using Windows");
        f.setSize(300,150);
        f.setBackground(Color.yellow);
        f.setFont(new Font("Serif", Font.PLAIN, 20));
        f.setLayout(new FlowLayout(FlowLayout.CENTER));
        f.add(b);
        b.addActionListener(this);
        f.setVisible(true);
        Close c = new Close( );
        f.addWindowListener(c);
    }
    public void actionPerformed(ActionEvent e) {
        f.dispose( );              //close the window
    }
    public class Close extends WindowAdapter {
        public void windowClosing(WindowEvent e) {
        //come here when the close icon is clicked
            f.dispose( );          //close the window
        }
    }//end of the Close class
}
```

Some of the most often used methods of this class are listed in table 12.2.

Table 12.2 *The key methods of the* **Frame** *class.*

Method	Description
void dispose( )	Closes the frame releasing all its system resource.
Image getIconImage( )	Returns the icon image for the frame.
MenuBar getMenuBar( )	Returns the menu bar for the frame.
String getTitle( )	Returns the title of the frame.
boolean isResizable( )	Returns **true** if the frame can be resized.
void remove(MenuComponent)	Removes the specified menu item from the frame.
void setIconImage(Image)	Specifies the icon to display when the frame is iconized.
void setMenuBar(MenuBar)	Sets the menu bar to that specified.
void setResizable(boolean)	If true, the frame can be resized.
void setTitle(String)	Sets the title to that specified.

Some of the methods listed in table 12.2 are concerned with managing the menu which can be added to frames. In the next section we are going to see how to create menus and to handle the events which are produced when menu items are selected.

The MenuBar class

Frames can have a menu bar attached to them. To create the menu bar the **MenuBar** class must be used. There is only one constructor for this class which is passed no parameters. When you have instantiated the **MenuBar** object, it is added to the **Frame** object with the **setMenuBar** method.

The headings which appear on the menu bar are instances of the **Menu** class. The items which appear under each heading when you click on it are **MenuItem** objects and are added using the **add** method.

To respond to the selection of a menu item, an **ActionListener** must be added to the **Menu** object. When an item is selected the **actionPerformed** method is called. This method is passed an **ActionEvent** object which describes the event which has occurred and where it originated from. To allow you to take different actions depending on which menu item was selected the **getActionCommand** method returns the source of the event.

To see how this works in practice we are going to develop an application which has a menu bar with two items on it. The first item is the style of text which is displayed in a **TextField**, and can be either bold, italic or plain. The second item is a range of sizes for the text, either 20, 30 or 40. The running application is shown in figure 12.5.

Fig. 12.5 The running applet with a menu.

The class we are using is called *UsingMenus*, it extends the **Frame** class and implements the **ActionListener** interface. It has three instance variables, the **TextField** where the text is displayed, *t*, and two integers, *textSize* and *textStyle*, which represent the size and style of the text:

```
public class UsingMenus extends Frame implements ActionListener{
    TextField t = new TextField("Chameleon",10);
    int textSize = 40;
    int textStyle = Font.PLAIN;
```

The command for instantiating the **MenuBar** and adding it to the **Frame** is:

```
// create a menu bar
    MenuBar m = new MenuBar( );
    setMenuBar(m);
```

The next stage is to instantiate the first menu heading (which is a **Menu** object), add it to the **MenuBar** and add an **ActionListener**.

```
// instantiate the "style" object and add to the menu bar
    Menu style = new Menu("Style");
    m.add(style);
// add a listener to the style menu
    style.addActionListener(this);
```

The individual items listed below the *Style* heading are added next:

```
// add a items to the style menu
    style.add(new MenuItem("Italic"));
    style.add(new MenuItem("Bold"));
    style.add(new MenuItem("Plain"));
```

The *Size* menu items are added in the same way.

When a menu item is selected the **actionPerformed** method is called. It checks to see which menu item was selected and changes the *textStyle* instance variable.

```
public void actionPerformed(ActionEvent e) {
    String command = e.getActionCommand( );
// get the style selected
    if (command.equals("Italic")) textStyle = Font.ITALIC;
    else if (command.equals("Bold")) textStyle = Font.BOLD;
    else if (command. equals("Plain")) textStyle = Font.PLAIN;
```

A similar set of tests is made to see if the size has changed and the *textSize* instance variable is assigned a new value. The **setFont** method for the **TextField** is called to change the font to the new style and size. The **repaint** method redraws the **TextField** with the new font:

```
// change the font style and size
    t.setFont(new Font("Serif", textStyle, textSize));
    repaint( );
```

To complete the application a new inner class is created which handles the window closing event which occurs when the close icon is clicked. The complete application is shown below:

```
import java.awt.*;
import java.awt.event.*;
public class UsingMenus extends Frame implements ActionListener{
    TextField t = new TextField("Chameleon",10);
    int textSize = 40;
    int textStyle = Font.PLAIN;
```

```
public UsingMenus(String title) {
    t.setFont(new Font("Serif", textStyle, textSize));
    setTitle(title);
    setSize(300,150);
// create a menu bar
    MenuBar m = new MenuBar( );
    setMenuBar(m);
// instantiate the "style" object and add to the menu bar
    Menu style = new Menu("Style");
    m.add(style);
// add a listener to the style menu
    style.addActionListener(this);
// add a items to the style menu
    style.add(new MenuItem("Italic"));
    style.add(new MenuItem("Bold"));
    style.add(new MenuItem("Plain"));
// instantiate the "size" object
    Menu size = new Menu("Size");
    m.add(size);
    size.addActionListener(this);
// add a listener to the size menu
    size.add(new MenuItem("20"));
    size.add(new MenuItem("30"));
    size.add(new MenuItem("40"));
// add the text field
    add(t);
// display the frame
    setVisible(true);
// create an instance of the Close class to handle window close events
    Close c = new Close( );
    addWindowListener(c);
}
public void actionPerformed(ActionEvent e) {
    String command = e.getActionCommand( );
// get the style selected
    if (command.equals("Italic")) textStyle = Font.ITALIC;
    else if (command.equals("Bold")) textStyle = Font.BOLD;
    else if (command. equals("Plain")) textStyle = Font.PLAIN;
// get the size selected
    if (command.equals("20")) textSize = 20;
    else if (command.equals("30")) textSize = 30;
    else if (command.equals("40")) textSize = 40;
// change the font style and size
    t.setFont(new Font("Serif", textStyle, textSize));
    repaint( );
```

```
        }
        public class Close extends WindowAdapter {
            public void windowClosing(WindowEvent e) {
        //come here when the close icon is clicked
                    dispose( );              //close the window
                    System.exit(0);          //exit the application
            }
        }//end of the Close class
        public static void main(String args[ ]) {
            UsingMenus f = new UsingMenus("Changing text size and style");
        }
    }
```

The Dialog class

The **Dialog** class is a subclass of the **Window** class, as the **Frame** class is, but it plays a slightly different role. **Dialog** objects are temporary windows which display a message and take some input from the user. There are seven constructors for this class:

- **Dialog(Dialog, String, boolean)** constructs a dialog attached to another **Dialog**, with the specified title. If the **boolean** parameter is the **true** the **Dialog** is modal.
- **Dialog(Dialog, String)** constructs a **Dialog** with a title.
- **Dialog(Dialog)** constructs a **Dialog** without a title.
- **Dialog(Frame, String, boolean)** constructs a **Dialog** attached to a **Frame** with its title and modality specified.
- **Dialog(Frame, String)** constructs a **Dialog** with a title.
- **Dialog(Frame, boolean)** constructs a **Dialog** with the specified modality.
- **Dialog(Frame)** constructs a **Dialog** without a title.

A **Dialog** can be either modal or non-modal. A modal **Dialog** does not allow you to do anything else in the application until you have responded to it. The default is non-modal, that is you can switch to other frames or dialogs before closing the current **Dialog**.

One of the most common uses of a **Dialog** object is to display a warning message when a problem occurs. In the next application, two **double** values are typed into the top two **TextField** components. The first is divided by the second and the result displayed in the bottom **TextField** component. Before the division a check is made to see if the second value is zero; if it is, a warning dialog is displayed and the division is not attempted. The running application is shown in figure 12.6.

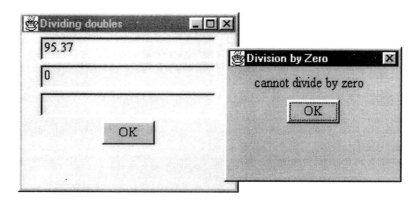

Fig. 12.6 Displaying a warning dialog.

The *UsingDialogs* class extends the **Frame** class and implements the **ActionListener** interface so that it can respond to the clicking of the buttons on both the **Frame** and the **Dialog**:

> *class UsingDialogs extends Frame implements ActionListener {*

The **TextField** and **Button** objects are instance variables of this class. The **Dialog** called *d* is also an instance variable:

> *private Dialog d = new Dialog(this, "Division by Zero", true);*

The **Dialog** is attached to the current **Frame**, with a title of *Division by Zero*. It is modal.

An **ActionListener** is added to the button on the **Frame** and on the **Dialog**. When a button is clicked the **actionPerformed** method is called.

An inner class called *Close* handles the closing of the **Frame** and the application when the close icon in the top right corner is clicked.

The complete application is shown below:

```
import java.awt.*;
import java.awt.event.*;
class UsingDialogs extends Frame implements ActionListener {
    private TextField text1 = new TextField(25);
    private TextField text2 = new TextField(25);
    private TextField text3 = new TextField(25);
    private TextField answer = new TextField(20);
    private Button okButton = new Button("  OK  ");
    private Button dialogButton = new Button("  OK  ");
    private Dialog d = new Dialog(this, "Division by Zero", true);
    public UsingDialogs(String title) {
    // set-up the frame
        setTitle(title);
        setSize(250,200);
```

```
        setFont(new Font("Serif", Font.PLAIN, 15));
        setLayout(new FlowLayout(FlowLayout.CENTER));
        setBackground(Color.yellow);
        add(text1);
        add(text2);
        add(text3);
        add(okButton);
        okButton.addActionListener(this);
        setVisible(true);
// set-up the error dialog
        d.setSize(200,150);
        d.setLayout(new FlowLayout(FlowLayout.CENTER));
        d.add(new Label(" cannot divide by zero"));
        d.add(dialogButton);
        dialogButton.addActionListener(this);
        Close c = new Close( );
        addWindowListener(c);
        d.addWindowListener(c);
}
public class Close extends WindowAdapter {
// if the close icon on the dialog is clicked close the dialog
// if the close icon on the main frame is clicked close the application
        public void windowClosing(WindowEvent e) {
                if (e.getSource( ) == d) d.dispose( ); else  //close the dialog
                System.exit(0);              //end the application
        }
} //end of the Close class
public void actionPerformed(ActionEvent e) {
// if the button on the dialog has been clicked close the dialog
        double value1, value2;
        if (e.getSource( ) == dialogButton) {
                text2.setText("");
                d.setVisible(false);
        }
// if the OK button on the main window has been clicked, convert the
// Strings in text2 and text3 to double, check for division by zero
// and either display the error dialog or the result
                else if (e.getSource( ) == okButton)    {
// the doubleValue method converts a String to a Double
// the valueOf method converts a Double to a double
                value1 = Double.valueOf(text1.getText( )).doubleValue( );
                value2 = Double.valueOf(text2.getText( )).doubleValue( );
                if (value2 == 0) {       // division by zero
                text3.setText("");   //clear text3
                d.setVisible(true);  //display the dialog
```

```
              } else text3.setText(String.valueOf(value1/value2)) //display result
          }
      }
      public static void main(String args[ ]) {
          UsingDialogs f = new UsingDialogs("Dividing doubles");
      }
  }
```

The characters typed into the **TextField** components are stored as a **String**. They can be accessed using the **getText** method. Before any mathematical operations can be carried out, these **String** values must be converted to **double** values; this is done in two stages. First the **String** is first converted to a **Double** object using the **Double.valueOf** method (that is the **valueOf** method in the **Double** class). Second the **Double** class has a method called **doubleValue**, which converts a **Double** object to a **double**. The **Double** class contains a single **double** field that effectively provides an object wrapper around the primitive **double** data type.

In common with the **Frame** class, the **Dialog** class inherits many methods from the **Window, Container** and **Component** classes, but the most often used methods specific to this class are shown in table 12.3.

Table 12.3 The key methods of the Dialog class.

Method	Description
String getTitle( )	Returns the title of the **Dialog**.
boolean isModal( )	Returns **true** if the **Dialog** is modal.
boolean isResizable( )	Returns **true** if the **Dialog** is resizable. By default, a **Dialog** is resizable.
void setModal(boolean)	If the parameter is **true** the **Dialog** is modal. The default is non-modal.
void setResizable(boolean)	If the parameter is **true** the **Dialog** is resizable.
void setTitle(String)	Changes the title to the specified **String**.
void show( )	Shows the **Dialog**. If the **Dialog** is visible, but underneath another **Dialog** or **Frame** it is brought to the front.

The FileDialog class

The **FileDialog** class displays a special type of **Dialog** which allows you to browse your file system and select a file. There are three constructors for this class:

- **FileDialog(Frame, String, int)** creates a **FileDialog** attached to the specified **Frame,** with a title. The **int** parameter specifies whether to display a dialog for loading or saving a file. This parameter can be either **FileDialog.LOAD** or **FileDialog.SAVE**.

- **FileDialog(Frame, String)** creates a **FileDialog** attached to the specified **Frame** with a title.
- **FileDialog(Frame)** creates a **FileDialog** attached to the specified **Frame**.

A **FileDialog** is always modal. This class has a set of methods which allow you to find the file and directory which is selected. To see how to use this class we are going to develop the application shown in figure 12.7.

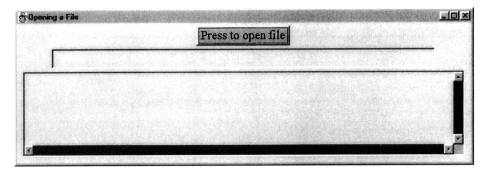

Fig. 12.7 The running application.

This application displays a **Frame** with a **Button**, **TextField** and **TextArea** objects. When the button is clicked the **FileDialog** as shown in figure 12.8 is displayed and you can browse through your file system and select a file. The **FileDialog** is system dependent and if you are not using Windows 98 it will have a different appearance.

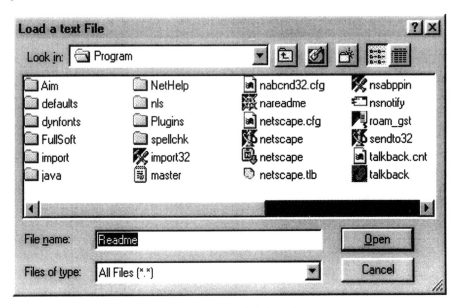

Fig. 12.8 The FileDialog class.

The application is capable of reading a text file and displaying it in the **TextArea** component. When a file is selected from the **FileDialog** it is read and displayed. The name of the file is shown in the **TextField** just above the **TextArea,** as shown in figure 12.9.

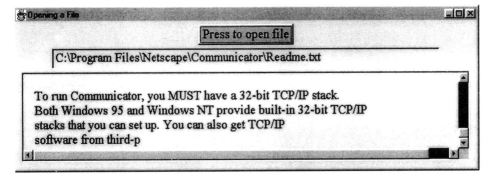

Fig. 12.9 The running application.

If there is an error in opening or reading the file, an input/output problem occurs and an **IOException** object will be generated. This is caught and the dialog shown in figure 12.10 is displayed.

Much of this application is similar to applications we have already looked at, so we are going to focus on the aspects which relate to the **FileDialog.**

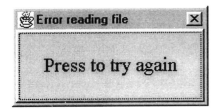

Fig. 12.10 An IOException occurs when running the application.

The application begins with importing some packages:

import java.awt.*;
import java.awt.event.*;
import java.io.*;

Note that the **java.io.*** package must be imported. This contains the classes needed for reading from a file.

The application starts in the **main** method where an instance of the *UsingFileDialogs* class is instantiated.

```
public static void main(String args[ ]) {
        UsingFileDialogs d = new UsingFileDialogs( );
}
```

The *UsingFileDialogs* class is a subclass of **Frame** and implements the **ActionListener** interface to handle the clicking of buttons, both the open file button on the main frame and the button on the error dialog. The instance variables are also defined after the class definition:

```
class UsingFileDialogs extends Frame implements ActionListener{
    TextField displayFilename = new TextField(60);        //displays the filename
    TextArea fileContent = new TextArea(5, 70);           //displays the text read
    FileDialog f = new FileDialog(this, "Load a text File", FileDialog.LOAD);
    Dialog IOError = new Dialog(this, "Error reading file", true);
    Button openButton = new Button("Press to open file");    // on Frame
    Button errorButton = new Button("Press to try again");   // on error dialog
```

The **TextField** is used to display the name of the file which has been read. The **TextArea** object displays the contents of that file. The **FileDialog** is to be used for loading (reading) a file. The error dialog which is displayed when an error occurs is also defined.

The constructor for the *UsingFileDialogs* class adds the AWT components to the **Frame** and adds a listener to the window close event for the **Frame**, using an inner class called *Close* which we have seen in previous applications:

```
public UsingFileDialogs( ) {
//add the Button, TextField and TextArea objects to the Frame
    add(openButton);
    openButton.addActionListener(this);
    add(displayFilename);
    displayFilename.setFont(new Font("Serif", Font.PLAIN, 20));
    add(fileContent);
    setLayout(new FlowLayout(FlowLayout.CENTER));
    setFont(new Font("Serif", Font.PLAIN, 20));
    setTitle("Opening a File");
    setSize(750, 250);
    setBackground(Color.cyan);
    setVisible(true);
    Close c = new Close( );
    addWindowListener(c);
}
```

The constructor method displays the initial **Frame**. The next stage is to respond to the clicking of the button on the **Frame** which displays the **FileDialog** and gets the file which is selected. When a button is clicked the **actionPerformed** method is called.

```
public void actionPerformed(ActionEvent e) {
    if (e.getSource( ) == openButton) {
//if the open file button on the Frame is clicked come here
        f.setDirectory("C:\\Program Files\\Netscape\\Communicator");
        f.setVisible(true);
        String s = f.getDirectory( );
        s += f.getFile( );
```

```
        displayFilename.setText(s);
        readFile(s);
// else if the button on the error dialog is clicked come here
    } else if (e.getSource( ) == errorButton) IOError.dispose( );
}
```

A check is made to see if the button on the **Frame** or the error dialog has been clicked using the **getSource** method of the **ActionEvent** object which is passed to this method. If the error dialog button was the source of the **ActionEvent**, the error dialog is closed using the **dispose** method and no other action is taken. The **setDirectory** method is used to specify the directory (or folder in Windows 98 jargon) which will be displayed first in the **FileDialog**. The **setVisible** method displays the **FileDialog**. The **getFile** and **getDirectory** methods return which file has been selected and where it is. Note that **getFile** only returns the file name and not its full path name. The text which is displayed in the **TextField** is the concatenation of the **String** returned by **getDirectory** and **getFile**. To read the text from the file the *readFile* method is called.

```
private void readFile(String filename) {
    byte[ ] myBuffer = new byte[1000];
    try {
// read the file into a byte array
        FileInputStream fis = new FileInputStream(filename);
        DataInputStream s = new DataInputStream(fis);
        s.read(myBuffer);
//display the information read
        fileContent.setText(new String(myBuffer));
    } catch (IOException e) {
//come here if an I/O error occurs
        IOError.setSize(200,100);
        IOError.add(errorButton);
        errorButton.addActionListener(this);
//display the error dialog
        IOError.setVisible(true);
    }
}
```

We have not covered much of the Java code in this method, particularly the opening and reading of files, which is covered in chapter 16, and dealing with exceptions which is covered in chapter 14. One way of handling exceptions, which are a form of run-time error is to use a **try** and **catch** construction. A **try** clause consists of the word **try** and some lines of Java within a { } pair. If an error occurs with a **try** clause, the program jumps to the following **catch** clause. In this case the **catch** clause is expecting an **IOException** to be generated (if any other type of exception is produced this **catch** clause is ignored). The opening and reading of up to 1000 bytes of the file is placed within the **try** clause. If an **IOException** is produced, the error dialog is displayed. If no exception occurs, the **catch** clause is ignored.

The complete listing for this application is shown below:

```
import java.awt.*;
import java.awt.event.*;
import java.io.*;
class UsingFileDialogs extends Frame implements ActionListener{
    TextField displayFilename = new TextField(60);    //displays the filename
    TextArea fileContent = new TextArea(5, 70);        //displays the text read
    FileDialog f = new FileDialog(this, "Load a text File", FileDialog.LOAD);
    Dialog IOError = new Dialog(this, "Error reading file", true);
    Button openButton = new Button("Press to open file");    // on Frame
    Button errorButton = new Button("Press to try again");    // on error dialog
    public UsingFileDialogs( ) {
    //add the Button, TextField and TextArea objects to the Frame
        add(openButton);
        openButton.addActionListener(this);
        add(displayFilename);
        displayFilename.setFont(new Font("Serif", Font.PLAIN, 20));
        add(fileContent);
        setLayout(new FlowLayout(FlowLayout.CENTER));
        setFont(new Font("Serif", Font.PLAIN, 20));
        setTitle("Opening a File");
        setSize(750,250);
        setBackground(Color.cyan);
        setVisible(true);
        Close c = new Close( );
        addWindowListener(c);
    }
    public void actionPerformed(ActionEvent e) {
        if (e.getSource( ) == openButton) {
    //if the open file button on the Frame is clicked come here
            f.setDirectory("C:\\Program Files\\Netscape\\Communicator");
            f.setVisible(true);
            String s = f.getDirectory( );
            s += f.getFile( );
            displayFilename.setText(s);
            readFile(s);
    // else if the button on the error dialog is clicked come here
        } else if (e.getSource( ) == errorButton) IOError.dispose( );
    }
    private void readFile(String filename) {
        byte[ ] myBuffer = new byte[1000];
        try {
    // read the file into a byte array
            FileInputStream fis = new FileInputStream(filename);
```

```
        DataInputStream s = new DataInputStream(fis);
        s.read(myBuffer);
//display the information read
        fileContent.setText(new String(myBuffer));
    } catch (IOException e) {
//come here if an I/O error occurs
        IOError.setSize(200,100);
        IOError.add(errorButton);
        errorButton.addActionListener(this);
//display the error dialog
        IOError.setVisible(true);
    }
}
public class Close extends WindowAdapter {
//close the Dialog when the close icon is clicked
    public void windowClosing(WindowEvent e) {
        dispose( );
        System.exit(0);
    }
} //end of the Close class
public static void main(String args[ ]) {
    UsingFileDialogs d = new UsingFileDialogs( );
}

}
```

The key methods for the **FileDialog** class, most of which we have seen in action are listed in table 12.4.

Table 12.4 *The key methods of the FileDialog class.*

Method	Description
String getDirectory( )	Returns the selected directory.
String getFile( )	Returns the name of the currently selected file, or null if no file is selected.
int getMode( )	Indicates if the dialog is to be used for saving or loading a file; the returned value can be either **FileDialog.LOAD** or **FileDialog.SAVE**.
void setDirectory(String)	Changes to the specified directory.
void setFile(String)	Changes the current file to the one specified.
void setMode(int)	The mode specified may be either **FileDialog.LOAD** or **FileDialog.SAVE**.

The Panel class

The **Panel** class is the simplest of the container classes. It has two constructors:

- **Panel( )** creates a **Panel** with the default **FlowLayout** layout manager.
- **Panel(LayoutManager)** creates a Panel with the specified **LayoutManager**.

A **Panel** provides an area onto which you can add other components. In the application shown in figure 12.11, a **GridLayout** is used to divide the applet drawing area (itself a **Panel**) into four rectangles. A **Panel** with a different colour is added to each of the rectangles.

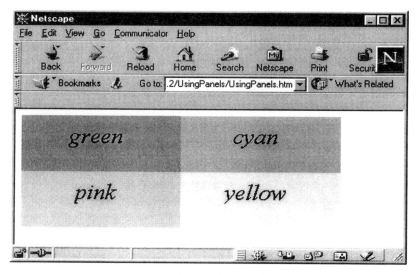

*Fig. 12.11 The **Panel** class.*

The Java code used to produce this applet is shown below:

```java
import java.applet.*;
import java.awt.*;
public class UsingPanels extends Applet {
    public UsingPanels() {
        setFont(new Font("Serif", Font.ITALIC, 30));
        setLayout(new GridLayout(2,2));
        Panel p1 = new Panel();
        p1.setBackground(Color.green);
        p1.add(new Label("green"));
        Panel p2 = new Panel();
        p2.setBackground(Color.cyan);
        p2.add(new Label("cyan"));
        Panel p3 = new Panel();
        p3.setBackground(Color.pink);
        p3.add(new Label("pink"));
        Panel p4 = new Panel();
        p4.setBackground(Color.yellow);
        p4.add(new Label("yellow"));
```

```
            add(p1);
            add(p2);
            add(p3);
            add(p4);
        }
    }
```

13

The Swing Components

Introduction

The Swing components are intended to extend but not replace the AWT components. Like the AWT, Swing is used to create graphical user interfaces for Java programs. Since this is the role of the AWT, why do we need Swing? Swing offers a number of advantages over the AWT components. There are more Swing components than AWT components including some high level components such as a tree-view and tabbed panels. Where the Swing and AWT components seem to overlap, such as the classes which represent buttons, the Swing component offers greater functionality than their AWT counterparts.

You can mix AWT and Swing components, and it is often necessary to do so since most IDEs do not support Swing, those which do, usually do not offer the full range of Swing components.

There are some problems if you want to write applets using the Swing components since, in Spring 1999, Swing-compatible browsers are not available. There are two solutions to this problem, you can use the applet viewer from Sun to run your applets, or download an extension to your browser from the Sun Web site which will extend its capabilities.

The introduction of the Swing components has been a major extension to the Java API and it is not possible to look at all of the components in this chapter, but we are going to look at some of the most important Swing components and in particular how they differ from the AWT components.

Differences between Swing and AWT components

When you write an application, the user interface is very important in making the user feel comfortable. When you create a GUI with Swing you can choose to give the program the feel and appearance of the platform on which it is running. If, for example, you are running under Windows, the program can take on the look and feel of a program written specifically for this platform. You can make your application look like a Win32 application, a Motif application or a Mac application. Sometimes, however, you may want a program to have the same GUI irrespective of its platform. In this case, you can specify a Java look and feel. You can even change the look and feel of Swing components at run time. Many Swing components seem to mirror existing AWT components, however the Swing components generally offer improved performance and extra functionality.

Swing is based on the JDK 1.1 Lightweight User Interface Framework Swing components, and unlike the AWT components are written from scratch and do not use any native code from the platforms on which they run. If there is not a suitable Swing component for your program you can create your own.

The Swing components

Swing is part of the Java Foundation Classes (JFC). The Swing packages are shown in figure 13.1.

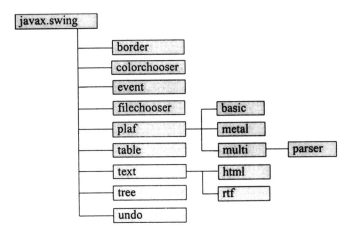

Fig. 13.1 The Java Swing packages.

You will need to import the Swing packages if you want to use them in your programs.

The Swing container classes

There are four Swing container components which extend from the corresponding AWT classes as shown in figure 13.2. **JFrame, JDialog, JWindow** and **JApplet** are heavyweight components which extend AWT components, while **JInternalFrame** is a lightweight component.

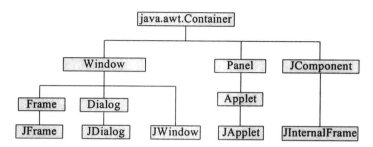

Fig. 13.2 *Swing container classes and the AWT classes they extend.*

These five Swing containers all implement the **RootPaneContainer** interface and delegate many operations to an instance of the **JRootPane** class. The **JRootPane** class contains:

- **glassPane** is an instance of **Component**, which covers the entire area of the **JRootPane** (including the menu if there is one) and can be used for drawing lines and images. It is also able to intercept mouse events. By default the **glassPane** is not visible.

- **layeredPane** is an instance of **JLayeredPane**, which allows you to add components in different layers. It is particularly useful when one component has to overlay another, for example when using pop-up menus.

- **contentPane** is an instance of **Container**. Instead of adding and deleting components directly to the **JRootPane**, you should add them to the **contentPane**. Similarly when you want to change the layout manager for components, you have to change the layout manager for the **contentPane**.

- **menuBar** is an instance of **JMenuBar**. It is optional.

To see the effect of using the Swing containers rather than the AWT containers, we are going to see how they are used and interact with the other Swing components.

The AbstractButton class

This abstract class defines the common behaviour for the **JButton, JToggleButton**, **JCheckbox** and **JRadioButton** classes. It extends the **JComponent** class, the base class for all Swing components and implements the **ItemSelectable** and **SwingConstants** interfaces.

The first **AbstractButton** subclass we are going to look at is **JButton**. In particular, we are going to look at the differences between the **java.awt.Button** class and the **javax.swing.JButton** class.

The Swing and AWT buttons

The Swing components are used in a very similar way to the AWT components, but there are some important differences. We are therefore going to look at an application using AWT components and the changes which must be made to use the Swing components. The working application using AWT components is shown in figure 13.3.

Fig. 13.3 *Using AWT components.*

When you click on the button labelled *First*, the message *Pressed first* is displayed, when the other button is pressed, the text *Pressed second* is displayed. When you click on the close icon on the top right corner of the frame the application ends.

We looked at applications like this in chapter 10, which covered the AWT components and event handling. The class we have created extends the **Frame** class and implements the **ActionListener** interface. Listeners are added to the two buttons. In the **actionPerformed** method a check is made to see from which button the event originated and the **setText** method of the **Label** component is used to change the text. An inner class is created called *ClosingWindow* which extends the **WindowAdapter** class and handles the clicking of the close icon on the window by closing the application. The **FlowLayout** manager is used to position the components. The complete listing of this application is shown below.

```
import java.awt.*;
import java.awt.event.*;
public class AWTButton extends Frame implements ActionListener {
    Button first, second;
    Label myLabel;
    public AWTButton( ) {
        setTitle("Using AWT Buttons");
        first = new Button("First");
        second = new Button("Second");
        myLabel= new Label("No button pressed yet");
        setLayout(new FlowLayout(FlowLayout.CENTER));
        add(first);
        add(second);
        add(myLabel);
        first.addActionListener(this);
        second.addActionListener(this);
        pack( );
        setVisible(true);
        ClosingWindow close = new ClosingWindow( );
        addWindowListener(close);
    }
    public void actionPerformed(ActionEvent evt) {
        if (evt.getSource( ) == first) myLabel.setText("Pressed first");
```

```
        else if (evt.getSource( ) == second) myLabel.setText("Pressed second");
    }
    public class ClosingWindow extends WindowAdapter {
        public void windowClosing(WindowEvent e) {
            System.exit(0);  // end the program
        }
    } // end of the ClosingWindows inner class
    public static void main(String args[ ]){
        AWTButton button = new AWTButton( );
    }
}
```

If we wish to change this application to use the Swing components, the class we have created must extend the **JFrame** class rather than the **Frame** class. The **Button** components are replaced by **JButton** components and the **Label** component is replaced with a **JLabel** component. In addition there are some changes we must make since the **JFrame** class is not completely compatible with the **Frame** class even though the **JFrame** class extends the **Frame** class. The **JFrame** class adds additional support for receiving events and for painting on the frame. The new application is called the *SwingJButton* class and is functionally the same as the previous program except for the following changes:

- The **javax.swing.*** package is imported.
- The *SwingJButton* class extends the **JFrame** class not the **Frame** class.
- A **JLabel** component is used in place of a **Label** component.
- **JButton** components are used in place of **Button** components.
- To change the layout of components we must change the layout manager on the **contentPane** from its default of **BorderLayout**, that is:

getContentPane( ).setLayout(new FlowLayout(FlowLayout.CENTER));

- Similarly to add the first component to the **contentPane** we must use:

getContentPane( ).add(first)

This produces the output shown in figure 13.4. Visually it is slightly different from that produced by the AWT components and has the default cross-platform look and feel.

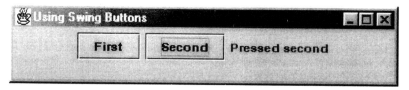

Fig. 13.4 *Using Swing components, cross-platform look and feel.*

Functionally this application behaves in the same way as the previous one. The complete listing is shown below:

```
import javax.swing.*;
import java.awt.*;
import java.awt.event.*;
public class SwingJButton extends JFrame implements ActionListener {
    JButton first, second;
    JLabel myLabel;
    public SwingJButton( ) {
        setTitle("Using Swing Buttons");
        first = new JButton("First");
        second = new JButton("Second");
        myLabel= new JLabel("No button pressed yet");
        getContentPane().setLayout(new FlowLayout(FlowLayout.CENTER));
        getContentPane().add(first);
        getContentPane().add(second);
        getContentPane().add(myLabel);
        first.addActionListener(this);
        second.addActionListener(this);
        pack( );
        setVisible(true);
        ClosingWindow close = new ClosingWindow( );
        addWindowListener(close);
    }
    public void actionPerformed(ActionEvent evt) {
        if (evt.getSource( ) == first) myLabel.setText("Pressed first");
        else if (evt.getSource( ) == second) myLabel.setText("Pressed second");
    }
    public class ClosingWindow extends WindowAdapter {
        public void windowClosing(WindowEvent e) {
            System.exit(0);  // end the program
        }
    } // end of the ClosingWindows inner class
    public static void main(String args[ ]){
        SwingJButton button = new SwingJButton( );
    }
}
```

Changing the look and feel

If you want to change the look and feel of your application from the default, you can use the **UIManager** class which allows you to find out the current look and feel of the application, and to change it. The two overloaded **setLookAndFeel** methods change the application's look and feel:

- **void setLookAndFeel(LookAndFeel)** is passed a **LookAndFeel** object.
- **void setLookAndFeel(String)** is passed the name of the class as a **String** which represents the required look and feel.

The first method may throw the first exception listed below, the second method may throw any of the exceptions:

- **UnsupportedLookAndFeelException** - the specified **LookAndFeel** class is not supported. You can check to see if a **LookAndFeel** class is supported by using the **boolean isSupportedLookAndFeel** method which returns a **false** value if it is not.
- **ClassNotFoundException** - the specified class could not be found.
- **InstantiationException** - the new instance of the class could not be created.
- **IllegalAccessException** - the specified class is not accessible.

The most common way of using this method is when you want to change from the cross-platform (metal) look and feel to the system look and feel. You do this with the **getCrossPlatformLookAndFeelClassName** or **getSystemLookAndFeelClassName** methods which both return a class name as a **String.** This can be passed to a **setLookAndFeel** method. If you insert the code shown below into the **main** method, before the instantiation of the *SwingJButton* class, the application will have the Windows appearance since it is running on a Windows 98 platform.

```
try {
    UIManager.setLookAndFeel(UIManager.getSystemLookAndFeelClassName( ));
}
catch(Exception e) {
    System.err.println("Error occurred in setting look and feel");
}
```

The output produced by this application is shown in figure 13.5.

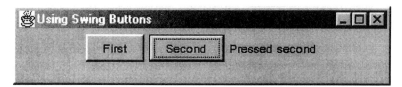

Fig. 13.5 *Using Swing components, system look and feel.*

The functionality is exactly the same as when the cross platform look is used or when the AWT components are used.

If you want to know what **LookAndFeel** classes are available on the system on which the application is running, there are a number of classes and of methods to assist you. The next application, shown in figure 13.6 displays a list of what is available.

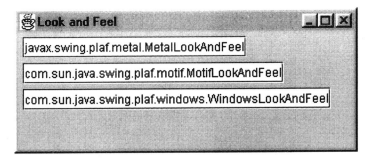

***Fig. 13.6** Displaying the available looks.*

The **UIManager** class has a method called **getInstalledLookAndFeels** that returns an array of **UIManager.LookAndFeelInfo** objects. These objects have a **getClassName** method which returns a **String** with the full name of the **LookAndFeel** classes. The application which displays a list of the **LookAndFeel** classes imports three packages:

import javax.swing.*;
import java.awt.*;
import java.awt.event.*;

The *UsingLandF* class is a subclass of the **JFrame** class:

***public class** UsingLandF **extends JFrame** {*

The maximum number of **LookAndFeel** classes which can be handled by this application is 10:

***static final int** max = 10;   //maximum number of look and feels*

In the constructor for the *UsingLandF* class, the layout manager is changed. An array of **JTextField** objects and an array of **UIManager.LookAndFeelInfo** objects is created:

***public** UsingLandF( ) {*
getContentPane( ).setLayout(new FlowLayout(FlowLayout.LEFT));
JTextField lookAndFeels[ ] = new JTextField[max];
UIManager.LookAndFeelInfo[] lk=new UIManager.LookAndFeelInfo[max];

An instance of the **UIManager** class is created and its **getInstalledLookAndFeels** method is used to fill the *lk* array:

UIManager m = new UIManager( );
lk = m.getInstalledLookAndFeels( );

The **JTextField** objects are instantiated and their constructor is passed the name of a **LookAndFeel** class, which is given by the **getClassName** method of the *lk* objects, so that the **LookAndFeel** class name is displayed in the **JTextField**. This is placed within a **try** clause. When an attempt is made to refer to a **LookAndFeelInfo** object which does not exist an **ArrayIndexOutOfBoundsException** occurs and control passes to the following **catch** clause, which takes no action. Exceptions are covered in detail in the next chapter.

```
try {
        for (int c = 0; c < max; c++) {
                lookAndFeels[c] = new JTextField(lk[c].getClassName( ));
                getContentPane( ).add(lookAndFeels[c]);
        }
    } catch (ArrayIndexOutOfBoundsException e) {
//come here when all of the installed LookAndFeel classes have been displayed.
    }
```

The remainder of the application handles the displaying of the frame and the closing of the application. The full application is shown below:

```
import javax.swing.*;
import java.awt.*;
import java.awt.event.*;
public class UsingLandF extends JFrame {
    static final int max = 10;   //maximum number of look and feels
    public UsingLandF( ) {
    getContentPane( ).setLayout(new FlowLayout(FlowLayout.LEFT));
    JTextField lookAndFeels[ ] = new JTextField[max];
    UIManager.LookAndFeelInfo[] lk=new UIManager.LookAndFeelInfo[max];
    UIManager m = new UIManager( );
//get the look and feel details as an array of LookAndFeelInfo objects the
//getClassName method of LookAndFeel class returns the full look and feel name
    lk = m.getInstalledLookAndFeels( );
    try {
            for (int c = 0; c < max; c++) {
                    lookAndFeels[c] = new JTextField(lk[c].getClassName( ));
                    getContentPane( ).add(lookAndFeels[c]);
            }
        } catch (ArrayIndexOutOfBoundsException e) {
//come here when all of the installed LookAndFeel classes have been displayed.
    }
    setTitle("Look and Feel");
    setSize(400,150);
    setVisible(true);
    ClosingWindow close = new ClosingWindow();
    addWindowListener(close);
    }
    public class ClosingWindow extends WindowAdapter {
            public void windowClosing(WindowEvent e) {
                    System.exit(0);   // end the program
            }
```

```
    } // end of the ClosingWindows inner class
    public static void main(String args[ ]){
        new UsingLandF( );
    }
}
```

The JButton class

This class inherits over 60 methods from the **AbstractButton** class, over 100 from **JComponent**, over 40 from **java.awt.Container** and over 100 from **java.awt.Component**, so it is not possible to review them all here. In fact the actual behaviour and use of this component is virtually identical to the AWT **Button** class. The main difference is that **JButton** supports icons as well as text on its face. To support this, it has four constructors rather than the two which **Button** has:

- **JButton( )** creates a button with a blank face.
- **JButton(Icon)** creates a button with an icon.
- **JButton(String)** creates a button with the specified text on its face.
- **JButton(String, Icon)** creates a button with the specified text and icon.

In the application shown below, three **ImageIcon** objects are created using three GIF files. One of these images is assigned to be the normal face of the button using the **JButton** constructor. The second **ImageIcon** object is displayed when the button is pressed, this is specified using the **setPressedIcon**. Finally rollover is enabled and a third icon is displayed using the **setRolloverIcon** method, so that when the mouse moves over the button a new image is displayed.

This application is shown below:

```
import javax.swing.*;
import java.awt.*;
import java.awt.event.*;
public class SwingButtonWithIcons extends JFrame {
    JButton manyFacedButton;
    public SwingButtonWithIcons( ) {
        ImageIcon normalFace = new ImageIcon("Images/normal.gif");
        ImageIcon pressedFace = new ImageIcon("Images/pressed.gif");
        ImageIcon rolledOverFace = new ImageIcon("Images/rollOver.gif");
        manyFacedButton = new JButton(normalFace);
        manyFacedButton.setPressedIcon(pressedFace);
        manyFacedButton.setRolloverIcon(rolledOverFace);
        manyFacedButton.setRolloverEnabled(true);
        manyFacedButton.setToolTipText("SwingButton with 3 different faces");
        manyFacedButton.setHorizontalAlignment(AbstractButton.LEFT);
        getContentPane().setLayout(new FlowLayout(FlowLayout.CENTER));
        getContentPane().add(manyFacedButton);
```

```
            pack( );
            setVisible(true);
            ClosingWindow close = new ClosingWindow();
            addWindowListener(close);
    }
    public class ClosingWindow extends WindowAdapter {
        public void windowClosing(WindowEvent e) {
            System.exit(0);   // end the program
        }
    } // end of the ClosingWindows inner class
    public static void main(String args[ ]){
        SwingButtonWithIcons button = new SwingButtonWithIcons( );
    }
}
```

In the **ImageIcon** constructor, the location and name of the GIF files must be specified. In this example the files are in a sub-directory (*Images*) directory containing the application. You could also specify a full path-name or a URL.

In addition to the three icons shown in the previous example, you can specify different icons for a wide variety of situations using the methods shown in table 13.1.

Table 13.1 *Methods for displaying icons on **JButton** components.*

Method	Description
void setIcon(Icon)	Sets the default image which is displayed when the button is neither pressed nor selected.
void setDisabledIcon(Icon)	Set the image when the button is disabled.
void setPressed(Icon)	Sets the image when the button is pressed.
void setSelectedIcon(Icon)	Sets the image when the button is selected.
void setDisabledSelectedIcon(Icon)	Sets the image when the button is both disabled and selected.
void setRolloverIcon(Icon)	Sets the image when the mouse moves over the button.
void setRolloverSelectedIcon(Icon)	Sets the image when the button is selected and the mouse is moved over it.

There are corresponding get methods which return an **Icon** object.

You can display both text and images at the same time on a **JButton** component. There are some useful methods shown, in table 13.2 for managing this text.

*Table 13.2 Methods for managing text on **JButton** components.*

Method	Description
void setText(String)	Puts new text on the button face.
void setHorizontalAlignment(int)	The permissible horizontal position of the image is defined in the **SwingConstants** interface, that is **LEFT**, **RIGHT** or **CENTER** (the default).
void setVerticalAlignment(int)	The permissible vertical position of the image, defined in **SwingConstants** interface, either **TOP**, **BOTTOM** or **CENTER** (the default).
void setHorizontalTextPosition(int)	Sets the horizontal position of the text relative to the image, either **LEFT**, **CENTER** or **RIGHT** (the default).
void setVerticalTextPosition(int)	Sets the vertical position of the text relative to the image as either **TOP**, **BOTTOM** or **CENTER** (the default);

The JToggleButton, JRadioButton and JCheckBox classes

JToggleButton is the superclass of **JRadioButton** and **JCheckBox** and defines their common functionality. Radio buttons and check boxes are used where you have to make a boolean yes/no, true/false choice. The difference between them is that radio buttons are usually grouped so that only one of the group can be **true**. When another member of the group is made **true**, the others automatically become **false**. If you want to have no buttons in the group selected, you can add an invisible radio button to the group and set its selected state to **true**. Radio buttons are logically grouped using the **ButtonGroup** class.

Seven **JRadioButton** constructors are shown below:

- **JRadioButton( )**
- **JRadioButton(Icon, boolean)**
- **JRadioButton(Icon)**
- **JRadioButton(String, boolean)**
- **JRadioButton(String, Icon, boolean)**
- **JRadioButton(String, Icon)**
- **JRadioButton(String)**

The **String** parameter is the text displayed adjacent to the button. The **Icon** parameter specifies an image. The **boolean** parameter gives the initial selection state of the button, the default selection state is **false.**

It is usual to show visually that radio buttons or check boxes are grouped by placing them on a container component such as a **JPanel** component and adding a border as shown in figure 13.7. Whenever one radio button is checked the others are set to **false**.

The processor chosen is displayed in a **JTextField** component on the right of the radio buttons.

Fig. 13.7 *Using radio buttons and button groups.*

The application is shown below. The particular points to note are:

- We need to import **javax.swing.border.*** since we are using the **LineBorder** class.
- The radio buttons are added to an instance of the **ButtonGroup** class to ensure that they behave as a group and only one can be checked at any time.
- The buttons are added to an instance of a **JPanel** component to ensure that they appear visually as a group when the application is run.
- A border is added to the panel to show that the components it contains are a group.
- The panel containing the radio buttons and a **JTextField** component is added to the **contentPane**.
- The **ItemListener** interface is implemented to handle events coming from the radio buttons. When a radio button is checked the **itemStateChanged** method is called to change the text displayed.

```
import javax.swing.*;
import javax.swing.border.*;
import java.awt.*;
import java.awt.event.*;
public class SwingToggleButton extends JFrame implements ItemListener {
    JRadioButton p266, p300, p350, p400, p450;
    JTextField title = new JTextField("Please choose a processor");
    public SwingToggleButton() {
        setTitle("Using Swing Radio Buttons");
//instantiate the radio buttons and button group
        p266 = new JRadioButton("PII 266");
        p300 = new JRadioButton("PII 300");
        p350 = new JRadioButton("PII 350");
        p400 = new JRadioButton("PII 400");
        p450 = new JRadioButton("PII 450");
        ButtonGroup b = new ButtonGroup();
//add the radio buttons to the button group
        b.add(p266);
        b.add(p300);
        b.add(p350);
        b.add(p400);
```

```
        b.add(p450);
//instantiate the panel, give it flowlayout and a border
        JPanel processor = new JPanel( );
        processor.setLayout(new FlowLayout(FlowLayout.LEFT));
        processor.setBorder(new LineBorder(Color.black));
//add the radio buttons and the text field to the panel
        processor.add(p266);
        processor.add(p300);
        processor.add(p350);
        processor.add(p400);
        processor.add(p450);
        processor.add(title);
//give the ContentPane a flowlayout
        getContentPane().setLayout(new FlowLayout(FlowLayout.CENTER));
//add the panel (containing the radio buttons) to the ContentPane
        getContentPane( ).add(processor);
//add the listeners for the radio buttons
        p266.addItemListener(this);
        p300.addItemListener(this);
        p350.addItemListener(this);
        p400.addItemListener(this);
        p450.addItemListener(this);
//don't forget to give the Swing frame a size and to display it
        setSize(500, 100);
        setVisible(true);
//handle the window closing event using the inner class calls close
        ClosingWindow close = new ClosingWindow( );
        addWindowListener(close);
    }
    public void itemStateChanged(ItemEvent evt) {
//come here when a radio button is clicked
        String choice = "You have chosen a PII ";
        if (evt.getSource( ) == p266) choice += "266";
        else if (evt.getSource( ) == p300) choice += "300";
        else if (evt.getSource( ) == p350) choice += "350";
        else if (evt.getSource( ) == p400) choice += "400";
        else if (evt.getSource( ) == p450) choice += "450";
//change the text to display the processor chosen
        title.setText(choice);
    }
    public class ClosingWindow extends WindowAdapter {
        public void windowClosing(WindowEvent e) {
            System.exit(0);  // end the program
        }
    } // end of the ClosingWindows inner class
```

```
    public static void main(String args[ ]){
// use the cross platform look and feel
        SwingToggleButton button = new SwingToggleButton( );
        }
    }
```

JCheckBox components behave in a similar manner to radio buttons and even have constructors with the same set of parameters as **JRadioButton** components. The main difference is that any number of the check boxes can be checked, therefore they do not need to be placed in a **ButtonGroup** component, however it is still usual to place related check boxes in a container such as **JPanel** component and add a border to visually link them. A set of **JCheckBox** components is shown in figure 13.8. The items selected are displayed in the text field below the check boxes.

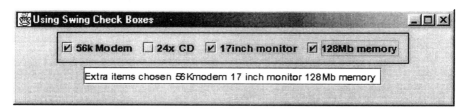

Fig. 13.8 *Using check boxes.*

The Java code needed to produce this application is very similar to that used in the radio button example. The main difference is that the check boxes are not added to a **ButtonGroup**. The same event handler method **itemStateChanged** is used, but the Java code is different. A check is made to see if each of the **JCheckBox** objects (called *modem*, *monitor*, *cd* and *memory*) is checked using the **isSelected** method. If it is, that item is added to the **String** choice which is displayed in the **TextField** component (called *title*) shown in figure 13.8. The application is shown below:

```
import javax.swing.*;
import javax.swing.border.*;
import java.awt.*;
import java.awt.event.*;
public class SwingCheckBox extends JFrame implements ItemListener {
        JCheckBox modem, cd, monitor, memory;
        JTextField title = new JTextField(40);
        public SwingCheckBox( ) {
                setTitle("Using Swing Check Boxes");
//instantiate the radio buttons and button group
                modem = new JCheckBox("56k Modem");
                cd = new JCheckBox("24x CD");
                monitor = new JCheckBox("17inch monitor");
                memory = new JCheckBox("128 MB memory");
//instantiate the panel, give it flowlayout and a border
                JPanel extras = new JPanel( );
```

```
                extras.setLayout(new FlowLayout(FlowLayout.LEFT));
                extras.setBorder(new LineBorder(Color.black));
//add the radio buttons and the text field to the panel
                extras.add(modem);
                extras.add(cd);
                extras.add(monitor);
                extras.add(memory);
//give the ContentPane a flowlayout
                getContentPane().setLayout(new FlowLayout(FlowLayout.CENTER));
//add the panel (containing the radio buttons) to the ContentPane
                getContentPane().add(extras);
                getContentPane().add(title);
//add the listeners for the radio buttons
                modem.addItemListener(this);
                monitor.addItemListener(this);
                memory.addItemListener(this);
                cd.addItemListener(this);
//don't forget to give the Swing frame a size and to display it
                setSize(500,100);
                setVisible(true);
//handle the window closing event using the inner class calls close
                ClosingWindow close = new ClosingWindow( );
                addWindowListener(close);
        }
    public void itemStateChanged(ItemEvent evt) {
//come here when a check box is clicked
                String choice = "Extra items chosen ";
                if (modem.isSelected( )) choice += "56Kmodem ";
                if (monitor.isSelected( )) choice += "17 inch monitor ";
                if (cd.isSelected( )) choice += "24x CD ";
                if (memory.isSelected( )) choice += "128 MB memory ";
//change the text to display the extras chosen
                title.setText(choice);
        }
    public class ClosingWindow extends WindowAdapter {
        public void windowClosing(WindowEvent e) {
                System.exit(0);   // end the program
        }
    } // end of the ClosingWindows inner class
    public static void main(String args[ ]){
        new SwingCheckBox( );
    }
}
```

Displaying text

We have already seen the **JLabel** and **JTextField** components in action, now we are going to take a closer look at them and their relationship to the other components which are used mainly to display text but may also display images.

The JLabel class

The **JLabel** components inherits directly from **JComponent**. It is the simplest of the components and displays text, an image or both. Since the contents of a **JLabel** cannot be changed at run time by the user, there are no keyboard events to handle for this component, and it cannot gain the focus when the application is running. You can specify the horizontal and vertical alignment of the text and image displayed and also their position relative to each other.

Six constructors for the **JLabel** class are shown below:

- **JLabel( )** creates a blank label.
- **JLabel(Icon, int)** creates a label with the specified image and horizontal alignment. The alignment can be either **JLabel.LEFT, JLabel.RIGHT** or **JLabel.CENTER**.
- **JLabel(Icon)** creates a label with the specified icon.
- **JLabel(String, Icon, int)** creates a label with the specified text, image and horizontal alignment.
- **JLabel(String, int)** creates a label with the specified text and horizontal alignment.
- **JLabel(String)** creates a label with the specified text.

Although **JLabel** is one of the most straightforward of the Swing classes to use, there are still some features which are different from the AWT **Label** class, in particular the ability to display icons. Figure 13.9 shows an application which displays four **JLabel** objects on a **JFrame** object. The top three **JLabel** objects have both an icon and text. The bottom label displays details of the look and feel used.

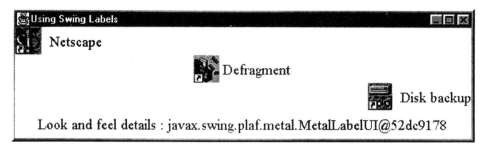

*Fig. 13.9 Using **JLabel**.*

This application imports four packages:

```
import javax.swing.*;
import javax.swing.plaf.*;
import java.awt.*;
import java.awt.event.*;
```

The *SwingLabel* class extends the **JFrame** class:

public class SwingLabel **extends JFrame**

This class has a single constructor. The first thing to be done is to sets up the size and title of the **JFrame** object:

```
public class SwingLabel extends JFrame {
    public SwingLabel( ) {
//set the JFrame title and size
        setTitle("Using Swing Labels");
        setSize(700,200);
```

The three files which are displayed are JPG files. The **ImageIcon** class is a concrete class which implements the **Icon** interface. The name of the JPG files are passed as a parameter to the **ImageIcon** constructor. The files are in the same directory as the running application:

```
ImageIcon Netscape = new ImageIcon("Netscape.jpg");
ImageIcon Defrag = new ImageIcon("Defrag.jpg");
ImageIcon Backup = new ImageIcon("Backup.jpg");
```

For each of the three **JLabel** objects which display both icons and text, the **JLabel** constructor which takes three parameters is used:

- The text to be displayed.
- An **Icon** object (An **ImageIcon** object can be used since this class implements the **Icon** Interface).
- The horizontal alignment.

The vertical alignment and the gap between the icon and text are also specified:

```
JLabel app1 = new JLabel("Netscape", Netscape, JLabel.LEFT);
app1.setVerticalAlignment(JLabel.TOP);
app1.setIconTextGap(10);
```

The **JLabel** objects *app2* and *app3* are defined in a similar way to display the defragmentation and backup icons. The horizontal alignment of these objects is **CENTER** and **RIGHT**.

The next stage is to create a Swing panel, that is a **JPanel** object to which the **JLabel** objects can be added:

```
JPanel p = new JPanel( );
p.setLayout(new GridLayout(4,1));
p.setBackground(Color.white);
```

The panel is given a **GridLayout** and is white. The three labels *app1*, *app2* and *app3* are added to this panel:

```
p.add(app1);
p.add(app2);
p.add(app3);
```

The **JLabel** object displayed at the bottom of the frame displays the look and feel of the *app1* label (the default look and feel has been used for all the labels). The look and feel of *app1* is found using the **getUI** method. The **toString** method converts this into a **String**. This label is added to the **Panel**.

```
JLabel lookAndFeel = new JLabel( );
lookAndFeel.setText("Look and feel details:"+app1.getUI( ).toString( ));
lookAndFeel.setHorizontalAlignment(JLabel.CENTER);
lookAndFeel.setFont(app1.getFont( ));
p.add(lookAndFeel);
```

The **JPanel** object, *p*, is assigned to the content pane of the frame, and the frame itself is displayed:

```
setContentPane(p);
setVisible(true);
```

The remainder of the application consists of a listener and an inner class which handles the clicking of the close icon in the top right corner of the **Frame** to end the application as we have seen earlier in many other applications. The **main** method creates an instance of the *SwingLabel* class and initiates the application.

The complete application is shown below:

```
import javax.swing.*;
import javax.swing.plaf.*;
import java.awt.*;
import java.awt.event.*;
public class SwingLabel extends JFrame {
    public SwingLabel( ) {
//set the JFrame title and size
        setTitle("Using Swing Labels");
        setSize(700,200);
//convert the 3 jpg files into Icon objects
        ImageIcon Netscape = new ImageIcon("Netscape.jpg");
        ImageIcon Defrag = new ImageIcon("Defrag.jpg");
        ImageIcon Backup = new ImageIcon("Backup.jpg");
//create a JLabel object containing some text, the Netscape icon
//and with left horizontal alignment
        JLabel app1 = new JLabel("Netscape", Netscape, JLabel.LEFT);
        app1.setVerticalAlignment(JLabel.TOP);
        app1.setIconTextGap(10);
```

```
//create a JLabel object containing some text, the Defrag icon
//and with CENTER horizontal alignment
        JLabel app2 = new JLabel("Defragment", Defrag, JLabel.CENTER);
        app2.setVerticalAlignment(JLabel.CENTER);
        app1.setIconTextGap(10);
//create a JLabel object containing some text, the Disk backup icon
//and with right horizontal alignment
        JLabel app3 = new JLabel("Disk backup", Backup, JLabel.RIGHT);
        app3.setVerticalAlignment(JLabel.BOTTOM);
        app3.setIconTextGap(10);
//create a panel
        JPanel p = new JPanel( );
        p.setLayout(new GridLayout(4,1));
        p.setBackground(Color.white);
//change the font of the three labels
        app1.setFont(new Font("Serif", Font.PLAIN, 18));
        app2.setFont(app1.getFont( ));
        app3.setFont(app1.getFont( ));
//add the labels to the panel
        p.add(app1);
        p.add(app2);
        p.add(app3);
//create a label to display the look and feel
        JLabel lookAndFeel = new JLabel( );
        lookAndFeel.setText("Look and feel details:"+app1.getUI().toString( ));
        lookAndFeel.setHorizontalAlignment(JLabel.CENTER);
        lookAndFeel.setFont(app1.getFont( ));
        p.add(lookAndFeel);
//the panel becomes the content pane
        setContentPane(p);
//display the frame
        setVisible(true);
//handle the clicking of the close icon on the frame
        ClosingWindow close = new ClosingWindow( );
        addWindowListener(close);
    }
    public class ClosingWindow extends WindowAdapter {
        public void windowClosing(WindowEvent e) {
            System.exit(0);   // end the program
        }
    } // end of the ClosingWindows inner class
    public static void main(String args[ ]){
        SwingLabel button = new SwingLabel( );
    }
}
```

In common with all Swing components this class has many methods. Some of the most commonly-used ones are given in table 13.3.

Table 13.3 The key methods of the JLabel class.

Method	Description
int getHorizontalAlignment( )	Returns the alignment of the label's contents along the horizontal axis: **LEFT, CENTER, RIGHT, LEADING** or **TRAILING.**
Icon getIcon( )	Returns the label's glyph or icon.
int getIconTextGap( )	Returns the amount of space between the text and the icon.
String getText( )	Returns the text that the label displays.
int getVerticalAlignment( )	Returns the alignment of the label text and icon along the vertical axis. This is either **TOP, CENTER** or **BOTTOM**
void setHorizontalAlignment(int)	Sets the horizontal alignment of the label's content to **LEFT, CENTER, RIGHT, LEADING** or **TRAILING.** The default for text only labels is **LEFT,** for image only labels it is **CENTER.**
void setIcon(Icon)	Defines the icon which is displayed.
void setIconTextGap(int)	Sets the amount of space between the text and the icon.
void setText(String)	Changes the text displayed to that specified.
void setVerticalAlignment(int)	Sets the alignment along the vertical axis to **TOP, BOTTOM** or **CENTER.** The default is **CENTER.**

The JTextField class

The **JTextField** component is used for entering and editing a single line of text, in the same way as the **java.awt.TextField** component.

Unlike the **TextField** class it does not have **setEchoChar** and **getEchoChar** methods which are used to specify and get a character which will be echoed whatever key is pressed. This is essential if you wish to input a password which you do not want displayed. The **JPasswordField** class extends the **JTextField** class and has this capability. This class has a **getPassword** method rather than **getText** method for returning the text which has been typed.

You can make the horizontal alignment left justified, centred or right justified using the **setHorizontalAlignment** method with the parameter **LEFT_ALIGNMENT, CENTER_ALIGNMENT** or **RIGHT_ALIGNMENT.** The **getHorizontal** method returns the current alignment.

The JTextArea class

This is a component which allows you to display one or more lines of text. It is very similar to the **java.awt.TextArea** class, but there are some important differences. The **JTextArea** class, unlike the **TextArea** class, is not able to scroll directly, but it does implement the **Scrollable** interface, so that it can be placed in a **JScrollPane** object if scrolling is needed.

In the application shown in figure 13.10, a **JTextArea** component is added to a **JScrollPane** to provide an editable scrollable multi-line text area.

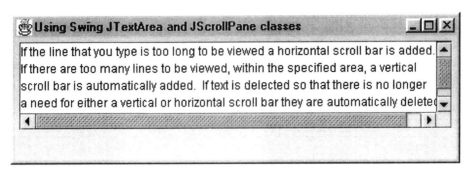

Fig. 13.10 *Using the JTextArea and JScrollPane components.*

The complete application is shown below:

```
import javax.swing.*;
import java.awt.event.*;
public class SwingTextArea extends JFrame {
    public SwingTextArea( ) {
//set the JFrame title and size
        setTitle("Using Swing JTextArea and JScrollPane classes");
        setSize(460, 150);
//create a JPanel and JTextArea
        JPanel p = new JPanel( );
        JTextArea text = new JTextArea(5,40);
//create a ScrollPane object and add the JTextArea object to it
        JScrollPane scroll = new JScrollPane(text);
//add the JScrollPane object to the JPanel.
        p.add(scroll);
//the panel becomes the content pane
        setContentPane(p);
//display the frame
        setVisible(true);
//handle the clicking of the close icon on the frame
        ClosingWindow close = new ClosingWindow( );
        addWindowListener(close);
    }
```

```
public class ClosingWindow extends WindowAdapter {
    public void windowClosing(WindowEvent e) {
        System.exit(0);   // end the program
    }
} // end of the ClosingWindows inner class
public static void main(String args[ ]){
    new SwingTextArea( );
}
}
```

The JList class

This is similar to the **List** class in the AWT package, but there are some important differences. The contents of the list are managed by a separate class called **ListModel**. The usual way of putting the list items into a **JList** is to define an array of strings and pass this to the **JList** constructor. This automatically creates a **ListModel** object which has some useful methods for managing list items, for example:

```
JList colorList;
String[ ] colors = {"red", "blue", "green", "orange", "yellow"};
colorList = new JList(colors);
```

This Java code creates a new **JList** object which contains a list of colours. You can use the **getElementAt** method of the **ListModel** class to find an item selected in the list:

```
String s;
s = colorList.getModel( ).getElementAt(colorList.getSelectedIndex( )).toString( );
```

The **getSelectedIndex** method returns the value of the selected item in the list. This value is used as an **int** parameter for the **getElementAt** method which returns an object of type **Object**. This is converted to a **String** by the **toString** method.

An alternative and simpler way of doing this is used in the next example. As before the **String** *s* is assigned the text representing the selected item:

```
String s = (colorList.getSelectedValue( )).toString( );
```

The **getSelectedValue** method returns the selected list item which is converted to a **String** by the **toString** method.

The event handling when a new list item is selected is handled by the **ListSelectionListener** interface which has a single method called **valueChanged** which is passed a **ListSelectedEvent** object.

To see the event handling and a few of the methods of the **JList** class in action the next application, shown running in figure 13.11, displays a list of colours. When a colour is selected either by clicking on a new entry with the mouse or scrolling with the up and down arrow keys the colour of the background changes to the colour chosen and the selected item is displayed in the **TextField**.

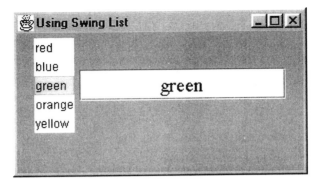

Fig. 13.11 *Using the JList component.*

This application is similar to the previous example in that the public class, called *SwingList*, extends the **JFrame** class and has its components added to a **JPanel** which is displayed on the **JFrame**. The handling of the event caused by clicking in the top right corner of the frame on the close icon is dealt with by an inner class.

This class implements the **ListSelectionListener** interface. When a new list item is selected the **valueChanged** method, shown below, is called:

```
public void valueChanged(ListSelectionEvent e) {
//come here when a new list item is selected
//display the color in the TextField
    colorName.setText((colorList.getSelectedValue( )).toString( ));
    switch (colorList.getSelectedIndex( )) {
        case 0 : p.setBackground(Color.red);
            break;
        case 1 : p.setBackground(Color.blue);
            break;
        case 2 : p.setBackground(Color.green);
            break;
        case 3 : p.setBackground(Color.orange);
            break;
        case 4 : p.setBackground(Color.yellow);
    }
}
```

The currently selected item is found using the **getSelectedValue** method, this is converted to a string and displayed in the **TextField**. If the index of the selected item is zero, that is, the first item in the list, the colour of the **JPanel** on which the components are displayed is changed to red, and so on for all of the other colours in the list.

The complete application is shown below, note that four packages must be imported:

```
import javax.swing. *;
import javax.swing.event. *;
import java.awt.event. *;
import java.awt. *;
```

```java
public class SwingList extends JFrame implements ListSelectionListener {
    JPanel p;
    JList colorList;
    JTextField colorName;
    public SwingList( ) {
//set the JFrame title and size
        setTitle("Using Swing List");
        setSize(300,300);
//create a panel
        p = new JPanel( );
//create a list of the entries for the list
        String[ ] colors = {"red", "blue", "green", "orange", "yellow"};
//add the entries to the list and add the list to the panel
        colorList = new JList(colors);
        p.add(colorList);
//add a listener to pick up changes in the item selected in the list
        colorList.addListSelectionListener(this);
//instantiate a TextField, change the font and make the text alignment central
        colorName = new JTextField(15);
        colorName.setFont(new Font("Serif", Font.PLAIN, 20));
        colorName.setHorizontalAlignment(
                            (int)TextField.CENTER_ALIGNMENT);
        p.add(colorName);
//the panel becomes the content pane
        setContentPane(p);
//display the frame containing the panel
        setVisible(true);
//handle the clicking of the close icon on the frame
        ClosingWindow close = new ClosingWindow( );
        addWindowListener(close);
    }
    public void valueChanged(ListSelectionEvent e) {
//come here when a new list item is selected
//display the color in the TextField
        colorName.setText((colorList.getSelectedValue( )).toString( ));
        switch (colorList.getSelectedIndex( )) {
            case 0 : p.setBackground(Color.red);
                break;
            case 1 : p.setBackground(Color.blue);
                break;
            case 2 : p.setBackground(Color.green);
                break;
            case 3 : p.setBackground(Color.orange);
                break;
            case 4 : p.setBackground(Color.yellow);
```

```
            }
        }
        public class ClosingWindow extends WindowAdapter {
            public void windowClosing(WindowEvent e) {
                System.exit(0);   // end the program
            }
        } // end of the ClosingWindows inner class
        public static void main(String args[ ]){
            new SwingList( );
        }
    }
```

The **JList** class does not support scrolling directly. You need to use the **JScrollPane** class if you want to provide scrolling behaviour.

You may only select more than one item from the list if multiple selection is enabled with the **setSelectionMode** method. The selection mode determines what items can be selected; there are three options:

- **SINGLE_SELECTION** - Only one item may be selected.
- **SINGLE_INTERVAL_SELECTION** - Only one contiguous set of items may be selected.
- **MULTIPLE_INTERVAL_SELECTION** - There are no restrictions on what may be selected.

The **void** method **addListSelectionListener** takes a **ListSelectionListener** object as a parameter. When a new item is selected the **valueChanged** method is called.

The most widely used methods of the **JList** class are shown in table 13.4:

Table 13.4 *The key methods of the JList class.*

Method	Description
void clearSelection( )	Deselects all items.
int getMaxSelectedIndex( )	The largest index of the selected items.
int getMinSelectedIndex( )	The small index of the selected items.
int getSelectedIndex( )	Returns the first selected index.
int[ ] getSelectedIndices( )	Returns an array of selected items.
Object getSelectedValue( )	Returns the first selected value.
Object[ ] getSelectedValues( )	Returns an array of the selected values.
int getSelectionMode( )	Returns the current selection mode.
void setSelectedIndex(int)	Selects one item.
void setSelectedIndices(int[ ])	Selects one or more items.
void setSelectionMode(int)	Changes the selection mode.

The JColorChooser class

Most of the Swing components we have looked at so far are similar to AWT components, but there are some components which do not have a related AWT components.

The **JColorChooser** class is designed to allow you to choose a colour visually, rather than using the **Color** class and specifying the red, green and blue components or using one of the pre-defined colours from that class. This is very useful, since it is difficult to visualise what a colour will look like until you actually see it.

The **JColorChooser** class has three constructors:

- **JColorChooser( )** creates a color chooser with an initial colour of white.
- **JColorChooser(Color)** creates a color chooser with the specified initial colour.
- **JColorChooser(ColorSelectionModel)** creates a color chooser with the specified selection model.

In the next application, a **JColorChooser** and two **JButton** objects are added to a **JPanel** which is displayed on a **JFrame** object. When a colour is chosen and the *OK* button is clicked, the background colour of the panel changes. Clicking on the *Exit* button ends the application. The running application is shown in figures 13.12, 13.13 and 13.14. The **JColorChooser** allows you to select the colour in three different ways.

The swatches page, shown in figure 13.12, gives a set of alternative colours and also lists the most recent colours chosen.

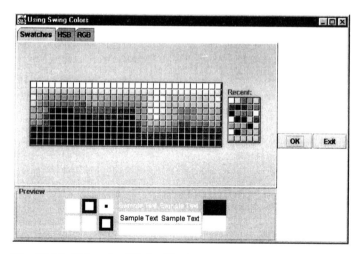

Fig. 13.12 Using the JColorChooser component, swatches page.

The RGB page, shown in figure 13.13, allows you to select the individual red, green and blue components of the colour. All colours can be specified by varying proportions of these colours.

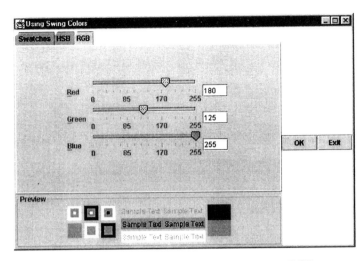

Fig. 13.13 *Using the **JColorChooser** component, RGB page.*

The HSB page, shown in figure 13.14, allows you to select a colour using the alternative hue, saturation and brightness model for colours rather than the more widely used red, green and blue model.

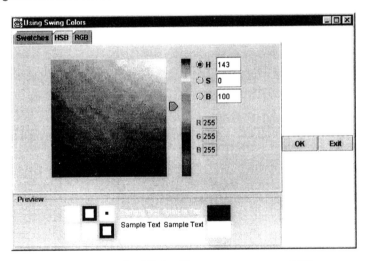

Fig. 13.14 *Using the **JColorChooser** component, HSB page.*

Three packages need to be imported for this application:

import javax.swing.*;
import java.awt.*;
import java.awt.event.*;

The *SwingColor* class extends the **JFrame** class and implements the **ActionListener** interface so that it can catch the events which occur when the buttons are clicked:

public class *SwingColor* **extends JFrame implements ActionListener {**

This class has four instance variables, the **JColorChooser**, the **JPanel** and the two **JButton** objects:

> **JColorChooser** *color;*
> **JPanel** *p;*
> **JButton** *ok, exit;*

The **JPanel** object is instantiated and is given a new layout manager called **BoxLayout:**

> *p =* **new JPanel( );**
> *p.setLayout(new* **BoxLayout(p, BoxLayout.X_AXIS));**

The **BoxLayout** class is a layout manager which allows you to display components in a horizontal row or a vertical column. In this example they are displayed in a row, to display them stacked vertically one above the other specify **BoxLayout.Y_AXIS** in the constructor.

The **JColorChooser** object, called *color*, is instantiated and added to the **JPanel** object:

> *color =* **new JColorChooser(Color.red);**
> *p.add(color);*

The buttons and their listeners are also added to the **JPanel** object as we have seen before.

The **JPanel** object is assigned to the content pane and the **JFrame** is displayed:

> *setContentPane(p);*
> *setVisible(true);*

When a button is clicked the **actionPerformed** method is called. If the *ok* button has been clicked the **getColor** method is used to find the current colour selected by the color chooser and this is used to change the background colour of the panel. If the *exit* button is clicked the application ends:

> **public void actionPerformed(ActionEvent e) {**
> *//come here when a button is clicked*
> > **if** *(e.getSource( ) ==* ok) p.setBackground(color.getColor( ));* else
> > **if** *(e.getSource( ) ==* exit) System.exit(0);*
> *}*

An inner class is added to handle the closing of the frame and the end of the application and a **main** method is used to initiate the application. The complete application is shown below:

> **import** *javax.swing.*;*
> **import** *java.awt.*;*
> **import** *java.awt.event.*;*
> **public class** *SwingColor* **extends JFrame implements ActionListener {**

```
        JColorChooser color;
        JPanel p;
        JButton ok, exit;
        public SwingColor( ) {
//set the JFrame title and size
            setTitle("Using Swing Colors");
            setSize(600,400);
//create a panel
            p = new JPanel( );
//use the BoxLayout for the panel
            p.setLayout(new BoxLayout(p, BoxLayout.X_AXIS));
            color = new JColorChooser(Color.red);
//add the JColorChooser object to the panel
            p.add(color);
//add the ok, exit buttons and listeners for events
            ok = new JButton(" OK ");
            p.add(ok);
            ok.addActionListener(this);
            exit = new JButton( " Exit ");
            p.add(exit);
            exit.addActionListener(this);
//the panel becomes the content pane
            setContentPane(p);
//display the frame containing the panel
            setVisible(true);
//handle the clicking of the close icon on the frame
            ClosingWindow close = new ClosingWindow( );
            addWindowListener(close);
        }
        public void actionPerformed(ActionEvent e) {
//come here when a button is clicked
            if (e.getSource( ) == ok) p.setBackground(color.getColor( )); else
            if (e.getSource( ) == exit) System.exit(0);
        }
        public class ClosingWindow extends WindowAdapter {
            public void windowClosing(WindowEvent e) {
                System.exit(0);   // end the program
            }
        } // end of the ClosingWindows inner class
        public static void main(String args[ ]){
            new SwingColor( );
        }
    }
```

It is not necessary to add the **JColorChooser** object to a **Panel** object. You can create a dialog directly using the **showDialog** method, which displays the color chooser and three buttons as shown in figure 13.15. Clicking on *OK* selects the colour and closes the dialog, *Cancel* does not assign the colour and closes the dialog, *Reset* selects the original colour and does not close the dialog.

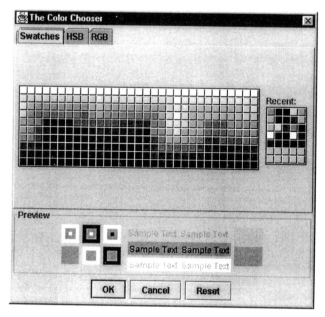

Fig. 13.15 The JColorChooser component with buttons.

The previous application shown in figures 13.12, 13.13 and 13.14 can be amended to use the dialog shown in figure 13.15. The statement adding the **JColorChooser** to the **JPanel** (shown below) must be removed:

p.add(color);

and the **actionPerformed** method changed as shown below:

```
public void actionPerformed(ActionEvent e) {
//come here when a button is clicked
    if (e.getSource( ) == ok) {
        Color c = color.showDialog(p, "The Color Chooser", Color.pink);
        p.setBackground(c);
        } else
    if (e.getSource( ) == exit) System.exit(0);
}
```

When the *OK* button on the panel is clicked, this method is called. The **showDialog** method is used to display the dialog. This is passed three parameters, the name of the parent component for the dialog, that is the **JPanel** object, the title of the dialog, and an initial color. It returns the colour chosen.

The JFileChooser class

The **JFileChooser** class is an extremely useful Swing class which has no equivalent among the AWT classes. It allows you to browse through your file system and to select a file.

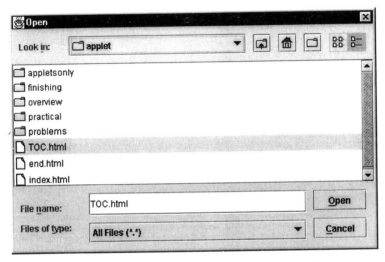

*Fig. 13.16 The open file form of a **JFileChooser** object.*

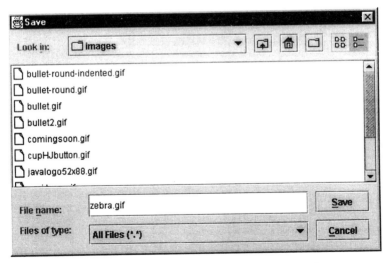

*Fig. 13.17 The save file form of a **JFileChooser** object.*

There are two slightly different forms depending on whether you wish to display an open file dialog or a save file dialog, as shown in figures 13.16 and 13.17.

This class has an extensive set of fields and methods which gives great flexibility. It is only possible to cover a small set of the most widely used facilities of this class. There are six constructors; the following three are most often used:

- **JFileChooser( )** creates a **JFileChooser** object which points to the home directory.
- **JFileChooser(String)** the parameter specifies the initial path.
- **JFileChooser(File)** the **File** parameter specifies the initial path.

There are over sixty methods in this class, not including those inherited from the **JComponent**, **Container** and **Component** classes which allow you to control every feature of the file selection process. A few of these methods are listed in table 13.5, and we will see some of them in action in the next application.

Table 13.5 The key methods of the JFileChooser class.

Method	Description
void approveSelection( )	Called when the *approve* button, that is the *Open* or *Save* button, is clicked.
void cancelSelection( )	Called when the *Cancel* button is clicked.
void changeToParentDirectory( )	Changes the current directory to the parent of that directory.
String getApproveButtonText( )	Returns the text on the *approve* button.
File getCurrentDirectory( )	Returns the current directory.
String getDescription(File)	Returns a description of the file.
FileFilter getFileFilter( )	Returns the current file filter.
String getName(File)	Returns the name of the specified file.
File getSelectedFile( )	Returns the selected file.
File[ ] getSelectedFiles( )	Returns a list of the selected files if multi-selection is enabled.
void setApproveButtonText(String)	Sets the text on the *approve* button.
void setCurrentDirectory(File)	Sets the current directory to that specified.
void setMultiSelectionEnabled(boolean)	If the boolean is **true**, multi-selection is allowed.
int showOpenDialog(Component)	Displays the open file dialog and returns either **CANCEL_OPTION** or **APPROVE_OPTION**.
int showSaveDialog(Component)	Displays the save file dialog and returns either **CANCEL_OPTION** or **APPROVE_OPTION**.

To see some of these methods in action we are going to look at an application which displays a **JFrame** object containing two **JButton** objects and a **JTextField** object. The initial frame of the running application is shown in figure 13.18. When the *Open File* button is clicked the **JFileChooser** is displayed. You can browse through your file system and select a file. The **JFileChooser** dialog has two buttons. Clicking the *Open* button returns the name of the file which can be displayed in the **JTextField** (the left image in figure 13.18). Clicking the *Cancel* button does not return any file details and the message *Operation cancelled* is displayed in the **JTextField** (the right image in figure 13.18).

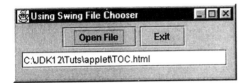 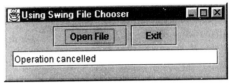

Fig. 13.18 The SwingFile application.

The *SwingFile* class extends the **JFrame** class and implements the **ActionListener** interface to detect the button events on the initial **JFrame**. The application is very similar to the previous example except that an instance variable *file* of type **JFileChooser** is defined:

    JFileChooser file;

This is instantiated in the *SwingFile* constructor and a listener added:

    *file = **new JFileChooser( );***
    *file.**addActionListener(this);***

When the **JFileChooser** has been displayed and a button is clicked on it, the **actionPerformed** method is called:

```
public void actionPerformed(ActionEvent e) {
//come here when a button is clicked
    if (e.getSource( ) == openFile) file.showOpenDialog(p); else
    if (e.getSource( ) == exit) System.exit(0); else
// if the "open" button was pressed e.getActionCommand
// will be "ApproveSelection"
    if (e.getActionCommand( ) == "ApproveSelection")
        jText.setText(file.getCurrentDirectory( ) + "\\"
                + file.getSelectedFile( ).getName( )); else
//if the "cancel" button was pressed e.actionCommand will be "CancelSelection"
    if (e.getActionCommand( ) == "CancelSelection")
                jText.setText("Operation cancelled");
}
```

The *openFile* button is on the initial **JFrame** and displays the open file dialog. The *exit* button is also on the initial **JFrame** and closes the application.

If the *open* button is clicked on the open file dialog, the **getActionCommand** method will return the **String** *ApproveSelection*. The name of the directory is returned by the **getCurrentDirectory** method and the name of the selected file is returned by the **getSelectedFile** method. These are displayed in the **JTextField** separated by a \ character. Note that to specify this character you need to enter \\, as shown.

If the *Cancel* button on the file dialog is clicked, the **getActionCommand** method returns *CancelSelection* and the text in the **JTextField** is set to *Operation cancelled*.

The complete application is shown below:

```
import javax.swing.*;
import java.awt.event.*;
public class SwingFile extends JFrame implements ActionListener {
    JFileChooser file;
    JPanel p;
    JButton openFile, exit;
    JTextField jText = new JTextField(25);
    public SwingFile() {
//set the JFrame title and size
        setTitle("Using Swing File Chooser");
        setSize(300,100);
//create a panel
        p = new JPanel();
//create a FileChooser and add an listener
        file = new JFileChooser();
        file.addActionListener(this);
//add the open file and exit buttons and listeners for events
        openFile = new JButton(" Open File ");
        p.add(openFile);
        openFile.addActionListener(this);
        exit = new JButton( " Exit ");
        p.add(exit);
        exit.addActionListener(this);
        p.add(jText);
//the panel becomes the content pane
        setContentPane(p);
//display the frame containing the panel
        setVisible(true);
//handle the clicking of the close icon on the frame
        ClosingWindow close = new ClosingWindow();
        addWindowListener(close);
    }
    public void actionPerformed(ActionEvent e) {
//come here when a button is clicked
        if (e.getSource() == openFile) file.showOpenDialog(p); else
        if (e.getSource() == exit) System.exit(0); else
```

```
// if the "open" button was pressed e.getActionCommand
// will be "ApproveSelection"
        if (e.getActionCommand( ) == "ApproveSelection")
            jText.setText(file.getCurrentDirectory( ) + "\\"
                + file.getSelectedFile( ).getName( )); else;
//if the "cancel" button was pressed e.actionCommand will be "CancelSelection"
        if (e.getActionCommand( ) == "CancelSelection")
                    jText.setText("Operation cancelled");

        }
    public class ClosingWindow extends WindowAdapter {
        public void windowClosing(WindowEvent e) {
            System.exit(0);   // end the program
        }
    } // end of the ClosingWindows inner class
    public static void main(String args[ ]){
        new SwingFile( );
    }
}
```

14
Java Exceptions

Introduction

Every application that we write or use has errors. In most circumstances these bugs are not so major that the application is impossible to use. Some errors which occur when an application runs are so serious that the application cannot continue, for example running out of memory or a failure of the hardware, however sometimes problems do occur when an application runs that we can anticipate and take some corrective action. If, for example, we try to open a file which does not exist an error will occur. You can catch this, display an error message and ask for another filename to be specified.

When an error of this type occurs an exception is generated and Java provides a set of language constructs which allow you to handle them. In this chapter we are going to look at the **Exception** class and how to handle exceptions when they occur.

The Exception class

All exceptions are subclasses of the **Exception** class. There are about 200 exceptions defined in the Java 2 API. You can also create your own exceptions if you cannot find an existing one which is suitable.

The try and catch clauses

If you want to take some action when an exception occurs, you must enclose the Java code where the exception may occur within a **try** clause. The **try** clause is followed by one or more **catch** clauses. More than one type of exception may occur within a **try** clause and if you want to distinguish between the different types you can have a series of different **catch** clauses. The basic layout of **try** and **catch** clauses are as follows:

```
try {
       //the code where the exceptions may occur
       //is placed within this try clause
} //end of try clause
catch (FirstException e1) {
       //the code to handle the exception goes here
} //end of the first catch clause
catch (SecondException e2) {
       //the code to handle the second exception goes here
} //end of the second catch clause
```

You can have as many **catch** clauses as you wish. A **catch** clause has to specify which exception it is catching. If you have more than one **catch** clause you must catch a subclass exception before the superclass of that exception. The **FileNotFoundException** is a subclass of **IOException** and its **catch** clause must be placed before the clause to catch the **IOException**.

The **Exception** class is the superclass of all exceptions, therefore the clause to catch this exception must come last, if you have more than one **catch** clause. We are going to see how this works in practice in the next example, shown running in figure 14.1. Two numbers are input into two **TextField** objects and the first is divided by the second. The result is displayed in the third **TextField**. There are a number of exceptions which can be produced. If the text in either the first or second **TextField** cannot be converted into a floating point number a **NumberFormatException** is thrown. If the division produces an error, an **ArithmeticException** may be thrown. If an exception is produced an error message is displayed as shown in figure 14.1, where the second value input is not a valid number.

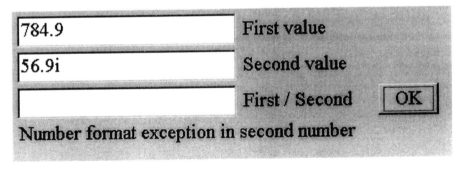

Fig. 14.1 Catching exceptions.

The complete listing for this applet is shown below:

```
import java.applet.*;
import java.awt.*;
import java.awt.event.*;
public class ExceptionHandling extends Applet implements ActionListener {
       private TextField first = new TextField(20);
```

```java
private TextField second = new TextField(20);
private Button ok = new Button(" OK ");
private TextField answer = new TextField(20);
private Label error = new Label(" ");
private double top, bottom; // the two numbers to be divided
public ExceptionHandling( ) {
    setFont(new Font("Serif", Font.PLAIN, 20));
    setLayout(new FlowLayout(FlowLayout.LEFT));
    add(first);
    add(new Label("First value       "));
    add(second);
    add (new Label("Second value   "));
    add(answer);
    answer.setEnabled(false);    // answer is read only
    add (new Label("First / Second "));
    add(ok);
    ok.addActionListener(this);
    add(error);
}
public void actionPerformed(ActionEvent evt)   {
    error.setText("");   //clear any error message
    error.setSize(400,20);
    try {
        top = Double.valueOf(first.getText( )).doubleValue( );
    }
    catch(NumberFormatException e) {
        error.setText("Number format exception in first number");
        answer.setText("");//clear the answer fields
        return;
    }
    try {
// the doubleValue method converts a String to a Double
// the valueOf method converts a Double to a double
        bottom = Double.valueOf(second.getText( )).doubleValue( );
    }
    catch(NumberFormatException e) {
        error.setText("Number format exception in second number");
        answer.setText("");//clear the answer fields
        return;
    }
    try {
        answer.setText(String.valueOf(top / bottom));
    }
    catch(ArithmeticException e) {
        error.setText("Arithmetic exception occurred in calculation");
```

```
    }
    catch(Exception e) {
        error.setText("Unspecified exception occurred in calculation");
    }
}
}
```

When the button is clicked the **actionPerformed** method is called. The first action in this method is to erase any previous error messages. Next, a **try** clause is opened and an attempt is made to convert the text in the first **TextField** into a **double** floating point number. If this cannot be done a **NumberFormatException** is thrown which is caught by the following **catch** clause which displays the message *Number format exception in first number*. The second number is converted from a **String** to a **double** in the same way. The division of the first number by the second is placed within a **try** clause. If an **ArithmeticException** is thrown, it is collected by the following **catch** clause. There is a second **catch** clause for exceptions in the **Exception** class which is guaranteed to catch any exceptions thrown by the division which are not **ArithmeticException** exceptions. Since all exceptions are either members of the **Exception** class or members of its subclasses any exception thrown by the previous **try** clause which has not already been caught will be trapped by this **catch** clause.

A **catch** clause for a particular exception class will catch any exception which is a member of the specified class or one of its subclasses, therefore it is essential that the **catch** clause for **ArithmeticException** exceptions is placed before the **catch** clause for **Exception** exceptions.

Throwing an exception

One of the surprising features of this application is that if you attempt to perform a division by zero an exception is not produced and the result *Infinity* is displayed. If you want to display an error message you can explicitly throw an error. The code replaces the existing **try** clause which divides the two numbers:

```
try {
    answer.setText(String.valueOf(top / bottom));
    if (bottom == 0.0) {
        answer.setText("");
        throw new ArithmeticException();
    }
}
```

If the bottom value is zero, the third **TextField,** which displays the result, is cleared and an **ArithmeticException** is explicitly thrown. This is caught by the **ArithmeticException catch** clause.

Creating new exceptions

The application could be improved if we created our own exception so that division by zero could be distinguished from other exceptions. To do this we must create a new class which extends an existing exception class. Since our new exception called *DivideByZeroException* is a type of arithmetic exception it is sensible to subclass the **ArithmeticException** class:

```
public class DivideByZeroException extends ArithmeticException {
    public DivideByZeroException( ) {
    }
}
```

This class does nothing except ensure that the *DivideByZeroException* exception can be thrown and therefore caught. To catch this exception we need to change the **try** clause where the division occurs to throw this exception and to add the **catch** clause:

```
try {
    answer.setText(String.valueOf(top / bottom));
    if (bottom == 0.0) {
        throw new DivideByZeroException( );
    }
}
catch(DivideByZeroException e) {
    error.setText("Division by zero");
}
```

The **catch** clause displays the message *Division by zero* when it is called. It is followed by the **catch** clauses for **ArithmeticException** and **Exception**.

Throwing without catching

If you do not want to handle an exception in a method with **try** and **catch** clauses you can throw it to the calling method. If there is not an exception handler in that method it is thrown further up the line and so on. To throw an exception you must list the exceptions to be thrown at the start of the method after **throws**, for example:

public void actionPerformed(ActionEvent evt) throws NumberFormatException {

If you do not include your own exception handling, Java will display an error message for you and usually end your application, however it is poor programming practice not to handle a problem when it occurs and to rely on a calling method which may have been written by someone else who was expecting methods to handle their own problems.

15

Writing Threaded Applications

Introduction

Operating systems such as UNIX, Windows 95 and Windows 98 are able to run more than one application at the same time. At any one moment however, if you have only one processor, you are actually executing only one of those applications, but by switching between them quickly your computer is able to give the impression that it is working simultaneously on more than one of the applications. This can be a very efficient use of computer time, since if one application is updating a database it will spend a lot of its time waiting for the disk which is slow compared to the speed of the processor. This waiting time can be used to run a second application without slowing down the first. The scheduling of different applications is a feature of the operating system of your computer and you usually do not have a great deal of control over how it works.

Sometimes a single application may want to do more than one activity at the same time, if for example you are downloading a large page from the Web, you want to be able to read and use the part that you have already downloaded without waiting for the whole of the page. An application which behaves in this way is said to have different threads of control or to be multi-threaded.

Java is able to produce multi-threaded applications, which often form a part of applications including animations.

Pre-emptive scheduling

If you are writing a multi-threaded application you are dependent on the capabilities of the underlying operating system on which the application is run. Most modern operating systems can cope with multi-threading. Since only one of the threads can run at any particular time some decision must be made about which thread is to be run. Most operating systems use a type of scheduling called pre-emptive.

In pre-emptive scheduling a thread can be in one of three states:

- Running. The thread is actually being given CPU time by the computer and is executing.
- Ready. The thread is ready and able to run, but has been temporarily suspended by the operating system.
- Blocked, sometimes called waiting. The thread is not ready to run until something else happens, for example it is waiting for input from a disk or the network, or for another thread to take some action.

The transitions between these three states is shown in figure 15.1.

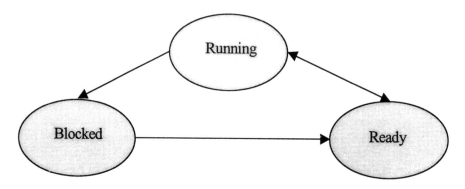

Fig. 15.1 Thread states in a pre-emptive scheduling system.

Only one thread is running at a time, assuming that you only have one processor on your computer. If you have a parallel, or multi-processor computer more than one thread can be running at once. When the operating system's scheduler decides that it has allocated enough time to a running thread, it puts that thread into the ready state. It then looks at the list of threads in the ready state. All of the threads in the ready state are able and willing to run. The scheduler chooses one, usually the one which has not been run for the longest time, puts it into the running state and starts executing it. Sometimes, before a thread has used up the time that the scheduler allocates to it, it finds that it has to wait, for example, for some information to come in from the network. In this situation the thread goes into the blocked state and the scheduler chooses another thread (which is in the ready state) to run. When the information from the network has arrived, the thread in the blocked state is transferred to the ready state indicating that it is ready to run.

The decision on which of the threads in the ready state is to run next is not always a straightforward one. All threads are not equal, some may need a higher priority than others.

There is a huge amount of theory behind the way in which schedulers work which is beyond the scope of this book, but it is important to know in overview what is going on in the background when you are using multiple threads, as some unexpected and baffling things can happen if you do not know about scheduling.

The Runnable interface

If you want a class to run within a thread the class must implement the **Runnable** interface or extend the **Thread** class, which implements the **Runnable** interface.

The **Runnable** interface has a single method called **run**. The class which implements the **Runnable** interface must therefore supply its own **run** method. Starting a thread causes the **run** method to be executed. This method is executed for a brief time and then another thread of the application is executed. This thread runs briefly and is then suspended so another thread can run and so on.

The first application we are going to look at calculates prime numbers. Approximately every second a thread runs which prints out how many seconds have elapsed. The stages in writing this application are as follows:

- Create a public class which implements the **Runnable** interface:

  public class TimeThreadAndPrime implements Runnable {

- Create a constructor for this class which creates a **Thread** object and calls its **start** method. This will call the **run** method:

  ```
  public TimeThreadAndPrime( ) {
      Thread FirstThread = new Thread(this);
      FirstThread.start( );
  }
  ```

- Create a **run** method which is executed when the thread is started, that is when the **start** method is called:

  ```
  public void run( ) {
      int elapsedTime = 0;
      while (true) {
          System.out.println("Time taken : " + elapsedTime + " seconds");
          elapsedTime++;
          try {
              Thread.sleep(1000);     //wait one second
          } catch (InterruptedException e) {
              System.out.println("Error - terminating application");
              System.exit(0);
          }
      }
  }
  ```

- Write the Java code for calculating and printing primes in the **main** method following the instantiation of the *TimeThreadAndPrime* class (which executes the constructor method).

The whole application is shown below:

```
public class TimeThreadAndPrime implements Runnable {
    public TimeThreadAndPrime( ) {
        Thread FirstThread = new Thread(this);
        FirstThread.start( );
    }
    public void run( ) {
        int elapsedTime = 0;
        while (true) {
            System.out.println("Time taken : " + elapsedTime + " seconds");
            elapsedTime++;
            try {
                Thread.sleep(1000);     //wait one second
            } catch (InterruptedException e) {
                System.out.println("Error - terminating application");
                System.exit(0);
            }
        }
    }
    public static void main (String args[ ]) {
        new TimeThreadAndPrime( );
    //calculate all the primes up to 1,000,000
        long sofar = 3;
        while (sofar < 1000000) {
            boolean prime = true;
            for (long c = 3; c < sofar/2; c += 2)
    // if c divides exactly into sofar, then sofar is not prime
                if ((sofar % c) == 0) prime = false;
                if (prime == true) System.out.println(sofar);
                sofar += 2;
        }
        System.out.println("Complete");
        System.exit(0);
    }
}
```

The **run** method has an endless **while** loop, which prints the value of the local variable *elapsedTime* and then increments that variable. The **sleep** method of the thread suspends the thread for 1000 milliseconds, that is one second and the loop is repeated. The **sleep** method may throw an **InterruptedException**, therefore it is placed within a **try** clause. The **catch** clause simply displays an error message and ends the application.

After the **main** method instantiates the *TimeThreadAndPrime* class (and therefore calls its constructor) it calculates and displays the prime numbers up to one million (this takes hours even on a fast computer). Approximately every second the printing of the primes is interrupted by the execution of the **run** method which prints out the approximate number of elapsed seconds.

A sample of the output from my computer is shown below:

187177
187181
Time taken 6337 seconds
187189
187193
Time taken 6338 seconds

The Thread class

In the next application we are going to have two threads running. One thread displays a list of car manufacturers, the other a list of motorbike manufacturers.

The *CarThread* class extends the **Thread** class and defines a list of car manufacturers. Each one is displayed in turn:

```
class CarThread extends Thread {
    String[ ] cars = {"Ford", "GM", "Volkswagen", "Mercedes", "BMW"};
    public void run( ) {
        for (int c=0; c<cars.length; c++)
            System.out.println(cars[c] + " make cars");
    }
}
```

The *BikeThread* class does exactly the same except that it prints a list of motorbike manufacturers. The **main** method instantiates each of these classes and executes their **start** methods. The complete application listing is shown below:

```
public class TwoThreads {
    public static void main (String args[ ]) {
        CarThread car = new CarThread( );
        BikeThread bike = new BikeThread( );
        car.start( );
        bike.start( );
    }
}
class CarThread extends Thread {
    String[ ] cars = {"Ford", "GM", "Volkswagen", "Mercedes", "BMW"};
    public void run( ) {
        for (int c=0; c<cars.length; c++)
            System.out.println(cars[c] + " make cars");
    }
}
class BikeThread extends Thread {
    String[ ] bikes = {"Harley", "Ducati", "Triumph", "Honda", "Yamaha"};
    public void run( ) {
```

```
        for (int c = 0; c <bikes.length; c ++)
            System.out.println(bikes[c] + " make bikes");
    }
}
```

The order in which the information is displayed is unpredictable, since we are not controlling the point at which we switch from one thread to another. On my computer the following text is displayed:

Ford make cars
Harley make bikes
GM make cars
Ducati make bikes
Volkswagen make cars
Triumph make bikes
Mercedes make cars
Honda make bikes
BMW make cars
Yamaha make bikes

On your computer the order in which the bikes are listed and the order in which the cars are listed will be the same, but it may display two car manufacturers followed by two bike manufacturers and so on.

Synchronizing threads

So far we have looked at applications where there is only one thread for a particular class. These threads behave fairly independently, with the Java virtual machine switching between the threads. As we have seen this can cause some problems since it is not known when a thread will be paused to allow another thread to run. It is a particular problem if you want to have more than one instance of a class which has a running thread.

In the following example shown below, we instantiate two instances of the *OneTwoThree* class:

```
public class ThreadSynchronized {
    OneTwoThree f1, f2;
    ThreadSynchronized( ) {
        f1 = new OneTwoThree(this);
        f2 = new OneTwoThree(this);
```

The constructor for the *OneTwoThree* class is passed the name of the current object (**this**). The constructor copies this object to an instance variable of the same type:

```
class OneTwoThree extends Thread {
    ThreadSynchronized currentObject;
    OneTwoThree(ThreadSynchronized thread) {
```

```
        currentObject = thread;
    }
```

The threads are started in the *ThreadSynchronized* class constructor using the **start** method which calls the **run** method.

```
f1.start( );
f2.start( );
```

The **run** method calls *printout*, a method in the *ThreadSynchronized* class five times:

```
public void run( ) {
    for (int c= 1; c < 5; c++)
        currentObject.printout( );
}
```

The *printout* method displays the text *One Two Three* on a single line:

```
void printout( ) {
    System.out.print("One ");
    System.out.print("Two ");
    System.out.println("Three");
}
```

The complete application is shown below:

```
public class ThreadSynchronized {
    OneTwoThree f1, f2;
    ThreadSynchronized( ) {
        f1 = new OneTwoThree(this);
        f2 = new OneTwoThree(this);
        f1.start( );
        f2.start( );
    }
    void printout( ) {
        System.out.print("One ");
        System.out.print("Two ");
        System.out.println("Three");
    }
    public static void main (String args[ ]) {
        new ThreadSynchronized( );
    }
}
class OneTwoThree extends Thread {
    ThreadSynchronized currentObject;
    OneTwoThree(ThreadSynchronized thread) {
        currentObject = thread;
    }
    public void run( ) {
```

```
    for (int c= 1; c < 5; c++)
        currentObject.printout( );
    }
}
```

As you would expect the point at which one thread is paused and another started is unpredictable. On my computer the following text is displayed:

One One Two Two Three
Three
One One Two Two Three
Three
One One Two Two Three
Three
One One Two Two Three
Three

The output may be different on your computer. To prevent one thread from interfering with the other the **synchronized** modifier can be used when defining the printout method:

synchronized void *printout( ) {*

If a method is synchronized it cannot be interrupted by another thread. Only when it has completed can another thread enter it. This produces the text *One Two Three* repeated eight times (four times for each thread).

The Thread class

A thread has a priority, which determines how much computer time it is given relative to other threads. The way in which this is calculated is dependent on the operating system of the computer. Priority can be either **Thread.MAX_PRIORITY**, **Thread.MIN_PRIORITY** or **Thread.NORM_PRIORITY**. If the priority of a thread is not explicitly specified, it is given the same priority as the thread which creates it.

All threads have a name, if you do not specify one explicitly one is created for you. The name is of the form *Thread-n*, where *n* is an integer.

The **Thread** class has been revised since the earlier versions of Java and there are numerous methods which have been deprecated. These changes are not simply to improve the API but to fix serious problems which may have occurred when threaded applications were written.

The **Thread** class has some useful methods which we have not looked at yet as shown in table 15.1.

*Table 15.1 The key methods of the **Thread** class.*

Method	Description
static Thread currentThread( )	Identifies the currently executing thread.
void destroy( )	Destroys the thread without any cleanup.
String getName( )	Returns the name of the current thread.
int getPriority( )	Returns the thread's priority.
boolean isAlive( )	Returns **true** if the thread is alive.
void join( )	Waits until the thread has died.
void join(long)	Waits at most for the specified number of milliseconds for the thread to die.
void join(long m, long n)	Waits at most for m milliseconds + n nanoseconds for the thread to die.
void setName(String)	Changes the name of the thread to that specified.
void setPriority(int)	Changes the thread priority to that specified.
static void sleep(long)	Temporarily suspends the execution of the thread for the specified number of milliseconds.
static void sleep(long m, long n)	Temporarily suspends the execution of a thread for m milliseconds + n nanoseconds.

Creating animation

An animation is usually created by displaying a series of successive images each slightly different from the last to create the impression of motion. If you wish to create animation in Java you must use threaded code to allow the Java Virtual machine time to update the screen. To see how this works in practice we are going to write an applet which has a small logo which rotates continually. The basic image shown in figure 15.2 can be created using any drawing package which has the capability to rotate the image by 45°. Each slightly rotated version of the image is stored as a GIF image. The first is called *zero.gif*, the second *fortyFive.gif*, the third *ninety.gif* and so on.

Fig. 15.2 The zero.gif image.

Eight image objects are specified, one for each of the eight GIF files to be displayed:

```
public class ThreadGraphics extends java.applet.Applet implements Runnable {
    Image zero, fortyFive, ninety, oneThirtyFive;
    Image oneEighty, twoTwentyFive, twoSeventy, threeFifteen;
    int angle = 0;
```

An instance variable called *angle* is defined with an initial value of zero.
In the **init** method, the images are loaded into the **Image** object from the files:

```
zero = getImage(getCodeBase( ), "zero.gif");
fortyFive = getImage(getCodeBase( ), "fortyFive.gif");
...
```

The thread is instantiated and started:

```
Thread twist = new Thread(this);
twist.start( );
```

Starting the thread calls the **run** method. This method loops endlessly, increasing
the *angle* instance variable by 45 each time until 360 is reached when it is zeroed. It
pauses for 100 milliseconds after every loop:

```
public void run( ) {
    while (true) {
        repaint( );
        angle += 45;
        if (angle >= 360) angle = 0;
        try {
            Thread.sleep(100);
        } catch (InterruptedException e) {
            System.exit(0);
        }
    }
}
```

If an exception occurs while the thread is sleeping the exception is caught and the
applet is ended. The **repaint** method is called, which in turn calls the **paint** method.
Depending on the value of angle a different image is displayed using the **drawImage**
method. The complete applet is shown below:

```
import java.applet.*;
import java.awt.*;
public class ThreadGraphics extends java.applet.Applet implements Runnable {
    Image zero, fortyFive, ninety, oneThirtyFive;
    Image oneEighty, twoTwentyFive, twoSeventy, threeFifteen;
    int angle = 0;
    public void init( ) {
        setBackground(Color.white);
//the images are in the same directory as the applet
        zero = getImage(getCodeBase( ), "zero.gif");
```

```
        fortyFive = getImage(getCodeBase( ), "fortyFive.gif");
        ninety = getImage(getCodeBase( ), "ninety.gif");
        oneThirtyFive = getImage(getCodeBase( ), "oneThirtyFive.gif");
        oneEighty = getImage(getCodeBase( ), "oneEighty.gif");
        twoTwentyFive = getImage(getCodeBase( ), "twoTwentyFive.gif");
        twoSeventy = getImage(getCodeBase( ), "twoSeventy.gif");
        threeFifteen = getImage(getCodeBase( ), "threeFifteen.gif");
        Thread twist = new Thread(this);
        twist.start( );
    }
    public void run( ) {
        while (true) {
            repaint( );
            angle += 45;
            if (angle >= 360) angle = 0;
            try {
                Thread.sleep(100);
            } catch (InterruptedException e) {
                System.exit(0);
            }
        }
    }
    public void paint(Graphics g) {
        Image img = zero;
        switch (angle) {
            case 0 :      img = zero;
                          break;
            case 45 :     img = fortyFive;
                          break;
            case 90 :     img = ninety;
                          break;
            case 135 :    img = oneThirtyFive;
                          break;
            case 180 :    img = oneEighty;
                          break;
            case 225 :    img = twoTwentyFive;
                          break;
            case 270 :    img = twoSeventy;
                          break;
            case 315 :    img = threeFifteen;
        }
        g.drawImage(img,100,100,img.getWidth(this),img.getHeight(this),this);
    }
}
```

The first parameter of the **drawImage** method is the **Image** object to be displayed. The second and third are the position of the top left corner of the image. The fourth and fifth are the width and height of the image. The sixth is the **ImageObserver**. This method implies that you can scale the image to any size you wish, in practice however there are problems with changing the image size from its default width and height (as specified by the **getWidth** and the **getHeight** methods). Some browsers have a problem in displaying re-scaled GIF images and will not display all re-scaled GIF images correctly. Netscape Communicator version 4.5 seems to handle this problem rather better than Internet Explorer 4.01. If you are writing an animation for the Web it is advisable to make sure that it behaves correctly with a variety of browsers.

The bouncing ball applet

One of the most common problems with animations when an image moves across the applet panel is that there is a lot of flicker when the image is updated, since when the **repaint** method is called the whole of the display area of the applet is redrawn. One successful way of reducing flicker in these situations is to reduce the amount of redrawing that the applet has to do by overwriting the old image with the colour of the background and then drawing the new image. To prevent the applet redrawing the whole area when **repaint** is called we must add a new **update** method which does not clear the panel and does nothing except call the **paint** method. To show this technique in action we are going to look at an applet which has a ball bouncing around the applet panel. The running applet with the direction of the bounce indicated is shown in figure 15.3.

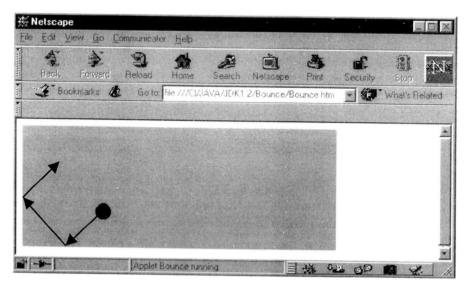

Fig. 15.3 The bouncing ball applet.

Since this is an applet which uses threaded code, it extends the **Applet** class and implements the **Runnable** interface:

public class Bounce extends Applet implements Runnable {

The position in which the ball is to be drawn is determined by the *x* and *y* instance variables. The previous position is given by *oldX* and *oldY*. The limit of the bounce in the x and y directions are defined by two static variables *xLimit* and *yLimit*, and the background colour by the static *backColor* variable:

```
double x, y, oldX, oldY;
static double xLimit = 300;
static double ylimit = 200;
static Color backColor = Color.lightGray;
```

The **init** method sets the background colour and instantiates and starts the thread:

```
public void init( ) {
    setBackground(backColor);
    Thread runner = new Thread(this);
    runner.start( );
}
```

The **run** method chooses random values for the change in *x* and *y* position every time that the ball is drawn, which are stored in *xChange* and *yChange* and random values are selected for the starting position, *x* and *y*. The main body of the method is an endless **while** loop which changes the values of *x* and *y* by *xChange* and *yChange*, calls **repaint** to draw the ball in its new position and sleeps for one millisecond. A check is made to see if the limit of the bouncing area has been reached. If it has, the direction of movement in that direction is reversed:

```
public void run( ) {
    double xChange = Math.random( );
    double yChange = Math.random( );
    x = Math.random( ) * xLimit;
    y = Math.random( ) * ylimit;
    oldX = x;
    oldY = y;
    while (true) {
        x += xChange;
        y += yChange;
        if ((x >= xLimit) | (x <= 0)) xChange = -xChange;
        if ((y >= ylimit) | (y <= 0)) yChange = -yChange;
        repaint( );
        try { Thread.sleep(1);}
        catch (InterruptedException e) { System.exit(0); }
    }
}
```

The **update** method which is called from repaint does nothing except call **paint**:

```
public void update(Graphics g) {
    paint(g);
}
```

Finally in the **paint** method, a ball is drawn in the same colour as the background in the position of the currently displayed ball, *oldX*, *oldY*, which effectively erases that ball. The colour is assigned to red and a new ball is drawn in the new position, *x*, *y*. The value of *x* and *y* are copied to *oldX* and *oldY*, so that this ball can be over-written the next time that **paint** is called:

```
public void paint(Graphics g) {
//erase the old ball by over-writing it
        g.setColor(backColor);
        g.fillOval((int)oldX, (int)oldY, 20, 20);
//draw the new ball
        g.setColor(Color.red);
        g.fillOval((int)x,(int)y,20,20);
//save the current co-ordinates so we can over-write this ball next time
        oldX = x;
        oldY = y;
    }
```

The complete listing of this applet is shown below:

```
import java.awt.*;
import java.applet.*;
public class Bounce extends Applet implements Runnable {
    double x, y, oldX, oldY;
    static double xLimit = 300;
    static double ylimit = 200;
    static Color backColor = Color.lightGray;
    public void init() {
        setBackground(backColor);
        Thread runner = new Thread(this);
        runner.start();
    }
    public void run() {
        double xChange = Math.random();
        double yChange = Math.random();
        x = Math.random() * xLimit;
        y = Math.random() * ylimit;
        oldX = x;
        oldY = y;
        while (true) {
            x += xChange;
```

```
                    y += yChange;
                    if ((x >= xLimit) | (x <= 0)) xChange = -xChange;
                    if ((y >= ylimit) | (y <= 0)) yChange = -yChange;
                    repaint( );
                    try { Thread.sleep(1);}
                    catch (InterruptedException e) { System.exit(0); }

              }
        }
        public void update(Graphics g) {
              paint(g);
        }
        public void paint(Graphics g) {
//erase the old ball by over-writing it
              g.setColor(backColor);
              g.fillOval((int)oldX, (int)oldY, 20, 20);
//draw the new ball
              g.setColor(Color.red);
              g.fillOval((int)x,(int)y,20,20);
//save the current co-ordinates so we can over-write this ball next time
              oldX = x;
              oldY = y;

        }
}
```

16

Files and Streams

Introduction

Many real-world application need access to large amounts of data, perhaps stored in a file or downloaded from a remote Web site. Java uses the concept of a stream of information which is a continuous flow of bytes between your application and an external source.

In this chapter we are going to look at the extensive set of classes Java provides for reading both streams of bytes and streams of characters (for reading text files). Reading from the keyboard is an important facility which we look at in detail in this chapter.

The File class

If you want to open a disk file to read or write information you can use the **File** class. There are three constructors for this class:

- **File(String)** the **String** is a file path name which is converted to an abstract path name.
- **File(File** parent, **String** child) the parent is a directory which contains the child file
- **File(String** parent, **String child)** the parent directory is specified as a **String** and contains the child file.

The child file is normally a data file, but can be a directory (which is a special form of file).

If you create a **File** object and use this constructor it does not guarantee that the file actually exists. Fortunately this class has a method called **exists** which you can use to check for a file's existence. In addition, there is a comprehensive set of methods for finding out details about the file, such as its length, whether it is hidden, if it is readable and so on. You can even create new files, and rename and delete files. The most often used methods are shown in table 16.1.

The absolute path name of a file is the full name including the drive, the directory path and the file name. The separator between directories in an absolute file name is system dependent, for example it is '/' on UNIX systems and '\' on Windows systems. Similarly, different systems use different characters to separate a list of file path names, for example ':' on UNIX systems and ';' on Windows systems. These two characters are returned by the **static String** fields **separator** and **pathSeparator** in the **File** class

Table 16.1 The key methods of the File class.

Method	Description
boolean canRead( )	Returns **true** if the file can be read.
boolean canWrite( )	Returns **true** if the file can be written to.
boolean createNewFile( )	Creates a new empty file if the specified file does not already exist. Returns **true** if a new file was created.
boolean delete( )	Deletes the file. If the file is a directory it must be empty to be deleted. Returns **true** if deletion occurs.
void deleteOnExit( )	Deletes the method when the virtual Java machine terminates. Once deletion has been requested it cannot be cancelled.
boolean exists( )	Returns **true** if the file exists.
String getAbsolutePath( )	Returns the full absolute path name of the file.
String getName( )	Returns the name of the file without its full path.
boolean isDirectory( )	Returns **true** if the file name is a directory (or folder in Windows 98 terminology).
boolean isFile( )	Returns **true** if the file is a normal file, that is not a directory or system file.
boolean isHidden( )	Returns **true** if the file is hidden according to the requirements of the underlying operating system.
long length( )	Returns the length of the file in bytes.
boolean mkdir( )	Creates a new directory. Returns **true** if successful.
boolean renameTo(File)	Renames a file to the specified name. Returns **true** if successful.
boolean setReadOnly( )	Makes a file read only. Returns **true** if successful.

In the next application we are going to see some of these methods in action. The application attempts to open a file called *Readme.txt*. Since the file name is specified without its path, it is assumed that the file exists in the same directory as the running application. If the file does not exist it is created and a **boolean** flag called *tempFile* is set to **true**. If the file exists or has just been created, the *displayDetails* method is called to display information about the file such as its name, its absolute path name and its size. If a file was created by the application it is deleted before the application ends. The complete application listing is shown below:

import java.io.*;
//open a file and display information about it.
//if the file does not exist create a temporary file of that name

```
//display information about it and then delete it.
public class FileClass {
    public FileClass( ) throws IOException {
        boolean tempFile = false, deleted = false;
        File f = new File("Readme.txt");
// if the file does not exist create a temporary file
        if (!f.exists( )) {
            tempFile = f.createNewFile( );
            System.out.println("Attempting to create temp file");
        }
        if (f.exists( )) displayFileDetails(f);
        else System.out.println("File does not exist and cannot be created");
//if a temporary file was created delete it
        if (tempFile) {
            deleted = f.delete( );
            if (deleted) System.out.println("Temp file deleted");
            else System.out.println("Temp file not deleted");
        }
    }
    private void displayFileDetails(File f) {
//display information about the opened file
        System.out.println("File name : " + f.getName( ));
        System.out.println("Path : " + f.getAbsolutePath( ));
        System.out.println("File length : " + f.length( ));
        if (f.isFile( )) System.out.println("File is normal");
        if (f.isHidden( )) System.out.println("File is hidden");
        else System.out.println("File is not hidden");
        if (f.isDirectory( )) System.out.println("File is a directory");
        if (f.canRead( )) System.out.println("File is readable");
        else System.out.println("File is not readable");
        if (f.canWrite( )) System.out.println("File is writeable");
        else System.out.println("File is not writeable");
        System.out.println("Path separator is " + f.pathSeparator);
        System.out.println("Name separator is " + f.separator);
    }
    public static void main(String args[ ]) throws IOException {
        new FileClass( );
    }
}
```

The **IOException** exception is thrown by **createNewFile** which is called in the constructor for *FileClass*. This exception is not handled in this application but is thrown by the constructor and the **main** method using throw clauses at the start of these methods.

For the file *Readme.txt* which is a normal non-hidden, readable and writeable text file on a Windows 98 system, the following information is displayed:

> File name : Readme.txt
> File path : C:\Java\Jdk1.2\Readme.txt
> File length : 109
> File is normal
> File is not hidden
> File is readable
> File is writeable
> Path separator is ;
> Name separator is \

The InputStream and OutputStream classes

The **File** class is able to open existing files and to create new files, however it does not have any methods for reading from or writing to files. To do this we have to create a stream between the application and the file. Java has a comprehensive set of stream classes with slightly different capabilities.

The **InputStream** class is an abstract input class which is the superclass of all the classes which represent a stream of bytes. It has numerous subclasses, as shown in figure 16.1, deprecated classes are not shown.

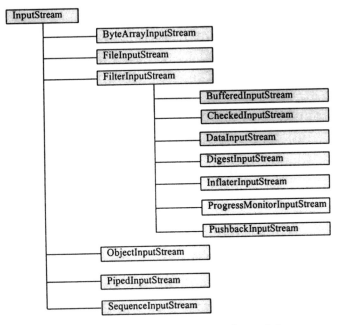

Fig. 16.1 The InputStream class and its subclasses

There is a corresponding set of classes which provide streams for output as shown in figure 16.2.

The **OutputStream** class is an abstract class which is the superclass of all classes which produce a stream of bytes.

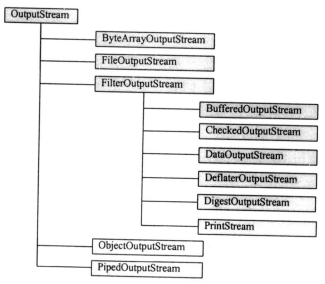

Fig. 16.2 The OutputStream class and its subclasses.

The **FileInputStream** class connects an outside file source to an application. The two most commonly-used constructors are:

- **FileInputStream(File)** - a **File** object is passed to the constructor.
- **FileInputStream(String)** - the name of the file is specified as a **String**.

This class has a number of useful methods for reading from a file as shown in table 16.2.

Table 16.2 The key methods of the FileInputStream class.

Method	Description
int available( )	Returns the number of bytes which can be read without blocking.
void close( )	Closes the stream and releases any resources.
int read( )	Reads a byte from the input stream.
int read(byte[ ])	Reads as many bytes as available or the length of the array, whichever is smaller
int read(byte[ ], int, int)	Reads from the specified offset the specified number of bytes.
long skip(long)	Skips over and ignores the specified number of bytes. The number of bytes skipped is returned.

All of these methods may throw **IOException** which must be handled in the usual way.

The corresponding **FileOutputStream** class is used for sending bytes from your application to a file. The most commonly-used three constructors are:

- **FileOutputStream(File)** creates an output stream to write to the file specified by the **File** object.
- **FileOutputStream(String)** creates an output stream to the specified file.
- **FileOutputStream(String, boolean)** creates an output stream to write to the specified file. If the boolean is **true**, bytes will be added to the end of the file, rather than overwriting existing bytes.

There are three methods for writing to the opened file as shown in table 16.3:

Table 16.3 *The key methods of the **FileOutputStream** class.*

Method	Description
void write(int)	Writes the specified byte to the output stream.
void write(byte[ ])	Writes the entire array to the output stream.
void write(byte[ ], int, int)	At the specified offset writes the specified number of bytes.

These methods may throw **IOException**. In the application shown below a file is opened for input and another for output. The entire contents of one file is then copied to the other:

```
import java.io.*;
public class FileCopying {
    public static void main(String args[ ]) {
        try {
            FileInputStream in = new FileInputStream("In.txt");
            FileOutputStream out = new FileOutputStream("Out.txt");
//read the first int
            int intRead = in.read( );
            while (intRead > 0){
//write to Out.txt
                out.write(intRead);
//display on the screen
                System.out.print((char)intRead);
//read the second and subsequent int
                intRead = in.read( );
            }
        }
        catch(Exception e) {
            System.out.println("Exception error - " + e.toString( ));
        }
```

```
    }
  }
```

The file being copied is a text file and so for confirmation that the file is being read the **int** read is converted to a **char** and then displayed using the **print** method.

One of the initially surprising features of these two classes is that they only has a set of methods for reading and writing bytes. This is sufficient for very simple applications where the data is unstructured, however if you want to read the data into the primitive data types such as **boolean, char, float** and **double** you must use the **DataInputStream** class.

The DataInputStream and DataOutputStream classes

There is only one constructor for the **DataInputStream** class which takes an **InputStream** object as its parameter:

- **DataInputStream(InputStream)**

Similarly if you wish to write the basic data types to a file you can use the **DataOutputStream** class. This also has only one constructor:

- **DataOutputStream(OutputStream)**

Both of these classes have a fairly comprehensive set of methods for reading and writing the primitive data types as shown in tables 16.4 and 16.5.

Table 16.4 The key methods of the DataInputStream class.

Method	Description
int read(byte[ ])	Reads as many bytes as available or the length of the array, whichever is smaller.
int read(byte[ ], int, int)	Reads from the specified offset the specified number of bytes.
boolean readBoolean( )	Reads a **boolean** from the stream.
byte readByte( )	Reads a single **byte**.
char readChar( )	Reads a single **char**.
double readDouble( )	Reads a **double**.
float readFloat( )	Reads a **float**.
int readInt( )	Reads an **int**.
long readLong( )	Reads a **long**.
short readShort( )	Reads a **short**.
int readUnsignedByte( )	Reads an unsigned **byte**.
int readUnsignedShort	Reads an unsigned **short**.
String readUTF( )	Reads a **String** in UTF format.

Note that there is no method for reading or writing a **String**, the nearest methods to this are **readUTF** and **writeUTF**. UTF is an encoding of the Unicode character set and saves the length of the **String** stored in addition to the **String** itself. You will notice if you examine a UTF format file in a simple text editor that the file contains some non-printable characters for this reason.

***Table 16.5** The key methods of the **DataOutputStream** class.*

Method	Description
int write(byte[ ], int, int)	At the specified offset writes the specified number of bytes.
boolean writeBoolean( )	Writes a **boolean** to the stream
byte writeByte( )	Writes a single **byte** from the stream.
char writeChar( )	Writes a **char** as a two byte value, high byte first.
double writeDouble( )	Writes a **double**.
float writeFloat( )	Writes a **float**.
int writeInt( )	Writes an **int**.
long writeLong( )	Writes a **long**.
short writeShort( )	Writes a **short**.
String writeUTF( )	Writes a **String** in UTF format.

All of the methods in these two tables may throw **IOException** which must be handled in the usual way.

Using the DataOutputStream class

To see how these methods are used in practice we are going to look at an application which opens a file which stores a few details about people. The running application is shown below in figure 16.3:

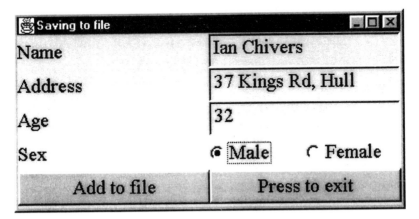

Fig. 16.3 Writing to a file.

For every person the following information is stored:

- The name of the person as a **String**
- The address of the person as a **String**
- The age of the person as an **int**
- The sex of the person as a **boolean**: **true** for male, **false** for female.

This application has a single class called *SaveToFile*. To write to the file, a **FileOutputStream** object is created, using a constructor which takes the name of the file to be opened. The **FileOutputStream** object is passed to the **DataOutputStream** constructor to create a **DataOutputStream** object. This object is declared as an instance variable:

> **DataOutputStream** *out;*

and is instantiated in the *SaveToFile* constructor:

```
try {
        out = new DataOutputStream(new FileOutputStream("Names.txt"));
}
catch(IOException e) {
        System.exit(0);
}
```

Since this instantiation can throw an **IOException** it is handled by a **try** and **catch** clause, which closes the application if it occurs.

Listeners are added to the two buttons. When either of them is clicked the **actionPerformed** method is called:

```
public void actionPerformed(ActionEvent e) {
        if (e.getSource( ) == write) {        //if the write button clicked
                try {
                        out.writeUTF(name.getText( ));
                        out.writeUTF(address.getText( ));
//convert the string to Integer and then to int
                        out.writeInt(Integer.valueOf(age.getText( )).intValue( ));
//if the "male" radio button is set write 'true' else write 'false'
                        if (male.getState( )) out.writeBoolean(true);
                        else out.writeBoolean(false);
//clear the textfields ready for the next input
                        name.setText("");
                        address.setText("");
                        age.setText("");
                }
                catch (IOException ex) {
                        System.exit(0);
                }
        } else if (e.getSource( ) == exit) System.exit(0); //exit button clicked
}
```

Clicking the *Press to exit* button closes the application. Clicking the *Add to File* button writes the present information displayed to the file, using the **writeUTF** method to write the name and address as strings, the **writeInt** method to write the age and the **writeBoolean** method to write the sex of the person. If the person is male the **writeBoolean** method writes **true** to the file, if female, **false** is written.

The complete application is shown below.

```
import java.awt.*;
import java.io.*;
import java.awt.event.*;
//This application writes four items to a file:
//(String)name, (String)address, (int)age), (boolean)sex
public class SaveToFile extends Frame implements ActionListener {
    private TextField name = new TextField(20);
    private TextField address = new TextField(20);
    private TextField age = new TextField(20);
    private CheckboxGroup g = new CheckboxGroup( );
    private Checkbox male = new Checkbox("Male", g, true);
    private Checkbox female = new Checkbox("Female", g, false);
    private Button write = new Button("Add to file");
    private Button exit = new Button("Press to exit");
    DataOutputStream out;
    public SaveToFile( ) {
        Panel p = new Panel( );
        try {
            out = new DataOutputStream(new FileOutputStream("Names.txt"));
        }
        catch(IOException e) {
            System.exit(0);
        }
        setLayout(new GridLayout(5,2));
        setFont(new Font("Serif", Font.PLAIN, 20));
//display all the components
        add(new Label("Name"));
        add(name);
        add(new Label("Address"));
        add(address);
        add(new Label("Age"));
        add(age);
        add(new Label("Sex"));
//add the Checkboxes to the panel and then add the Panel to the Frame
        p.setLayout(new GridLayout(1,2));
        p.add(male);
        p.add(female);
        add(p);
```

```
                p.setBackground(Color.yellow);
//add the "write" button to the Frame
                add(write);
//listen to the "write" button clicks
                write.addActionListener(this);
//add the "exit" button to the Frame
                add(exit);
//listen to the "exit" button clicks
                exit.addActionListener(this);
//specify the frame size and make it visible
                setBackground(Color.yellow);
                setTitle("Saving to file");
                setSize(400,200);
                setVisible(true);
        }
        public void actionPerformed(ActionEvent e) {
                if (e.getSource( ) == write) {      //if the write button clicked
                        try {
                                out.writeUTF(name.getText( ));
                                out.writeUTF(address.getText( ));
//convert the string to Integer and then to int
                                out.writeInt(Integer.valueOf(age.getText( )).intValue( ));
//if the "male" checkbox is set write "true" else write "false"
                                if (male.getState( )) out.writeBoolean(true);
                                else out.writeBoolean(false);
//clear the textfields ready for the next input
                                name.setText("");
                                address.setText("");
                                age.setText("");
                        }
                        catch (IOException ex) {
                                System.exit(0);
                        }
                } else if (e.getSource( ) == exit) System.exit(0); //exit button clicked
        }
        public static void main(String args[ ]) {
                new SaveToFile( );
        }
}
```

A **GridLayout** is used to display the AWT components. To ensure that the two **Checkbox** components are in the same grid square a **Panel** object is created. This **Panel**, called *p*, has a **GridLayout** with two horizontally adjacent grid squares. The two **Checkbox** components are added to this **Panel** and therefore appear side by side. The **Panel** containing these **Checkbox** components is then added to the **Frame**. The two **Checkbox** objects are in the same **CheckboxGroup** and therefore only one of them can be set to **true** at any one time.

Note that the application expects to find the file *Names.txt* in the same directory as the running application.

Using the DataInputStream class

The next application reads the file that we have just created. You can either copy the file *Names.txt* to the same directory as this new application, or specify a full path name when opening the file. The application reads sequentially through the file until the last record is reached, which causes an exception and terminates the application. The running application, called *ReadFromFile* is shown below in figure 16.4. It is visually almost identical to the application which writes to the file:

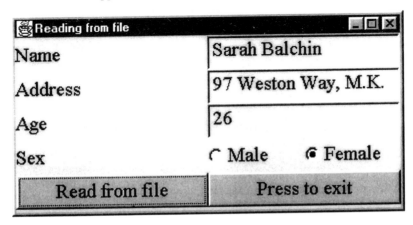

Fig. 16.4 Reading from a file.

A **DataInputStream** object is declared as an instance variable:

DataInputStream in;

In the *ReadFromFile* constructor, a **FileInputStream** object is created to connect the file *Names.txt* to the application. This is passed to the constructor for the **DataInputStream** object. Since this can throw an **IOException** it is handled using a **try** and **catch** clause:

```
try {
    in = new DataInputStream(new FileInputStream("Names.txt"));
}
catch(IOException e) {
    System.exit(0);
}
```

The **TextField** components are made read-only in the constructor using the **setEditable** method and the **Checkbox** components are disabled using the **setEnabled** method, to prevent the information which is displayed being changed:

```
//prevent the user from changing the displayed information
        name.setEditable(false);
        address.setEditable(false);
        age.setEditable(false);
        male.setEnabled(false);
        female.setEnabled(false);
```

The file is read when the *Read from file* button is clicked and the **actionPerformed** method is called. The *name* and *address* is read using the **readUTF** method. The *age* is read using the **readInt** method and the *sex* using the **readBoolean** method. An attempt to read past the end of the file produces an **IOException** which is caught and terminates the application. The complete application listing is shown below:

```
import java.awt.*;
import java.io.*;
import java.awt.event.*;
//The file Names.txt contains four pieces of date for every person:
///(string)name, (string)address, (int)age, (boolean)sex.
//The information is read sequentially until the end of the file is reached.
public class ReadFromFile extends Frame implements ActionListener {
        private TextField name = new TextField(20);
        private TextField address = new TextField(20);
        private TextField age = new TextField(20);
        private CheckboxGroup g = new CheckboxGroup( );
        private Checkbox male = new Checkbox("Male", g, true);
        private Checkbox female = new Checkbox("Female", g, false);
        private Button read = new Button("Read from file");
        private Button exit = new Button("Press to exit");
        DataInputStream in;
        public ReadFromFile( ) {
            Panel p = new Panel( );
            try {
                in = new DataInputStream(new FileInputStream("Names.txt"));
            }
            catch(IOException e) {
                System.exit(0);
            }
            setLayout(new GridLayout(5, 2));
            setFont(new Font("Serif", Font.PLAIN, 20));
//display all the components
            add(new Label("Name"));
            add(name);
```

```
                    add(new Label("Address"));
                    add(address);
                    add(new Label("Age"));
                    add(age);
                    add(new Label("Sex"));
//add the Checkboxes to the panel and then add the Panel to the Frame
                    p.setLayout(new GridLayout(1, 2));
                    p.add(male);
                    p.add(female);
                    p.setBackground(Color.yellow);
                    add(p);
//add the "read" button to the Frame
                    add(read);
//listen to the "read" button clicks
                    read.addActionListener(this);
//add the "exit" button to the Frame
                    add(exit);
//listen to the "exit" button clicks
                    exit.addActionListener(this);
//specify the frame size and make it visible
                    setTitle("Reading from file");
                    setBackground(Color.yellow);
                    setSize(400,200);
                    setVisible(true);
//prevent the user from changing the displayed information
                    name.setEditable(false);
                    address.setEditable(false);
                    age.setEditable(false);
                    male.setEnabled(false);
                    female.setEnabled(false);
            }
        public void actionPerformed(ActionEvent e) {
            if (e.getSource() == read) {      //if the read button clicked
                try {
                        name.setText(in.readUTF());
                        address.setText(in.readUTF());
//convert the int to String
                        age.setText(String.valueOf(in.readInt()));
//if the boolean read is true set the "male" checkbox else set the "female"
                        if (in.readBoolean()) male.setState(true);
                        else female.setState(true);
                }
                catch(IOException ex) {
                        System.exit(0);
                }
```

```
        } else if (e.getSource( ) == exit) System.exit(0); //exit button clicked
    }
    public static void main(String args[ ]) {
            new ReadFromFile( );
    }
}
```

Reading text files

One major omission from the classes we have looked at so far is that if you want to read of write a text file line by line there is no method available which allows you to do this. The **readLine** method in the **DataInputStream** class is now deprecated since it did not always properly convert bytes to characters. Fortunately there is a set of classes which have this capability. The **Reader** class is an abstract class which has a set of subclasses for reading text. The two subclasses we are going to look at are the **FileReader** class and the **BufferedReader** class.

The two most commonly-used constructors of the **FileReader** class are:

- **FileReader(File)** which creates a connection between the **File** specified and the application.
- **FileReader(String)** which connects the file with the specified name to the application

The **BufferedReader** class has a set of methods for reading from a character stream (such as a **FileReader** object). Characters which are read are buffered to increase efficiency. The **BufferedReader** class has two constructors:

- **BufferedReader(Reader)** creates a buffered character reading stream using the default buffer size.
- **BufferedReader(Reader, int)** creates a buffered character reading stream with the specified buffer size.

Both of these constructors may throw **FileNotFoundException**. This class has three methods for reading from the stream:

*Table 16.6 The key methods of the **BufferedReader** class.*

Method	Description
int read( )	Reads a single character.
int read(char[ ], int, int)	Reads from the specified offset the specified number of characters.
String readLine( )	Reads a line which is terminated by a line feed \n, a carriage return \r or a \r\n pair.

These methods may all throw **IOException**.

To see how these classes work, the next application opens a text file, reads it a line at a time and displays that line until the end of the file is reached.

```
import java.io.*;
//This application reads a text file a line at a time and displays it
public class FileReading {
    public static void main (String args[ ]){
        try{
            FileReader fr = new FileReader("Readme.txt");
            BufferedReader br = new BufferedReader(fr);
//read the first line
            String stringRead = br.readLine( );
//read until the end of the file is reached
            while (stringRead != null) {
                System.out.println(stringRead);
//read the second and subsequent lines
                stringRead = br.readLine( );
            }
        }
        catch(FileNotFoundException e){
            System.out.println("File not found");
            System.exit(0);
        }
        catch(IOException f) {
            System.out.println("IOException while reading file");
            System.exit(0);
        }
    }
}
```

An instance of the **FileReader** class is created using the name of the file to be read. This object is passed to the **BufferedReader** constructor. Since this may produce a **FileNotFoundException**, it is placed within a **try** clause with a corresponding **catch** clause.

The reading of the text file a line at a time is performed by the **readLine** method. Since this method may produce an **IOException** there is also a **catch** clause for this exception. When the end of the file is reached the **readLine** method returns a **null**.

There are a corresponding set of methods for writing to a text file using the **FileWriter** class

Reading from the keyboard

When an application starts, there is a pre-defined object called **System.in** which is a **BufferedInputStream** object and represents a stream from the keyboard. If we want to use this to read strings from the keyboard we have to use the **BufferedReader** class, but we cannot do this directly, since this class does not have a constructor which takes a **BufferedInputStream** object (that is **System.in**) as a parameter. We first have to create an **InputStreamReader** object and use this to create a **BufferedReader** object. In Java this sequence looks like this:

> *InputStreamReader isr = new InputStreamReader(System.in);*
> *BufferedReader br = new BufferedReader(isr);*

Now that we have created a **BufferedReader** object we can use its **readLine** method to read lines from the keyboard. The following application reads a line from the keyboard and then prints it again to confirm that it has been read. The application ends when Return is pressed on its own.

> *import java.io.*;*
> *//This application reads a line from the keyboard and echoes it*
> *public class ReadFromKeyboard {*
>   *public static void main (String args[ ]){*
>   *String stringRead;*
>   *try{*
>   *InputStreamReader isr = new InputStreamReader(System.in);*
>   *BufferedReader br = new BufferedReader(isr);*
> *//read until just return is pressed*
>   *do {*
>   *stringRead = br.readLine( );*
>   *System.out.println(stringRead);*
>   *} while (!stringRead.equals(""));   //while not just "return"*
>   *}*
>   *catch(IOException e) {*
>   *System.out.println("IOException while reading from keyboard");*
>   *System.exit(0);*
>   *}*
>   *}*
> *}*

The **readLine** method throws **IOException** which is handled in the usual way.

Java also creates a companion object to **System.in** called **System.out** which we have already used extensively. This is a **PrintStream** object and therefore has an extensive set of overloaded **print** and **println** methods for writing to the screen.

Converting strings to other data types

The **readLine** method is a good way to read a **String** from the keyboard, but if you want to read a different data type from the keyboard you have to do some additional processing to convert the **String** to another data type such as **int**, **float** or **double**. There are two stages, for example in converting a **String** to an **int**:

- Convert from a **String** using the **valueOf** method in the **Integer** class. This returns an object of type **Integer**.
- To create an **int** representation of **Integer** use the **intValue** method.

The process is similar to produce **float** and **double** variables as shown:

```
public class StringConversion {
    public static void main(String args[ ] ){
    String s = "1234";
    int intValue;
    float floatValue;
    double doubleValue;
//convert the string to Integer and then to int
    intValue = Integer.valueOf(s).intValue( );
//convert the string to Float and then to float
    floatValue = Float.valueOf(s).floatValue( );
//convert the string to Double and then to double
    doubleValue = Double.valueOf(s).doubleValue( );
//display the values to confirm
    System.out.println("Integer value is " + intValue);
    System.out.println("Float value is " + floatValue);
    System.out.println("Double value is " + doubleValue);
    }
}
```

As expected this displays the output:

```
1234
1234.0
1234.0
```

The **Integer**, **Double** and **Float** classes provide a wrapper around the primitive data types to create an object. An **Integer** object contains one field of type **int**. **Double** and **Float** also contain just one field each, of type **double** and **float**. All of these classes have a method for converting their objects to a primitive type.

Index